Network Security
JumpStart

Network Security JumpStart™

Matthew Strebe

SYBEX®

San Francisco ◆ London

Associate Publisher: Neil Edde

Acquisitions and Developmental Editors: Heather O'Connor, Maureen Adams

Editor: Colleen Wheeler Strand

Production Editors: Molly Glover, Kelly Winquist

Technical Editor: Donald Fuller

Graphic Illustrator: Jeff Wilson, Happenstance Type-O-Rama

Electronic Publishing Specialist: Kate Kaminski, Happenstance Type-O-Rama

Proofreaders: Nelson Kim, Emily Hsuan, Dave Nash, Laurie O'Connell, Yariv Rabinovitch

Indexer: Nancy Guenther

Book Designers: Maureen Forys and Kate Kaminski, Happenstance Type-O-Rama

Cover Designer: Archer Design

Cover Illustrator: Archer Design

Library of Congress Card Number: 2002104869

ISBN: 0-7821-4120-X

To Seanna Monet Strebe
You were born during Chapter 4.

Acknowledgments

My wife makes my life easy enough for such luxuries as writing, which isn't easy with a rambunctious two-year-old and a new baby. She deserves most of the credit for this book.

Maureen Adams kicked off this project, Heather O'Connor developed it, Kelly Winquist negotiated it through the production process, Colleen Strand (with help from Brianne Agatep) turned my incoherent ramblings into English, and Don Fuller checked the facts. I'd also like to extend my thanks to the "unsung" Sybex heroes: Kate Kaminski, Jeff Wilson, Nelson Kim, Emily Hsuan, Dave Nash, Laurie O'Connell, and Yariv Rabinovitch.

Contents

Contents

Introduction

Computer security is a broad and imposing subject. Hackers, the mysterious lurkers of the Internet, create a serious threat to the legitimate users of the Web. With so many different computers, operating systems, and applications out there, how could any one book cover such a broad topic?

Computer security is, at its core, simple. There are really only a few major concepts, a few successful strategies, and a few major families of problems. This book describes the basic computer security mechanisms, presents successful strategies, and teaches you about the major families of problems that exist. While it does not approach the details specific to particular applications, it does point you in the right direction and teach you how to find those answers yourself.

You'll find after reading this book that computer security isn't all that daunting. Most of the fear, uncertainty, and doubt surrounding computer security is just hype generated by people who don't really understand the problem. Like the fable of the three blind men and the elephant, seeing only a portion of the problem can be very misleading. This book shows you the Whole Elephant. It will dispel the myths and replace them with a concrete understanding of security in general. You can spend the rest of your career filling in the details as they emerge.

Who Should Read This Book?

This book was specifically written for people who want to get started in the field of network security, in a technical, managerial, or executive role, and for those users who want to keep their own computers safe from intrusion. You should be familiar with the operation of a computer before you read this book, but you don't have to be a computer technician or network administrator to understand it. This book would be just as useful for a home user as it would for a network administrator or a Chief Executive Officer.

About This Book

Computer and network security is a massive topic that no single book could hope to cover in any sort of detail. So this book doesn't try to.

This book is a broad overview of computer and network security, covering the major fields of security, the broad solutions to security problems, and the most important implementation details. Think of this book as a guidebook to computer security in general. It will teach you the major security concepts, show you the big picture, and point you in the right direction to find the details that you need from the experts who know them best.

Unlike a lot of topics, computer security is somewhat subjective, and there are legitimate differences of opinion on security matters amongst equally qualified experts. This book errs on the side of more security for the most part, and represents my opinions, which I've developed over the course of two decades of security related work, first as a hacker, then a military classified materials custodian, a defense contractor, and a network administrator and security consultant.

When reading this book, you will find yourself asking: "Yes, but how exactly do I implement your recommendations?" I have deliberately avoided providing specific instructions on how to implement security because security administration requires constant study and detective work on your part—any book that pretended to provide checklists you could use to secure your network would be obsolete by the time you read it. You will need to search the web constantly looking for security problems and their solutions in order to keep your network secure. This book is your roadmap to the research you should perform on the Internet, as no book could hope to keep up with the barrage of new threats appearing every day.

I have provided pointers to the Internet and to other relevant books throughout this book so you can quickly find detailed information about security topics. Of course, websites come and go, addresses change, and books don't. If you have a difficult time with any of the links provided in this book, use your favorite search engine to search on the key terms presented in the text, and you should have no problem finding even more up-to-date information.

I do on occasion provide some specific tips that aid in the understanding of a problem or concepts that are so fundamental and universally applicable that everyone needs to know them anyway, such as how to implement security permissions in Windows and Unix.

This book is platform agnostic. Both commercial and open source solutions are presented for most problems. Windows and Unix are given equal time as platforms because these two systems comprise 90% of all network servers and clients on the planet and are in pretty much a dead heat for market share. I have not mentioned anything specific about Novell NetWare or mainframe operating systems like AS/400, VMS, or anything older, because these systems are rapidly loosing market share and are being replaced by Windows and Unix. While Macintosh OS X is on the upswing, it is Unix underneath, so it's security posture and implementation are largely the same.

In any case, most of the information in this book applies no matter what operating system you are using.

Book Features

This book comprises 15 chapters that cover everything from the basic security concepts and the motivations of hackers to the specific security problems encountered by web and e-mail servers.

The first four chapters cover conceptual information and theory, such as security concepts, the motivation of hackers, encryption technology, and security administration.

Chapters 5 through 9 cover specific information about protecting your network from hackers, creating secure connections over the Internet, avoiding viruses, and implementing backups.

Chapters 10 through 12 contain specific information about Windows and Unix security, because these two operating systems are the most popular and the most frequently targeted operating systems on the planet. This book discusses only the Windows operating systems based on the Windows NT kernel: NT, 2000, XP, and .NET. Versions of Windows based on MS-DOS (3, 95, 98, and Me) are not securable and should be replaced as quickly as possible with a version that is—this book does not discuss them. For the Unix world, this book concentrates on BSD, System V version 4, and Linux; all modern Unix distributions are derived from one of these three variants.

Chapters 13 and 14 cover the special problems related to providing public Internet services with computers that cannot be completely secure because they server anonymous Internet users. Web and e-mail service are specifically discussed, but the concepts apply to any Internet-based service.

Finally, Chapter 15 discusses how to determine if you're being hacked and how to catch hackers in their tracks. It's presented last because the information in rest of the book leads up to the concepts presented here.

Throughout the book, you will find Terms to Know, key terms that will be defined in the chapters where they appear and compiled in the Glossary. There are also Review Questions at the end of each chapter, to help you solidify important concepts in your mind. Answers to the Review Questions are provided in Appendix A.

I can be reached at mbs+jumpstart@connetic.net. Please feel free to contact me to discuss security and security consulting, or simply to praise my writing skills or technical acumen. For the purpose of disagreeing with me, I can be reached at mbs+devnull@connetic.net.

Chapter

1

Security
Principles

Security is the sum of all measures taken to prevent loss of any kind. Loss can occur because of user error, defects in code, malicious acts, hardware failure, and acts of nature. Holistic computer security uses a number of methods to prevent these events, but is primarily focused on preventing user error and malicious acts.

Security is the antithesis of convenience—generally, the more secure something is, the less convenient it is. Think about this in the context of your life: think of how easy it would be if you could just walk up and push a button to start your car without worrying about keys—or paying for car insurance. But the risk of theft and accidents makes these two security measures mandatory. Meanwhile, advanced technology like remote key fobs for cars is making automotive security easier, just like biometric scanners can make logging on computers both more secure and less annoying at the same time.

Computer security is not complicated. It may seem that way, but the theory behind computer security is relatively simple. Hacking methods fall into just a few categories. And solutions to computer security problems are actually rather straightforward.

In this chapter, you will learn about:

 Why computers aren't secure

 The history of computer security

 The theoretical underpinnings of network security

Why Computers Aren't Secure

Most people question why computers are so insecure—after all, people have been hacking for a long time. The vast majority of hacking exploits occur because of one of the following pervasive problems:

Security is an annoyance.   Administrators often fail to implement security features in operating systems because doing so causes problems for users. Users also circumvent security—by choosing easy-to-use (easy-to-guess) passwords like "123456," never changing those passwords, disclosing those passwords to co-workers, or sharing user accounts.

Vendors ship software so that it will install in the most feature-filled configuration with its security features disabled so that unskilled users won't run into roadblocks and don't have to understand and configure software correctly before they use it. This means that the vast majority of installations are never properly secured.

The fact that strong security is an annoyance that requires extra learning on the part of everyone involved is the most common reason for security failures.

Features are rushed to market.   Vendors concentrate their efforts on adding features that make their software more useful, with little thought to security. A perfect example of this is the addition of scripting language support to Microsoft Outlook and Outlook Express.

When the Internet first took off, "e-mail **virus**" scares propagated around the Net via e-mail. Computer security experts ignored them, knowing that a virus required an execution environment like a computer language in order to actually propagate. They laughed at the possibility that anyone would actually tie a computer language to an e-mail system, since anyone with any security consciousness at all would never let this happen. Despite the warnings, and even though the scripting language support built in to Microsoft Office had already been exploited to create "macro" viruses embedded in Word and Excel documents, Microsoft ignored the signs and the explicit warnings of their own employees and incorporated a scripting language into their e-mail software. Even worse, they set it up to automatically execute code contained in e-mail messages, configured it to do so by default, and enabled features like "auto-preview" that even opened the messages upon arrival and executed their embedded code. To make matters even more egregious, they shipped this insecure software for free with every copy of their ubiquitous Windows operating system, thus ensuring that it would be widely deployed.

Thus, the plague that is e-mail viruses today arrived—well predicted, forewarned, and completely ignored by a vendor in order to implement a feature that less than 1% of legitimate users actually ever use. Microsoft simply didn't concern themselves with even a cursory study of the security implications of adding this feature to their software. They couldn't have done a better job of implementing a new hacking exploit if they had been doing it on purpose.

Vendors who spend time on security are eclipsed by the competition.
Customers don't truly value security. If they did, they would use older, well-tested, security-proven software that doesn't have all the bells and whistles of the latest versions. Companies like Microsoft that retrofitted their existing products to work on the Internet decimated their competition. Had they waited to do it securely, they would have been beaten to market by someone who didn't. The end result? The least secure products always get to market first and become standards.

Computers and software evolve very quickly.   Computers and networking technology have been evolving far faster than companies can predict what might go wrong with them. Moore's law states that computer hardware will double in power every two years. His prediction has been eerily accurate for over three decades now.

Protocols that were not developed to be secure were adapted to purposes that they were never intended for and then grew in popularity to a far wider audience than the original creators could have imagined.

Programmers can't accurately predict flaws.   Programmers rarely consider that the state of their functions might be externally changed to any possible value while the code is running, so they only check for values that they send to it themselves. Once the code passes its normal debugging checks, it's shipped without having been tested to pass a barrage of random data thrown at it. Even if they did attempt to predict flaws, the 10 programmers who created a project could never come up with the complete set of attacks that the million hackers who attempt to exploit it will.

There is little diversity in the software market.   The duopoly of the **Windows** and **Unix** operating systems has narrowed the targets of hackers to minor variations on just two operating systems. In most applications, just one or two products make up the lion's share of the market, so hackers only have to crack one product to gain wide access to many people. Two web servers, Apache and IIS, compose more than 90% of the web service market. Two closely related families of operating systems, Windows and Unix, compose more than 90% of the operating system market for PCs.

Vendors are not motivated to reveal potential flaws.   To avoid marketing fiascoes, vendors try to hide problems with their operating systems and thereby naturally discourage discussion of their flaws. Conversely, hackers publicize flaws they discover immediately to the entire world via the Internet. This dichotomy of discussion means that flaws are far more widely disseminated than the solutions to them are.

Windows
A family of single-user operating systems developed by Microsoft for small computers. The most recent version has incorporated enhancements to allow multiple users to run programs directly on the machine.

Unix
A family of multi-user operating systems that all conform completely to the POSIX (Portable Operating System Interface for Unix) specification and operate in very similar fashion, this includes Unix, BSD, Linux, and derivatives of these major versions.

Patches are not widely deployed and can cause problems when they are installed.   When security problems are found with a piece of software, the vendor will fix the problem, post a patch on the Internet, and send out an e-mail notice to registered customers. Unfortunately, not everyone gets the notice or installs the patch—in fact, the majority of users never install security patches for software unless they actually get hacked.

Even worse, vendors rush security patches to clients with unexposed bugs that can cause even more serious problems on their client's machines and even in the best cases require additional processing to find the flaws, thus slowing the systems. In many cases, the cure can be worse than the disease.

With these problems epidemic in the security market, you might wonder if the security problem will ever be solved. In fact, there will always be flaws in software. But there are many relatively easy things that can be done to fix these problems. Secure **protocols** can be layered on top of unsecured protocols or replace them outright. Border security with **firewalls** can prevent **hackers** from reaching most systems, thus making their security flaws unimportant. Compilers and computer languages can be modified to eliminate problems that programmers fail to check for. And vendors can find ways to make security more convenient, like filtering easily guessed passwords using spell-checker technology. And, as hackers continue to exploit systems, customers will demand proactive security and reward vendors who emphasize security rather than those who ship feature-filled, but poorly thought-out, products.

NOTE

Why can't vendors get it and make software secure out of the box? In truth, they can. The OpenBSD operating system hasn't been remotely hacked (hacked over the Internet) in over four years. Its developers have accurately predicted and proactively closed **hacking** exploits before they could be exploited. But OpenBSD is not very popular, because it doesn't have a lot of features—it's just a basic operating system, and once you add your own software, that software can still be exploited.

protocol
An agreed upon method of communicating between two computers.

firewall
A packet router that inspects the data flowing through it to decide which information to pass through based upon a set of programmed policies.

hacker
One who engages in hacking.

hacking
The act of attempting to gain access to computers without authorization.

The History of Computer Security

By understanding of the history of computer security, understanding why computers aren't secure becomes obvious.

Stories of major, nearly catastrophic, hacking exploits happen all the time. In 2001 alone, the Code Red **worm** spread unchecked through the Internet—and once it was patched, the Nimbda virus did almost exactly the same thing; e-mail viruses spread with regularity, and Microsoft shipped its newest flagship operating system, Windows XP, with a security flaw so egregious that hackers could literally exploit any computer running it with no serious effort at all; the Linux standard FTP and DNS services were exploited, allowing hackers to enter websites and deface their contents at will. It seems like hacking is just getting worse, even as organizations spend more money on the problem. In fact, widespread hacking is getting more common.

In 1988, the year in which reporting began, the Computer Emergency Response Team (CERT) at Carnegie Mellon University, which tracks Internet security incidents, reported six hacking incidents. In 1999, they reported nearly 10,000. In 2000, they reported over 22,000. In 2001, they reported over 52,000 incidents. Numbers like these can sound scary, but when you factor in the growth of the Internet by counting incidents per computers attached to the Internet, security incidents are rising at a rate of 50% per year (rather than the 100% per year that the raw numbers suggest) and have been since 1993, the first year for which reasonably reliable information is available about the overall size of the Internet.

The following sections are a quick reprisal of computer security since the dawn of time. (See graphic on next page.)

⌐1945

Computers didn't exist in any real sense before 1945. The original need for security (beyond prevention of outright theft of equipment) sprung from the need for secure military and political communication. **Codes** and **ciphers** were originally studied because they could provide a way to secure messages if messages were intercepted, and could allow for distance communication like smoke, mirror, or pigeon signaling.

---

worm
Any program that takes active measures to replicate itself onto other machines in a network. A network virus.

code
An agreed-upon set of symbols that represent concepts. Both parties must be using the same code in order to communicate, and only predetermined concepts can be communicated.

cipher
A mathematical function used to transform a plain message into a form that cannot be read without decoding it. Ciphers can encode any message.

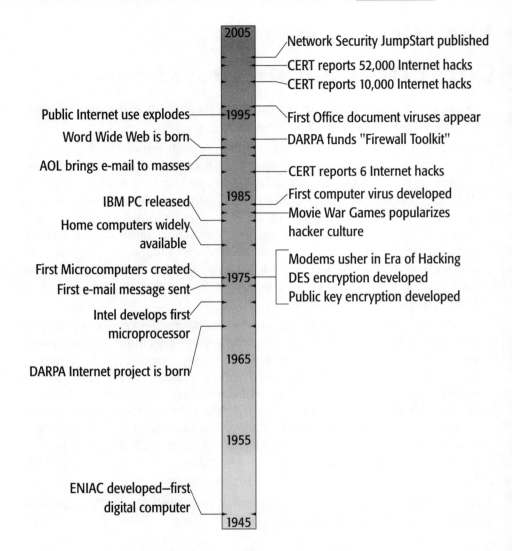

Before the advent of telegraphy, telephony, and radio communications, simply transmitting a message anywhere was extremely difficult. Wars were prosecuted slowly; intrigues were based on hunches, guesses, and paranoia, because real information was difficult to come by. Messages transmitted by post or courier were highly likely to be intercepted, and when they were, the consequences were disastrous for the war or political effort.

For that reason, codes, which are far easier to implement than ciphers, formed the backbone of secure communications prior to the advent of automated computing. Codes are simple substitution ciphers—one word is used to transmit another word, concept, or phrase. Both parties encode and decode their messages using a codebook, and generally the codes were chosen so that they made reasonable sense when read in their coded form in an attempt to hide the fact that they were encoded—similar to the modern concept of steganography, or hiding encrypted data as noise inside other content like a digital picture or sound file. (Most militaries still use codes and codebooks for operational messages over unencrypted radio links as a holdover from earlier times, but as computing power becomes cheap this practice is quickly fading into obscurity.) Unfortunately, both parties had to have the codebook, and its interception meant that all encoded communication could be decoded.

1945–1955

A half-century ago, the first electronic computers were being developed. These gargantuan machines operated on vacuum tubes and had considerably less computing power than today's $50 calculator. They cost many millions of dollars to build and operate, and every compute cycle was precious. Wasting computing time on such luxuries as security was unheard of—but since you had to have both physical access and substantial training to operate these machines, security was not a problem. With so many other problems to solve, computer security wasn't even on the research horizon at this time.

1955–1965

As computers moved into the business world in the sixties, computer security was limited only to making sure that the occasional disgruntled employee couldn't cause harm and that the competition had no access to the computers. Both measures still relied upon physical security for the environment rather than security measures in software. Accounts and passwords, when implemented, were simple and used merely for tracking which users performed which actions in the system rather than for any form of true security. There's not a single verified instance of remote malicious hacking activity occurring during or before this era.

1965–1975

During the late sixties and early seventies, as **mainframes** grew more powerful and the number of users attached to them reached into the thousands, accountability became more important. To limit what typical users could do, the concept of limited user accounts and unlimited administrative accounts came into practice. Typical users could not perform actions that might corrupt data or disrupt other users, while administrators could do anything necessary on the system.

mainframe
A large and powerful (in context) computer that many users share via terminal displays.

7

User accounts protected by passwords were used to discriminate between the various types of users. Most mainframes shipped from the factory with a default password that the administrators were relied upon to change once they received the machine—a practice that is still common with simple network devices.

operating system
The program that controls the overall operation of a computer.

Operating system research was beginning to take root in this period, and mainframe operating systems like Multics were beginning to be adapted to a much smaller breed of business-class machines, like minicomputers and the first single-user systems called workstations. The phone company was involved in a tremendous amount of operating research at the time, and developed a light version of Multics, called UNIX. At the same time, Digital Equipment was developing a more portable version of their operating system, called VMS, while IBM worked on their various mainframe operating systems.

Hacking in this era consisted of mere rumors of rogue programmers performing illicit hacks—like writing code that took the fractional remnants of rounded transactions and deposited them in their own bank accounts or writing backdoors into their code so that they could always gain access to systems (as the original developers of UNIX have insinuated that they did).

1975—1985

The lack of true security came to light in the seventies when companies started providing remote access to terminal users over modems that operated using the public telephone system. Modems allowed small offices to connect directly to central computers in the corporate headquarters. Companies also leased the newer digital phone circuits and began connecting remote offices directly to their systems over "leased lines" that did not require modems and could span the country—at great expense. And, since only direct connections could be made between mainframes and terminals, there was very little flexibility for routing information.

The military had been using computers for years at this point and had been chaffing at the lack of flexibility in sending messages between mainframes. In 1969, the Defense Advanced Research Projects Agency (DARPA) initiated a project to explore the promise of packet-based networks, where individual tiny messages could be transmitted between two end-systems and routed by intermediate systems connected in a loosely hierarchical method, thus allowing any participants on the network to communicate. These research efforts began to bear useful fruit in the late seventies.

The amount of computing power required to perform message (or packet) routing was impractical at the time, but it was clear that computers would quickly become powerful enough to make the problem trivial in the next few years.

Because message routing required intermediate systems to perform work that didn't directly involve them, security was antithetical in the early packet-based research systems; intermediate systems could not waste the time to authenticate every packet that went through them, and requiring security would have kept the system from getting off the ground. But in the military, physical security and accountability more than made up for the lack of systems security, and since no un-trusted users were attached to the system, security wasn't an issue.

But the government realized that security would become an issue, and began funding major initiatives to improve computer security. IBM developed the **Data Encryption Standard (DES)** for the government in 1975. And at nearly the same time, Whitfield Diffie and Martin Helman developed the concept of the **public key encryption (PKE)**, which solved the longstanding problem of secure key exchange. In 1977, Rivest, Shamir, and Adelman implemented PKE in the proprietary RSA encryption algorithm. These pioneering efforts in network encryption weren't widely deployed at the time, but they are the foundation of computer security today.

The development of the microprocessor by Intel in 1972 was beginning to reach the public by 1975. Hobbyists could build their own computers from parts available through catalogs, and by 1978 complete computer systems could be purchased off the shelf by end users in any town in the U.S.

They could be purchased with modems that were capable of communicating directly with corporate computers as well, and the art and practice of hacking was born.

Hacking in those days consisted of "war-dialing" a range of phone numbers automatically by leaving hobby computers running over night. Whenever a computer answered, the computer would typically print out the phone number. In any case, it would hang up immediately, causing numerous nuisance calls to people in the middle of the night. The hacker would then go through the list of found computers manually, looking for signs of computers that might be easy to break into, like mainframe computers whose default administrative **passwords** had never been changed.

After a few high-profile, apparently effortless cases of hackers breaking into computer systems occurred, the concept of **call-back security**, also known as dial-back security, was introduced. With call-back security, the answering computer (the system) accepts only a phone number from the calling computer (the client) and hangs up. The system then checks this phone number against an allowed list, and if it appears, the system calls back the client whose computer is set to listen for a call back. The fact that phone numbers can't easily be forged and that phone lines are somewhat difficult to tap made for all the security that was necessary in those days.

Data Encryption Standard (DES)
A secret key encryption algorithm developed by IBM, under contract to the U.S. government, for public use.

public key encryption (PKE)
A method of encryption that solves the problem of exchanging secret keys by using different but related ciphers for encoding and decoding.

password
A secret known to both a system and a user that can be used to prove a user's identity.

call-back security
Security that is implemented by having the main system call the remote user back, thus ensuring that the user attempting to gain access is an authorized one (so long as the phone system remains secure).

Hackers did have the ability to hack the telephone company's computers to reroute phone calls and manually direct where calls went, but hackers with these skills were extremely rare, and lacking any public discussion forum, every hacker pretty much had to learn these techniques on their own. By the mid-eighties, call-back security had solved the problem of computer security to the point that it was worth solving, and increased security by the public telephone companies made exploiting these systems very difficult.

bulletin-board system (BBS)
Use of a single central computer to which many computers have intermittent access to shared information.

1985–1995

In the mid-eighties, PC computers exploded in popularity, going from a novelty owned by geeks to an essential tool of nearly every desktop in the country in the span of 10 years. With the explosion in popularity grew the need to connect PC computers together directly, and so local area networks, pioneered in the previous decade, came out of the research closet and onto the desktop as well. These networks used business-grade versions of the military's packet-based networks that were optimized for small networks. By 1995, networked PCs were crucial to the business world.

At the same time, home computer enthusiasts with modems were creating online communities called **bulletin-board systems (BBS)**. By using a single expensive PC with a lot of modems or an obsolete mainframe as a central server, home users could dial in to chat with friends, send text messages, and participate in online discussion groups and games. Without exception these services were text based to make maximum use of the slow modem links and low processing power of the computers of the day.

Some of these BBSs became very large. CompuServe became the largest BBS at this time, linking millions of computer users by modem and allowing them to trade electronic mail and to "chat" or use text messages with one another in real time. Another company, America Online, took the BBS concept and put a graphical interface on it, making getting "on line" easy enough for computer novices.

BBSs allowed hackers to begin trading in information and to form distributed hacking cabals—usually targeting other BBSs, since most business computers had become locked down with the advent of dial-up security. Hacking in this period worked largely the same way that it had in the seventies, except that the targets were new phone companies, BBSs, and the occasional improperly secured corporate mainframe.

That is, unless you happened to be a student at a university. During these years, universities took over development of the military's original packet-routing protocols and developed them to solve real-world problems. Just like the military prototype, these systems relied on the fact that intermediate systems would route data without authentication in order to function. Security was a layer pasted on top, in the actual application that used the packet network, rather than at the network layer. This allowed clever students to watch data flowing through intermediate systems to gather passwords, and then use those passwords to gain access to other systems. Since military installations and academic research companies were also connected to this "Internetwork," early Net hackers had the chance to cause real mischief—but rarely actually did.

During this period, e-mail grew out of simple messaging systems that allowed only interoffice communication into a messaging system that could span companies and allow anyone attached to the Internet to trade real, human information. Other research projects like FTP and Gopher allowed people to trade computer files and documents over the Internet. In 1990, Gopher was merged with a research concept called HyperText (previously seen by the public in Apple's HyperCard product) to produce "browsable documentation" that contained embedded links to other documents that could be automatically downloaded when the link was selected. This technology, called the World Wide Web, allowed scientists to publish their scientific papers immediately, and was an immediate boon to the scientific and Internet computing communities.

The fact that hacking could occur on the nascent Internet didn't pass unnoticed, however. Every major entity attached to the Internet, including the military, universities, and companies like IBM and Digital, developed special intermediate systems that performed extra analysis of data flowing through them to determine if the data was legitimate and should be routed. These routers were called firewalls.

1995–2005

The Internet exploded on the public scene between late '94 and early '96 (we'll just call it '95). Borne largely by the twin utilities of universal e-mail and the World Wide Web, the Internet became so compelling that the owners of most BBSs began to connect their systems to the Internet, and the government turned over management of it to a consortium of Internet service providers (ISPs). Universities frequently allowed wide access to their Internet connections early on, and soon, phone companies began installing pure "modem banks" to answer phone connections and put them directly on the Internet. They all became Internet service providers, and within an amazingly short period of time, millions of people were connected directly to one another over the Internet. BBSs who didn't convert to ISPs, with the solitary exception of AOL (which provided a bridge to the Internet but maintains its proprietary BBS client software), became extinct almost overnight.

The Internet boom happened so fast that software vendors were caught completely off guard. Bill Gates, the chairman of Microsoft, said in 1994 that the Internet would blow over. His words merely echoed the typical response of most PC software developers. Some new companies, like Netscape, were formed from students who had been using the Internet at school and knew its potential, but these companies were few and far between.

By the next year, it was obvious that the Internet wasn't going to just blow over. In a telling incident, Mr. Gates called a meeting at his retreat and forced his entire company to abandon their current developments and refocus their efforts on making every one of their products "Internet Enabled." Other software companies couldn't react as quickly, and the Internet caused many of them to stumble, ship late, and become irrelevant. Only those who rushed to make their software and operating systems compatible with Internet protocols remained in the game. The very largest names in computer software at the time, like Borland, WordPerfect, Novell, IBM, and Lotus, were all simultaneously hobbled by the fact that Microsoft was able to make their products take advantage of this new technology in short order, while they chose to finish their current developments and wait for the next development cycle to make their products Internet-ready. By the time their next product revisions came out, nobody cared and Microsoft had completely eclipsed them all.

The rush to market, while a marketing coup for Microsoft, made security an afterthought. Microsoft actually believed their own hype about their flagship operating system, Windows NT, and felt that its office-grade security would make it the most secure operating system on the Internet. For their home use products like Windows 95, 98, and Me, security wasn't even attempted—you could gain access to the computer by clicking "cancel" at the log-in dialog, if one was even configured to appear. After all, if Microsoft had held up the development of these products to try to make them secure, end users would have just adopted somebody else's insecure products that were ready to go.

The Internet with its totally non-secure protocols was the fertilizer that the hacking world needed after the sparse desert of the late eighties. Once phone companies had locked down their systems, hacking had frankly become rather boring and routine. Anybody you could hack wasn't going to be interesting anyway, so there was little point in trying. But suddenly, everyone was attached to the same insecure network, ripe for the plucking.

Microsoft's dominance of the PC software market meant that hackers could concentrate their efforts on understanding just two operating systems: Unix, the native OS of the Internet, and Windows, the operating system of the masses. By creating exploits to hack these two operating systems remotely over the Internet, hackers gained almost unlimited access to information on the Internet. Vendors scrambled to patch security problems as soon as they were discovered, but the lag between discovery and response left weeks during which hackers could broadcast their discoveries and cause widespread damage.

Businesses clamped down by installing firewalls, evolved from early military and commercial security research efforts, onto their leased lines at the point where they attached to their ISP. Firewalls went a long way towards protecting interior systems from exploitation, but they still allowed users to circumvent security accidentally and did little to stop the exploitation of services that had to be allowed—like e-mail and web services. These two services now constitute the bulk of hacking targets because they can't be blocked while still operating correctly.

Toward the close of this era, **encryption** gained wide use as the savior of the Internet. By implementing security protocols that could hide data and prove someone's identity while preserving the ease-of-use and ubiquity that made the Internet popular, encryption, along with firewalling, is basically saving the Internet from abandonment due to security concerns.

encryption
The process of encoding a message using a cipher.

Hackers will continue to exploit insecure protocols, but as vendors learn to ship secure software or shore it up with integrated firewall code, and as implementers learn to secure their own systems, hacking is doomed to drift steadily towards the situation in the late eighties, when it was no longer that interesting because those remaining insecure users were trivial.

2005—

Hacking will drop off dramatically once Microsoft integrates strong firewalling software into all of its operating systems, which will occur late in 2004 when they realize that the adoption of their new e-commerce .NET services depends upon security rather than features. The Open Source community and their flag-ship Linux product have already integrated true firewalling years earlier, and Linux is seen as more secure than Windows—a situation that Microsoft will not tolerate for long. Apple will simply adapt the Open Source firewalling services into Mac OS X, which is based upon BSD Unix, to prevent its exploitation, and every other commercial version of Unix will be completely eclipsed and made obsolete by the free, faster moving, and more secure Linux or BSD Unix operating systems by this time.

E-mail forgery will become more popular briefly, until users begin to use the X.509 certificate-based encryption and digital signature capabilities already supported but rarely used. Someone (probably Microsoft) will set up a free certificate authority for private users and make Outlook automatically download certificates from it, as part of an online digital identity that will be used to enable secure e-commerce services. This may be used as an e-commerce payment-clearing house akin to a credit-card system, and could be called something like "Microsoft .NET Passport."

Once Microsoft and the Open Source community tighten down the hatches on their operating systems and services, hacking exploits will become fewer and farther between. The government will catch up with hacking activity after it tapers off and begin making examples of people again. Hacking as a hobby will taper down to trickle.

Until a researcher somewhere and somewhen discovers a fundamental mathematical flaw in the encryption software upon which all of these security measures are based…

Security Concepts

Computer security is based on the same concepts that physical security is: trust, knowledge of a secret to prove authenticity, possession of a key to open locks, and legal accountability. The metaphors are so apt that most computer security mechanisms even have the same names as their physical counterparts.

Trust

All computer security springs from the concept of inherent or original trust. Just like a child inherently trusts its parents, a secure computer system inherently trusts those who set it up. While this may seem rather obvious, it is an important concept because it is the origination of all subsequent security measures.

There's more inherent trust in computer security than simply the original establishment of a system. For example, you trust that there are no "backdoors" in the software you use that could be exploited by a knowledgeable person to gain access. You trust that the login screen that you are looking at is actually the system's true login screen and not a mimic designed to collect your password and then pass it to a remote system. Finally, you trust that the designers of the system have not made any serious mistakes that could obviate your security measures.

Authentication

Authentication is the process of determining the identity of a user. Forcing the user to prove that they know a secret that should be known only to the actual user proves that the user is who they say they are.

User accounts are associated with some form of secret, such as a password, PIN, biometric hash, or with a device like a **smart card** that contains a larger, more secure password than a human could remember. To the system, there is no concept of a human; there is only a secret, information tied to that secret, and information to which that secret has access.

Authentication is only useful in so far as it is accurate. Passwords are probably the least reliable form of authentication in common use today, but they're also the most easily implemented—they require no special hardware and no sophisticated algorithms for basic use. However, they are easily guessed, and even when they're carefully chosen it's still possible to simply guess the entire range of possible passwords on many systems in short order.

authentication
The process of determining the identification of a user.

user account
A record containing information that identifies a user, including a secret password.

smart card
An electronic device containing a simple calculator preprogrammed with a code that cannot be retrieved. When given a challenge, it can calculate a response that proves it knows the code without revealing what the code is.

A less common but more secure method of authentication is to physically possess a unique key. This is analogous to most physical locks. In computer security systems, "keys" are actually large numbers generated by special algorithms that incorporate information about the user and which are stored on removable media like smart cards. The problem with keys is that, like physical keys, they can be lost or stolen. However, when combined with a password they are very secure and difficult to thwart.

Another form of authentication provides inherent identification by using a physical property of the user. This is called biometric authentication, and it relies upon unique and unchangeable physical properties of a human, such as handwriting characteristics, fingerprints, facial characteristics, and so forth. Biometric authentication is the most reliable form of authentication because it's easy to use, nearly impossible to fake, and can't be circumvented by users even if they wanted to. Some forms of biometric authentication are easier to "forge" than others, and naïve implementations can sometimes be easily faked. But when well implemented, biometric authentication is the most secure form of authentication and the only form that can be truly said to uniquely and unmistakably identify a user.

Chain of Authority

During the installation of a security system, the original administrator will create the root or additional administrative accounts. From that original account, all other accounts, keys, and certificates spring. Every account on a system, even massive systems containing millions of accounts, spring from this chain of authority. The concept of chains of authority isn't often discussed because it is inherent in a secure system.

Certificate systems are also based on a chain of authority. Consider the case of separate businesses that do a lot of work together. It would be convenient if users from Business Alpha could automatically log on to computers at Business Beta. But because these two systems have two different chains of authority, there's no way for Business Alpha to trust that users who say they are from Business Beta actually are. This problem is solved by having both businesses trust a third-party **trust provider**, or a company that specializes in verifying identity and creating secure certificates that can be used to prove identity to foreign systems. As long as both businesses trust the same trust provider, they are rooted in the same chain of authority and can trust certificates that are generated by that trust provider. Trust Providers are the digital equivalent of a Notary Public. Examples of trust providers include VeriSign and Thawte.

trust provider
A trusted third party that certifies the identity of all parties in a secure transaction. Trust providers do this by verifying the identity of each party and generating digital certificates that can be used to determine that identity. Trust Providers perform a function analogous to Notaries Public.

Accountability

Accountability is where the secret meets the user. Users don't try to circumvent security because their identity would be known and they would be held legally accountable for their actions. It is accountability that prevents illegal behavior, rather than access controls.

In pure accountability-based systems, no access control mechanisms are present. Users simply know that their every action is being logged, and since their identity is known and their activities are tracked, they won't do things that could jeopardize their position (unless something happens to make them no longer care).

The problem with accountability-based systems is two-fold—they only work if identity can't be faked, and there are rare occasions where users lose their inhibitions. Without access control, these rare users can destroy the entire system. For these reasons, accountability-based security is normally used to augment access control systems rather than to replace them.

Access Control

Access control is the security methodology that allows access to information based on identity. Users who have been given permission or keys to information can access it—otherwise, access is denied.

Permissions-Based Access Control

Once the system knows the identity of an individual because they've been authenticated, the system can selectively allow or deny access to resources like stored files based on that identity. This is called "permissions-based security" because users are either granted or denied permission to access a **file** or other resource.

The question of who has access to which files is typically either defined by administrators when the system is implemented or created according to some set of default rules programmed into the system; for instance, the original creator (owner) of a file is the only user who can change it.

Access controls are typically implemented either as directory permissions that apply to all files within the directory or by an Access Control List, which is a component of a file that explicitly lists which users can access it. Typically, when a file is created, an ACL is automatically copied from the parent directory's ACL, so it is said to "inherit" permissions from the containing directory.

file
A sequence of related information referenced by a file name in a directory.

17

Unfortunately, none of these security controls works if the operating system can be circumvented. By shutting off the system and mounting its storage in another computer, a foreign system can read off all the files without interference because it's not asking for permission from the operating system. Essentially, permissions can be circumvented the same way a kid can disobey her parents—by simply not asking for permission in the first place.

private key
The key used to decode public key messages that must be kept private.

Encryption-Based Access Control (Privacy)

A totally different way to control access is to simply encrypt data using public key encryption. Access to the encrypted data is given to those who want it, but it's worthless to them unless they have the **private key** required to decode it. Using PKE to secure data works very well, but it requires considerably more processing power to encode and decode data.

TIP

Encryption is such an important topic in computer security that it requires its own chapter to be covered properly. If you don't understand the terms used in this section, just re-read it after you read Chapter 3.

Encryption-based access control is also dangerous because data can be irrevocably lost if the private key required to decrypt it is lost. For this reason, most practical systems store a copy of a resource's private key in a key repository that can be accessed by an administrator, which itself is encrypted using another key. The problem of potential loss of information doesn't go away, but the system includes more participants and therefore permanent loss less likely to happen.

Practical systems also don't encrypt files with a unique public key for each file or user—in fact, they encrypt files using a secret key registered to an entire group and then encrypt the list of secret keys for the group using a private key. The private key is given to each member of the group (possession of the private key makes one a member of the group). Thus, members of the group have the key to decrypt the store that contains the secret key required to decrypt the file. This way, when an account is deleted, no keys are irrevocably lost because other members still have the key.

In pure systems, the keys for a group are stored in a file that is encrypted using a user's smart card. By possessing the smart card, a user can decrypt the store that contains the keys for the groups they are members of, which in turn can be used to decrypt the store that contains the keys that are used to decrypt individual files. This is how a chain of authority is created using encryption, and systems that work this way are called Public Key Infrastructure (PKI) systems.

No common systems work this way yet, but support for PKI is being retrofitted into both Windows and Unix. Shortly, most systems will work this way.

Encryption-based access control solves the problem of requiring the operating system to arbitrate access to secure data. Even if the operating system has been circumvented, stored data is still encrypted. Encrypted data can be transmitted over public media like the Internet without concern for its privacy.

Review Questions

1. What is security?

   _____

2. What is the most common reason why security measures fail?

   _____

3. Why would vendors release a product even when they suspected that there could be security problems with the software?

   _____

4. How many operating systems make up 90% of the operating system market?

   _____

5. Factoring in the growth of the Internet, at what rate is the number of computer security incidents increasing?

   _____

6. Why weren't computers designed with security in mind from the beginning?

   _____

7. During what era did "hacking" begin to occur en masse?

   _____

8. In what year was Public Key Encryption developed?

   _____

9. Prior to the Internet, how did most hackers share information?

   _____

10. Why is it likely that applications (other than those designed to implement security) that concentrate on security will fail in the marketplace?

_____

_____

11. What is the process of determining the identity of a user called?

_____

_____

12. When a new computer is first set up, how does the system know that the person setting up the computer is authorized to do so?

_____

_____

13. What is the most secure form of authentication?

_____

_____

14. How can a hacker circumvent permissions based access control?

_____

_____

15. How can a hacker circumvent correctly implemented encryption-based access control?

_____

_____

Terms to Know
- ❑ operating system
- ❑ passwords
- ❑ private key
- ❑ protocols
- ❑ public key encryption (PKE)
- ❑ smart card
- ❑ trust provider
- ❑ Unix
- ❑ user accounts
- ❑ virus
- ❑ Windows
- ❑ worm

Chapter

2

Understanding
Hacking

Know thy enemy. Hackers are the reason you need to implement computer security, and an in-depth defense against any adversary requires an in-depth understanding of that adversary. This chapter describes hackers, their motivations, and their methods.

By knowing a hacker's motivations, you can predict your own risk level and adapt your specific defenses to ward off the type of hackers you expect to attack your network, while retaining as much usability as possible for your legitimate users.

In this chapter you will learn about:

 The types of hackers

 Vectors that hackers exploit

 How hackers select targets

 How hackers gather information

 The most common hacking methods

What Is Hacking?

Hacking is quite simply the attempt to gain access to a computer system without authorization. Originally, the term *hacker* simply referred to an adept computer user, and gurus still use the term to refer to themselves in that original sense. But when breaking into computer systems (technically known as *cracking*) became popular, the media used the term "hacker" to refer only to computer criminals, thus popularizing only the negative connotation. In this book, we refer only to that negative connotation as well.

Hacking is illegal. Title 18, United States Code, Section 1030, first enacted by Congress in 1984, criminalized hacking. Technically, the code requires that the perpetrator actually "do" something other than simply obtain access and read information—but then, if that's all they did you probably wouldn't know you'd been hacked anyway. The law specifically states that the perpetrator must "knowingly" commit the crime—thereby requiring that at least some sort of notification that unauthorized access is illegal be posted or that some authentication hurdle be established in order to make the activity prosecutable.

According to the FBI, for a computer-related crime to become a federal crime the attacker must be shown to have caused at least $5,000 worth of damage. This is why spammers who access open relay mail servers get away with transmitting their floods of e-mail through other people's mail servers without being prosecuted—they're not doing enough financial damage to any one victim to really be prosecutable, and the SMTP servers are not performing authentication so there's no reasonable expectation of security.

Types of Hackers

Learning to hack takes an enormous amount of time, as does perpetrating actual acts of hacking. Because of the time hacking takes to learn, there are only two serious types of hackers: the underemployed and those hackers being paid by someone to hack. The word "hacker" conjures up images of skinny teenage boys aglow in the phosphor of their monitors. Indeed, this group makes up the largest portion of the teeming millions of hackers, but they are far from the most serious threat.

Hackers fall quite specifically into these categories, in order of increasing threat:

- Security experts
- Script kiddies
- Underemployed adults
- Ideological hackers
- Criminal hackers
- Corporate spies
- Disgruntled employees

script kiddie
A novice hacker.

Security Experts

Most security experts (including me) are capable of hacking, but decline to do so for moral or economic reasons. Computer security experts have found that there's more money in preventing hacking than in perpetrating it, so they spend their time keeping up with the hacking community and current techniques in order to make themselves more effective in the fight against it. A number of larger Internet service companies employ ethical hackers to test their security systems and those of their large customers, and hundreds of former hackers now consult independently as security experts to medium-sized businesses. These experts often are the first to find new hacking exploits, and they often write software to test or exacerbate a condition. Practicing hackers can exploit this software just as they can exploit any other software.

Script Kiddies

Script kiddies are students who hack and are currently enrolled in some scholastic endeavor—junior high, high school, or college. Their parents support them, and if they have a job it's only part-time. They are usually enrolled in whatever computer-related courses are available, if only to have access to the computer lab.

These hackers may use their own computers, or (especially at colleges) they may use the more powerful resources of the school to perpetrate their hacks.

Script kiddies joyride through cyberspace looking for targets of opportunity and are concerned mostly with impressing their peers and not getting caught. They usually are not motivated to harm you, and in most instances, you'll never know they were there unless you have some alarming software or a firewall that logs attacks. These hackers constitute about 90% of the total hacking activity on the Internet.

If you considered the hacking community as an economic endeavor, these hackers are the consumers. They use the tools produced by others, stand in awe of the hacking feats of others, and generally produce a fan base to whom more serious script kiddies and underemployed adult hackers play. Any serious attempt at security will keep these hackers at bay.

Script kiddies hack primarily to get free stuff: software and music, mostly. They share pirated software amongst themselves, make MP3 compressed audio tracks from CDs of their favorite music, and trade the serial numbers needed to unlock the full functionality of demo software that can be downloaded from the Internet.

Underemployed Adult Hackers

Underemployed adults are former script kiddies who have either dropped out of school or failed to achieve full-time employment and family commitments for some other reason. They usually hold "pay the rent" jobs (often as computer support professionals). Their first love is probably hacking, and they are quite good at it. Many of the tools script kiddies use are created by these adult hackers.

Adult hackers are not intentional criminals in that they do not intend to harm others. However, the same disrespect for law that makes them hackers makes nearly all of them software and content pirates. Adult hackers often create the "crackz" applied by other hackers to unlock commercial software. This group also writes the majority of the software viruses. These are the hackers who form the notorious hacking cabals.

Adult hackers hack for notoriety in the hacking community—they want to impress their peers with exploits, gain information, and make a statement of defiance against the government or business. These hackers hack for the technical challenge. This group constitutes only about a tenth of the hacking community if that much, but they are the source for the vast majority of the software written specifically for hackers.

The global nature of the Internet means that literally anyone anywhere has access to your Internet-connected machines. In the old days, it cost money or talent to reach out and hack someone. These days, there's no difference between hacking a computer in your neighborhood and one on the other side of the world. The problem is that in many countries, hacking is not a crime because intellectual property isn't strongly protected by law. If you're being hacked from outside your country, you wouldn't be able to bring the perpetrator to justice (even if you found out who it was) unless they also committed some major crime, like grand theft of something besides intellectual property. Underemployed adult hackers are a risk if your company has any sort of intellectual property to protect.

Ideological Hackers

Ideological hackers are those who hack to further some political purpose. In the last three years, ideological hacking has gone from just a few verified cases to a full-blown information war. Ideological hacking is most common in hot political arenas like environmentalism and nationalism.

These hackers take up the standard of their cause and (usually) deface websites or perpetrate **denial-of-service attacks (DoS)** against their ideological enemies. They're usually looking for mass media coverage of their exploits, and because they nearly always come from foreign countries and often have the implicit support of their home government, they are impervious to prosecution and local law.

While they almost never direct their attacks against targets that aren't their enemies, innocent bystanders frequently get caught in the crossfire. Examples of ideological hacking are newspaper and government sites defaced by Palestinian and Israeli hackers (both promulgating their specific agendas to the world) or the hundreds of thousands of IIS web servers exploited by the recent "Code Red" worm originating in China (which defaced websites with a message denigrating the U.S. Government).

This sort of hacking comes in waves whenever major events occur in political arenas. While it's merely a nuisance at this time, in the future these sorts of attacks will consume so much bandwidth that they will cause chaotic "weather-like" packet storms. Ideological hackers are of little risk because they are really only spraying the computer version of graffiti as far and wide as possible.

Criminal Hackers

Criminal hackers hack for revenge, to perpetrate theft, or for the sheer satisfaction of causing damage. This category doesn't bespeak a level of skill so much as an ethical standard. Criminal hackers are the ones you hear about in the paper—those who have compromised Internet servers to steal credit card numbers, performed wire transfers from banks, or hacked the Internet banking mechanism of a bank to steal money.

denial-of-service attack (DoS)
A hacking attack in which the only intended purpose is to crash a computer or otherwise prevent a service from operating.

These hackers are as socially deformed as any real criminal—they are out to get what they can from whomever they can regardless of the cost to the victim. Criminal hackers are exceedingly rare because the intelligence required to hack usually also provides ample opportunity for the individual to find some socially acceptable means of support. Criminal hackers are of little risk to institutions that do not deal in large volumes of computer-based financial transactions.

Corporate Spies

Actual corporate spies are very rare, because it's extremely costly and legally very risky to employ these tactics against competing companies. Who does have the time, money, and interest to use these tactics? Believe it or not, these tactics are usually employed against high technology businesses by foreign governments. Many high technology businesses are young and naive about security, making them ripe for the picking by the experienced intelligence agencies of foreign governments. These agencies already have budgets for spying, and taking on a few medium-sized businesses to extract technology that would give their own national corporations an edge is commonplace.

Nearly all high-level military spy cases involve individuals who have incredible access to information, but as public servants don't make much money. This is a recipe for disaster. Low pay and wide access is probably the worst security breach you could have.

Disgruntled Employees

Disgruntled employees are the most dangerous—and most likely—security problem of all. An employee with an axe to grind has both the means and the motive to do serious damage to your network. These sorts of attacks are difficult to detect before they happen, but some sort of behavioral warning generally precipitates an attack.

Unfortunately, there's very little you can do about a disgruntled employee's ability to damage your network. Attacks range from the complex (a network administrator who spends time reading other people's e-mail) to the simple (a frustrated clerk who takes a fire-axe to your database server).

It's most effective to let all employees know that the IT department audits all user activity for the purpose of security. This prevents problems from starting, since hacking attempts would be a dead giveaway, and since you know the identity of all the users.

Vectors That Hackers Exploit

There are only four ways for a hacker to access your network:

- ◆ By connecting over the Internet
- ◆ By using a computer on your network directly
- ◆ By dialing in via a Remote Access Server (RAS)
- ◆ By connecting via a non-secure wireless network

There are no other possible vectors. This small number of possible vectors defines the boundaries of the security problem quite well, and as the following sections show, makes it possible to contain them even further. The graphic below shows all the vectors that a hacker could potentially use to gain access to a computer.

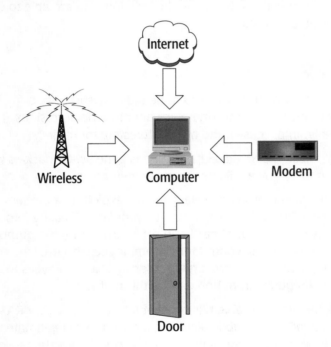

Direct Intrusion

Hackers are notoriously nonchalant and have, on numerous occasions, simply walked into businesses, sat down at a local terminal or network client, and began setting the stage for further remote penetration.

In large companies, there's no way to know everyone by sight, so an unfamiliar worker in the IS department isn't uncommon or suspicious at all. In companies that don't have ID badges or security guards, it isn't anybody's job to check credentials, so penetration is relatively easy. And even in small companies, it's easy to put on a pair of coveralls and pretend to be with a telephone or network wiring company or even pose as the spouse of a fictitious employee. With a simple excuse like telephone problems in the area, access to the server room is granted (oddly, these are nearly always co-located with telephone equipment). If left unattended, a hacker can simply create a new administrative user account. In less than a minute, a small external modem can be attached and configured to answer, without even rebooting your server.

Solving the direct intrusion problem is easy: Employ strong physical security at your premises and treat any cable or connection that leaves the building as a security concern. This means putting firewalls between your WAN links and your internal network, or behind wireless links. By employing your firewalls to monitor any connections that leave the building, you are able to eliminate direct intrusion as a vector.

Dial-Up

Dial-up hacking, via modems, used to be the only sort of hacking that existed but it has quickly fallen to second place after Internet intrusions. (Hacking over the Internet is simply easier and more interesting for hackers.)

This doesn't mean that the dial-up vector has gone away—hackers with a specific target will employ any available means to gain access.

Although the dial-up problem usually means exploiting a modem attached to a Remote Access Server, it also includes the problem of dialing into individual computers. Any modem that has been set to answer for the purpose of allowing remote access or remote control for the employee who uses the computer presents a security concern. Many organizations allow employees to remotely access their computers from home using this method.

Containing the dial-up problem is conceptually easy: Put your RAS servers outside your firewall in the public security zone, and force legitimate users to authenticate with your firewall first to gain access to private network resources. Allow no device to answer a telephone line behind your firewall. This eliminates dial-up as a vector by forcing it to work like any other Internet connection.

Internet

Internet intrusion is the most available, most easily exploited, and most problematic vector of intrusion into your network. This vector is the primary topic of this book. If you follow the advice in this section, the Internet will be the only true vector into your network.

You already know that the Internet vector is solved by using firewalls so there's no point in belaboring the topic here. The remainder of this book is about solving the Internet intrusion vector.

Wireless

Wireless, especially the extremely popular **802.11b** protocol that operates at 11Mbs and is nearly as cheap as standard Ethernet adapters and hubs, has taken root in the corporate world and grown like a weed. Based on the earlier and much less popular 802.11 standard, 802.11b allows administrators to attach **Wireless Access Points (WAPs)** to their network and allow roaming wireless users (usually attached to laptops) to roam the premises without restriction. In another mode, two WAPs can be pointed at one another to form a wireless bridge between buildings, which can save companies tens of thousands of dollars in construction or circuit costs.

802.11b came with much a touted built-in encryption scheme called the **Wired-Equivalent Privacy (WEP)** that promised to allow secure networking with the same security as wired networks. It sounded great. Too bad it took less than 11 hours for security experts to hack it. Nobody paid attention at first, so these same researchers released software that automatically hacked it. WEP is so thoroughly compromised at this point that it should be treated as a non-secure connection from the Internet. All wireless devices should be placed on the public side of your Internet, and users should have to authenticate with your firewall. The newer 128-bit WEP service is more secure, but it should still not be considered actually equivalent to wired security.

This leaves just one remaining problem: theft of service. You can take a laptop down the sidewalks of San Francisco at this very moment and authenticate with any one of over 800 (by a recent count published on Slashdot) of 802.11b networks. While you might be outside the corporate firewall, if you're just looking to browse the web, you're in luck. It's especially lucky if you're a hacker looking to hide your trail behind someone else's IP address.

802.11b
A very popular wireless networking standard that operates at 11Mbps and allows roaming computers to connect to a local area network.

Wireless Access Point (WAP)
An 802.11b wireless network hub.

Wired-Equivalent Privacy (WEP)
A flawed encryption protocol used by the 802.11b wireless networking protocol.

Hacking Techniques

Hacking attacks progress in a series of stages, using various tools and techniques. A hacking session consists of the following stages:

⋄ Target selection

⋄ Information gathering

⋄ Attack

The hacker will attempt to find out more about your network through each successive attack, so the stages above actually feed back into the process as more information is gathered from failed attacks.

Target Selection

Target selection is the stage where a hacker identifies a specific computer to attack. To pass this stage, some vector of attack must be available, so the machine must have either advertised its presence or have been found through some search activity.

DNS Lookup

Hackers who are looking for a specific target use the same method that Internet browsers use to find a host: they look up the domain name using **Domain Name Service (DNS)**. While simple, and technically not qualified as an attack, you can actually defend against this target selection technique by simply not registering public domain names for any hosts except your mail and web servers. Then you've limited your major defense problem to just those servers.

For the interior of your network, use internal DNS servers that are not available to the Internet and which do not perform DNS zone transfers with public DNS servers. This is easily accomplished by registering your ".com" names with your ISP, and using Windows Active Directory or Bind in Unix on an interior server that is not reachable from the Internet to manage your interior names.

Network Address Scanning

Hackers looking for targets of opportunity use a technique called network address **scanning** to find them. The hacker will specify a beginning and ending addresses to scan, and then the hacker's computer program will send an ICMP echo message to each of those network addresses in turn. If a computer answers from any one of those addresses, then the hacker has found another target.

Domain Name Service (DNS)
The host name–to–IP address directory service of the Internet.

scan
A methodical search through a numerical space, such as an address or port range.

Address scans are being performed constantly on the Internet. If you have a computer connected to the public Internet, it's probably being address-scanned at least once per hour.

The best way to foil this kind of attack is to configure machines not to reply to ICMP echos. This prevents hackers from easily determining that your machine exists.

Port Scanning

Once a hacker has selected a target computer, the hacker will attempt to determine which operating system its running and which services it's providing to network clients. On a TCP/IP-based network (such as the Internet), services are provided on numbered connections called **ports**. The ports that a computer responds to often identify the operating system and supported services of the target computer.

There are a number of tools available on the Internet that a hacker can use to determine which ports are responding to network connection requests. These tools try each port in turn and report to the hacker which ports refuse connections and which do not. The hacker can then concentrate on ports corresponding to services that are often left unsecured or that have security problems.

Port scanning can reveal which operating system your computer is running, because each OS has a different set of default services. For example, by scanning the TCP ports between 0 and 150, a hacker can discern Windows hosts (by the presence of port 139 in the scan list), NT hosts (by the presence of port 135 in the list), and various Unix hosts (by the presence of simple TCP/IP services like port 23 (Telnet), which NT and Windows do not install by default. This information tells the hacker which tools to use to further compromise your network.

Port scans are direct evidence that an individual hacker is specifically targeting your network. As such, port scans should be responded to and investigated seriously.

Service Scanning

Internet worms, which are automated hacking attacks that are perpetrated by programs running on an exploited computers rather than by humans, operate by implementing a single attack and then searching for computers that are vulnerable to it. Invariably, this search takes the form of a port scan against just the one port that the attack exploits. Because the worm scans just a single port, it won't show up as either an address scan (because it's not ICMP) or a port scan (because it only hits a single port). In fact, there's no way to tell whether a single service scan is a legitimate connection attempt or a malicious service scan.

port
A parameter of a TCP stream that indicates which process on the remote should receive the data. Public servers listen on "well-known" ports established by convention to monitor specific processes like web or e-mail servers.

33

Typically, the service scan is either followed up by an architecture probe (if the worm is sophisticated) or simply by an attempted service-specific attack like a **buffer overrun**.

Information Gathering

Information gathering is the stage where the hacker determines the characteristics of the target before actually engaging it. This may be through publicly available information published about the target, or by probing the target using non-attack methods to glean information from it.

SNMP Data Gathering

The **Simple Network Management Protocol (SNMP)** is an essential tool for managing large TCP/IP networks. SNMP allows the administrator to remotely query the status of and control the operation of network devices that support SNMP. Unfortunately, hackers can also use SNMP to gather data about a network or interfere with the operation of the network.

Simple Network Management Protocol was designed to automatically provide the configuration details of network devices. As such, "leaky" devices on the public side of your network can provide a wealth of information about the interior of your network.

Nearly every type of network device, from hubs to switches to routers to servers, can be configured to provide SNMP configuration and management information. Interfaces like DSL adapters and cable modems are frequently SNMP configurable, as are many firewalls. Because of the ubiquitous nature of SNMP, it is frequently overlooked on devices that exist outside the public firewall, providing a source of information about your network and the possibility that a device could be remotely managed by a hacker. An example of this is a common brand of **Virtual Private Network (VPN)** controller that must be placed in parallel with a firewall and which exposes its SNMP information to the public interface so that it can be controlled by the service provider. These boxes leak a tremendous amount of information about the interior of your network.

Architecture Probes

Architecture **probes** work by "fingerprinting" the sorts of error messages that computers reply with when problems occur. Rather than attempting to perpetrate an attack, probes merely attempt to coax a response out of a system in order to examine that response; hackers may be able to determine the operating system running on the target machine based on the exact nature of the error message, because each type of operating system responds slightly differently.

buffer overrun
A hacking exploit that sends specifically malformed information to a listening service in order to execute code of the hacker's choice on the target computer, thus paving the way for further exploitation.

Simple Network Management Protocol (SNMP)
A protocol with no inherent security used to query equipment status and modify the configuration of network devices.

probe
An attempt to elicit a response from a host in order to glean information from the host.

Virtual Private Network (VPN)
An encrypted communications channel between two end systems through which other non-secure or non-routable protocols may be tunneled.

34

Hackers examine the responses to bad packet transmissions from a target host using an automated tool that contains a database of known response types. Because no standard response definition exists, each operating system responds in a unique manner. By comparing unique responses to a database of known responses, hackers can often determine which operating system the target host is running.

Assume hackers can determine which operating system your public host is running. Plan your defenses such that you do not rely upon security through obscurity. For example, you shouldn't assume a hacker couldn't tell you're running Windows NT Server on your machine because you've blocked identifying ports. You should still take all security measures to secure an operating system, even if you don't think a hacker knows which operating system it is.

Directory Service Lookups

The **Lightweight Directory Access Protocol (LDAP)** is yet another information-leaking service. By providing LDAP information to the public, which might include valuable clues into the nature of your network and its users, you provide a wealth of information to hackers. Hackers use the LDAP, as well as older directory services like Finger and Whois, to glean information about the systems inside your network and their users.

Sniffing

Sniffing, or collecting all the packets that flow over a network and examining their contents, can be used to determine nearly anything about a network. Sniffing is the computer form of wiretapping. While sniffing can collect encrypted packets, those packets are useless unless the collector has some means of decrypting them.

While sniffing is technically an information-gathering attack, it cannot be performed without either gaining physical access to the network or by having already successfully compromised a computer inside the network. It's not possible to remotely wiretap a connection, except by performing a successful man-in-the-middle attack against it. As such, these exploits are extremely rare.

Attacks

Hackers use a wide variety of attacks against various systems, most of which are custom tailored to exploit a specific network service. This section profiles the most common and most broadly applicable types of hacking attacks. The remainder of this book explains how to defend against them.

Lightweight Directory Access Protocol (LDAP)
A protocol that is used to read, modify, or write information about users, computers, and other resources on a network to a directory service.

---

sniffing
The process of wiretapping and recording information that flows over a network for analytical purposes.

These attacks are profiled in the order of how difficult they are to perpetrate.

Denial of Service

Networked computers implement a specific protocol for transmitting data, and they expect that protocol to transmit meaningful information. When the protocol is implemented incorrectly and the implementation of the protocol doesn't perform sufficient error checking to detect the error, a denial-of-service attack is likely to occur. In some cases, the attacked computer will crash or hang. In other cases, the service being attacked will fail without causing the computer to crash.

Perhaps the most ominous sounding of network layer attacks is the aptly named Ping of Death. A specially constructed ICMP packet that violates the rules for constructing ICMP packets can cause the recipient computer to crash if that computer's networking software does not check for invalid ICMP packets. Most operating systems perform this check, so this specific exploit is no longer effective, but many other service-specific denial-of-service attacks exist and more are being discovered all the time.

Many implementations of DNS, RPC, and WINS are particularly vulnerable to random information being sent to their ports. Some implementations of DNS also crash if they receive a DNS response without having first sent a DNS request.

The more complex a service is, the more likely it is to be subject to a denial-of-service attack. Denial-of-service attacks are the easiest and least useful form of a hacker's attack, and as such, most hackers eschew their use.

Floods

Floods are simple denial-of-service attacks that work by using up scarce resources like network bandwidth or computer processing power.

For example, SYN floods exploit the connection mechanism of TCP. When a TCP/IP session is opened, the requesting client transmits a SYN message to the host's requesting service, and the receiving server responds with a SYN-ACK message accepting the connection. The client then responds with an ACK message, after which traffic can flow over the established bi-directional TCP connection.

When a server receives the initial SYN message, it typically creates a new process thread to handle the client connection requests. This process thread creation requires CPU compute time and allocates a certain amount of memory. By flooding a public server with SYN packets that are never followed by an ACK, hackers can cause public servers to allocate memory and processor time to handle them, thus denying legitimate users those same resources. The practical effect of a SYN flood is that the attacked server becomes very sluggish and legitimate users' connections time out rather than be correctly serviced.

There's a scary future for SYN flood attacks. Since the SYN flood source machine isn't looking for a response, there's no reason why the SYN flood attack software can't simply use randomly generated IP addresses in the source field. This sort of SYN flood could not be discerned from the simple high volume of traffic and would be able to get past SYN flood filters.

Another type of flood attack, more aptly called an avalanche attack, preys on the direct broadcast addressing features of network layer protocols like IP and UDP. This causes an avalanche of responses to broadcast queries that are redirected to a host other than the hacker.

A simple avalanche attack proceeds by flooding a victim's host with ICMP echo request (ping) packets that have the reply address set to the broadcast address of the victim's network. This causes all the hosts in the network to reply to the ICMP echo request, thereby generating even more traffic—typically one to two orders of magnitude more traffic than the initial ping flood.

A more complex avalanche attack proceeds as above but with the source IP address of the echo request changed to the address of a third-party victim, which receives all the echo responses generated by the targeted subnet of hosts. This attack is useful to hackers because they can use a relatively slow link, like a modem, to cause an avalanche of ping traffic to be sent to any location on the Internet. In this way, a hacker with a slower link to the Internet than his ultimate victim can still flood the ultimate victim's pipe by avalanching a higher speed network.

Forged E-mail

Hackers can create e-mail that appears to be coming from anyone they want. In a variation of this attack, they can spoof the reply-to address as well, making the forgery undetectable.

Using a technique as simple as configuring an e-mail client with incorrect information, hackers can forge an e-mail address to an internal client. By claiming to be from someone the client knows and trusts, this e-mail uses a psychological attack to induce the reader to return useful information, including an installable **Trojan horse** or a link to a malicious website. This is the easiest way to gain access to a specific targeted network

Internet e-mail does not authenticate the identity of a sender, and many versions of e-mail programs do not log enough information to properly track the source of an e-mail message. By simply signing up for a hosted e-mail account with a false identity, a hacker can deftly hide their identity, even if the e-mail can be traced to its source.

Trojan horse
A program that is surreptitiously installed on a computer for the purpose of providing access to a hacker.

The only feasible defense against e-mail forgery (getting everyone in the world to use public key encryption for all e-mail is infeasible) is user awareness; make sure your users understand that e-mail forgery is possible and constitutes a likely attack mechanism in well-defended networks.

Most popular e-mail clients allow the installation of personal encryption certificate keys to sign e-mail from all internal users. All unsigned e-mail should be considered potentially suspect. Filter executable attachments, such as .exe, .cmd, and .bat files, out of e-mail at the firewall.

Automated Password Guessing

Once a hacker has identified a host and found an exploitable user account or services like **NetBIOS**, Telnet, or **Network File System (NFS)**, a successful password guess will provide control of the machine.

Most services are protected with an account name and password combination as their last line of defense. When a hacker finds an exploitable service running on a target machine, the hacker must still provide a valid account name and password in order to log in.

Automated password guessing software uses lists of common passwords, names, and words from the dictionary to attempt to guess high-profile or important account names, such as the root user password on Unix systems or the Administrator account in NT systems. The software typically takes a list of account names and a list of possible passwords and simply tries each account name with each password.

Hackers are using new "common password" lists to make these attacks faster. These lists are derived from the statistical analysis of stolen account information from exploited servers. By combining lists of stolen passwords and analyzing the lists for password frequency, hackers have created lists of passwords in order of how commonly they are used. This means that if any accounts on your network have relatively common passwords, hackers will get in, and quickly. I've used these lists to gain administrative access to servers in as little as 11 seconds over the Internet.

Trojan Horses

Trojan horses are programs that are surreptitiously installed on a target system either directly by a hacker, by a computer virus or worm, or by an unsuspecting user. Once installed, the Trojan horse either returns information to the hacker or provides direct access to the computer.

NetBIOS

Network Basic Input Output System. An older network file- and print-sharing service developed by IBM and adopted by Microsoft for use in Windows.

Network File System (NFS)

A widely supported Unix file system.

38

The most useful sorts of Trojan horses are called backdoors. These programs provide a mechanism whereby the hacker can control the machine directly. Examples include maliciously designed programs like NetBus, Back Orifice, and BO2K, as well as benign programs that can be exploited to give control of a system, like netcat, VNC, and pcAnywhere. Ideal backdoors are small and quickly installable, and they run transparently.

Trojan horses are usually carried by e-mail–borne viruses or sent as attachments to e-mail.

Buffer Overruns

Buffer overruns are a class of attacks that exploit a specific weakness common in software. Buffer overruns exploit the fact that most software allocates blocks of memory in fixed-size chunks to create a scratchpad area called a *buffer*, within which it processes inbound network information. Often these buffers are programmed to a fixed maximum size, or they are programmed to trust the message to correctly indicate its size.

Buffer overruns are caused when a message lies about its size or is deliberately longer than the allowed maximum length. For example, if a message says it's 240 bytes long, but it's actually 256 bytes long, the receiving service may allocate a buffer only 240 bytes long but then copy 256 bytes of information into that buffer. The 16 bytes of memory beyond the end of the buffer will be overwritten with whatever the last 16 bytes of the message contains. Hackers exploit these problems by including machine language code in the section of the message that is past the buffer end. Even more disturbing is the fact that software is often written in such a way that code execution begins after the end of the buffer location, thus allowing hackers to execute code in the security context of the running service.

By writing a short exploit to open a further security hole and postfixing that code to the buffer payload, hackers can gain control of the system.

New buffer-overrun attacks are found all the time. IIS has been hit with so many new buffer overrun attacks in 2001 that many corporations are moving away from it as a service platform. Automated worms that exploit common IIS buffer overruns have swamped the Net with scanning and copying activity as they search for victims and propagate.

Buffer overrun attacks are the most serious hacking threat at the moment and are likely to remain so for quite some time. Defend against them on public servers by staying up-to-date on the latest security bulletins for your operating system, or by using security proxies that can drop suspicious or malformed connections before they reach your server.

Source Routing

The TCP/IP protocol suite includes a little-used option for specifying the exact route a packet should take as it crosses a TCP/IP-based network (such as the Internet). This option is called **source routing**, and it allows a hacker to send data from one computer and make it look like it came from another (usually more trusted) computer. Source routing is a useful tool for diagnosing network failures and circumventing network problems, but it is too easily exploited by hackers and so you should not use it in your TCP/IP network. Configure your firewalls to drop all source-routed TCP/IP packets from the Internet.

The hacker can use source routing to impersonate a user who is already connected and inject additional information into an otherwise benign communication between a server and the authorized client computer. For example, a hacker might detect that an administrator has logged on to a server from a client computer. If that administrator is at a command prompt, the hacker could inject a packet into the communications stream that appears to come from the administrator and tells the server to execute the change password command; locking out the administrator account and letting the hacker in.

The hacker also might use source routing to impersonate a trusted computer and write DNS updates to your DNS server. This allows the redirecting of the network clients that rely on the DNS server to translate Internet names into IP addresses so that the client computers go instead to a hostile server under the control of the hacker. The hacker could then use the hostile server to capture passwords.

Session Hijacking

Hackers can sometimes **hijack** an already established and authenticated networking connection.

In order to hijack an existing TCP connection, a hacker must be able to predict TCP sequence numbers, which the two communicating computers use to keep IP packets in order and to ensure that they all arrive at the destination. This isn't necessarily as difficult as it might seem because most current TCP/IP implementations use flawed pseudorandom number generators (explained in Chapter 3) that generate somewhat predictable sequence numbers.

The hacker must also be able to redirect the TCP/IP connection to the hacker computer and launch a denial-of-service attack against the client computer, so that the client computer does not indicate to the server computer that something is wrong. In order to hijack an SMB session (such as a drive mapping to a NetBIOS share), the hacker must also be able to predict the correct NetBIOS

source routing
A test mechanism allowed by the IP protocol that allows the sender to specify the route that a packet should take through a network, rather than rely upon the routing tables built into intermediate routers.

hijack
A complex attack that subsumes an existing authenticated connection between two hosts, thereby allowing a hacker to assume the credentials of the account used to establish the connection.

Frame ID, Tree ID, and the correct user ID at the server level of an existing Net-BIOS communications link.

While an exploit of this nature is theoretically possible, tools for hijacking SMB connections are not readily available to the garden-variety hacker (as opposed to TCP hijacking tools, which can be downloaded from the Internet). A properly secured Internet site will not expose NetBIOS to the Internet anyway, however.

Man-in-the-Middle Attacks

Man-in-the-middle attacks are rare and difficult to perpetrate, but extraordinarily effective when they work. In a man-in-the-middle attack, the hacker operates between one computer and another on your network, or between a client computer on the Internet or other WAN network and your server computer in your secure LAN. When the client computer opens a connection to the server computer, the hacker's computer intercepts it through some means, perhaps via a DNS or DHCP impersonation attack, by rerouting the IP traffic from the client to a compromised computer, or perhaps by ARP redirecting an Ethernet switch. The hacker computer opens a connection to the server computer on the behalf of the client computer. Ideally (from the hacker's point of view), the client will think it is communicating with the server, and the server will think it is communicating with the client, and the hacker computer in the middle will be able to observe all of the communications between the client and the server and make changes to the communicated data.

Depending on the nature of the communications, the hacker computer may be able to use a man-in-the-middle attack to gain greater access to your network. For example, if the connection is an Administrator-level telnet into a server from a client computer, the hacker computer in the middle could (after passing through the log-on credentials to gain entry to the server) download the password file from the server to the hacker's computer. On an insecure network such as the Internet, it is difficult to defend against a man-in-the-middle attack. Fortunately, it is also difficult to construct a successful man-in-the-middle attack. The measures you take to protect your network against data gathering, denial-of-service, and impersonation will help protect you from a man-in-the-middle attack. Nevertheless, you should never connect to your network using an administrative account over an insecure network.

You can use encryption to create secure communications links over a TCP/IP network and you can use third-party authentication packages to ensure that your client computers are communicating directly with a trusted host computer (and vice versa.)

man-in-the-middle
Any of a broad range of attacks where an attacking computer redirects connections from a client through itself and then to the ultimate server, acting transparently to monitor and change the communication between the destinations.

Review Questions

Terms to Know
- ❏ 802.11b
- ❏ buffer overrun
- ❏ denial of service (DoS)
- ❏ Domain Name Service (DNS)
- ❏ floods
- ❏ hijack
- ❏ Lightweight Directory Access Protocol (LDAP)
- ❏ NetBIOS
- ❏ Network File System (NFS)
- ❏ man-in-the-middle
- ❏ port

1. What is the most common type of hacker?

2. Which type of hacker represents the most likely risk to your network?

3. What is the most damaging type of hacker?

4. What four methods can hackers use to connect to a network?

5. What is the most common vector used by hackers use to connect to networks?

6. What are the three phases of a hacking session?

7. What method would a hacker use to find random targets?

8. What type of target selection indicates that a hacker has specifically targeted your systems for attack?

9. Which method of target selection attack is employed by worms to find targets?

10. What activity does sniffing refer to?

_____

11. What is the simplest type of attack a hacker can perpetrate?

_____

12. What security mechanisms are implemented by e-mail to prevent forgery?

_____

13. What would a hacker use a Trojan horse for?

_____

14. Currently, what is the most serious hacking threat?

_____

Terms to Know
- ❑ probe
- ❑ scan
- ❑ scanning
- ❑ script kiddies
- ❑ Simple Network Management Protocol (SNMP)
- ❑ sniffing
- ❑ source routing
- ❑ Trojan horse
- ❑ Virtual Private Network (VPN)
- ❑ Wireless Access Point (WAP)
- ❑ Wired-Equivalent Privacy (WEP)

Chapter

3

Encryption and Authentication

Nearly all modern security mechanisms are based on keeping secrets private to certain individuals. Security systems use **encryption** to keep secrets, and they use **authentication** to prove the identity of individuals. These two basic security mechanisms are the foundation upon which nearly all security mechanisms are based.

In this chapter, you will learn about:

 Secret key encryption

 Hashes and one-way functions

 Public key encryption

 Password authentication

 Challenge/response authentication

 Sessions

 Public key authentication

 Digital signatures

 Certificates

 Biometric authentication

Encryption

The primary purpose of encryption is to keep secrets. It has other uses, but encryption was first used to protect messages so that only the person knowing the trick to decoding a message could read the message. Today, encryption allows computers to keep secrets by transforming data to an unintelligible form using a mathematical function.

Just like simple arithmetics, encryption functions take the message and the encryption key and produce an encrypted result. Without knowing the **secret key**, the result makes no sense.

For example, let's say I need to hide the combination to a lock. In this case, the combination (also called the *message*) is 9-19-69. To keep things simple, I'm going to add (adding is the "**algorithm**") 25 (which is the key) to each of the numbers to produce the encrypted value: 34-44-94. I can post this value right on the combination lock so I won't forget it, because that number won't do anyone who doesn't know how to use it any good. I just need to remember the algorithm and the key: subtract 25. The encrypted text is nearly worthless without the key. I can also simply tell my friends what the key and the algorithm are, and they can combine that knowledge with the encrypted data to decode the original combination.

You may have noticed that in this example we used the opposite mathematical operation to decode the encrypted text; we added 25 to encode and subtracted 25 to decode. Simple arithmetic algorithms are called **symmetrical algorithms** because the algorithm used to encode can be reversed in order to decode the data. Since most mathematical operations can be easily reversed, symmetrical algorithms are common.

Although this example may seem simplistic, it is exactly what happens with modern secret-key **cryptosystems**. The only differences are in the complexity of the algorithm and the length of the key. This example, despite its simplicity, shows exactly how all symmetric encryption systems work. Here is another example, using a slightly more complex key. Notice how the key is repeated as many times as necessary to encode the entire message.

authentication
The process of determining a user's identity in order to allow access.

encryption
The process of encoding a plain text message so that it cannot be understood by intermediate parties who do know the key to decrypt it.

secret key
A key which must be kept secret by all parties because it can be used to both encrypt and decrypt messages.

algorithm
A method expressed in a mathematical form (such as computer code) for performing a specific function or operation.

symmetrical algorithm
An algorithm which uses the same secret key for encryption as for decryption.

cryptosystem
A computing system that implements one or more specific encryption algorithms.

ENCRYPT

| D | E | A | R | | D | I | A | R | Y | , | | I | T | ' | S | | B | E | E |
+ | S | E | C | R | E | T | C | O | D | E | S | E | C | R | E | T | C | O | D | E |

| W | J | D | J | E | X | M | P | V | D | S | E | L | W | E | M | C | Q | I | J |

DECRYPT

| W | J | D | J | E | X | M | P | V | D | S | E | L | W | E | M | C | Q | I | J |
− | S | E | C | R | E | T | C | O | D | E | S | E | C | R | E | T | C | O | D | E |

| D | E | A | R | | D | I | A | R | Y | , | | I | T | ' | S | | B | E | E |

The most common use for encryption with computers is to protect communications between users and communications devices. This use of encryption is an extension of the role codes and **ciphers** have played throughout history. The only difference is that, instead of a human being laboriously converting messages to and from an encoded form, the computer does all the hard work.

Encryption isn't just for communication. It can also be used to protect data in storage, such as data on a hard drive. Most modern operating systems like Unix or Windows are configured to allow only authorized users to access files while the operating system is running, but when you turn your computer off, all those security features go away and your data is left defenseless. An intruder could load another operating system on the computer or even remove the hard drive and place it in another computer that does not respect the security settings of the original computer, and your data would be accessible. Encryption solves this problem by ensuring that the data is unintelligible if the correct key isn't provided, irrespective of whether the computer is still running in order to protect the data.

Secret Key Encryption

Our example in the last section was an example of **secret key encryption**. In secret key encryption, the same key is used to both encode and decode the message, so it is said to be symmetrical—because both keys are the same. Secret key encryption requires that both parties know the algorithm and the key in order to decode the message. Until the development of **public key encryption** by cryptographers in the 1970's, secret key encryption was the only type of encryption available.

Secret key encryption works well for keeping secrets, but both parties have to know the same secret key in order to decode the message. There's no secure way to transfer the key from one party to the other without going to extraordinary lengths, like having both parties meet in the same secluded area to exchange keys. There's certainly no way to exchange keys over an electronic medium without the possibility of a wiretap intercepting the key.

One-Way Functions (Hashes)

Hashes are used to verify the correctness of information, and are based on mathematical algorithms called one-way functions. Some mathematical functions cannot be reversed to retrieve the original number. For example, let's say that we're going to divide 46835345 by 26585. This results in 1761 with a remainder of 19160. So let's say that we have an algorithm that simply returns the remainder (19160) and discards the quotient (1761). Now, if we have just the remainder

cipher
Data that has been encrypted.

secret key encryption
Encryption by means of a secret key.

public key encryption
Encryption by means of a public key; an encryption methodology that allows the distribution of an encryption key which does not compromise the secrecy of the decrypting private key, due to the utilization of a related pair of one-way functions.

(called a modulus) and one of the original numbers, there's no way to reconstruct the other operand because the quotient has been discarded. The remainder alone does not retain enough information to reconstruct the original number.

The illustration below shows an extremely simple hash. In this algorithm, two numbers are added, and if the result is even, a binary "1" is the result. If the result is odd, a "0" is the result. The combination of binary digits forms the hash. Because the actual numbers are lost, the hash cannot be reconstructed, but it can be used to determine with reasonable certainty whether or not two plaintexts match. Simple hashes are often called *checksums*. This hashing algorithm is not appropriate for security because there are many other plaintexts that will produce the same result, so the probability of an accidental match is too risky.

one-way function
An algorithm that has no reciprocal function and cannot therefore be reversed in order to discover the data originally encoded.

HASH

D	E	A	R		D	I	A	R	Y	,		I	T	'	S		B	E	E
S	E	C	R	E	T	C	O	D	E	S	E	C	R	E	T	C	O	D	E

?

| 0 | 1 | 1 | 1 | 0 | 1 | 0 | 1 | 1 | 1 | 0 | 0 | 1 | 0 | 0 | 0 | 0 | 0 | 0 | 1 | = | 482433 |

DECODE

0	1	1	1	0	1	0	1	1	1	0	0	1	0	0	0	0	0	0	1
S	E	C	R	E	T	C	O	D	E	S	E	C	R	E	T	C	O	D	E

¿

| A | B | B | B | A | B | A | B | B | B | A | A | B | A | A | A | A | A | A | B |

Of course, since we can't reconstruct the original number, we can't use **one-way functions** to encode and decode information. But we can use them to be certain that two people know the same number without revealing what that number is. If two people were aware of the original dividend (46835345) in the above scenario, and you told them to divide the number they knew by 26585, discard the whole product, and tell you the remainder, they would both report 19160—thus proving that they knew the same original number or that they were amazingly lucky, because there is only a 1 in 26585 chance that they could have guessed the correct remainder. By simply making the number large enough that the odds of guessing the correct remainder are just as high as guessing the correct operand in the first place, you can use this one-way nonreversible function to prove that two parties know a number without ever revealing what that number actually is to anyone who might overhear you.

For example, let's say a system requires logon authentication, where a user provides their name and password in order to use a system. They could simply enter their name and password and the computer could check that against a list of stored passwords. If the passwords matched, the user would be allowed in.

But let's say that hackers gained access to the computer. They could steal the list and then have everyone's password. Once other people know a user's password, you can no longer hold that user accountable for their actions since you can't guarantee that they actually performed those actions on a system.

We can't use secret key encryption to encrypt the password file because the secret key would need to be stored on the system in order for the system to decode the password file. Since we've already stipulated that hackers have access to the system, they would also have access to the secret key and could use that to decrypt the password file.

This is a situation where one-way functions work well. Rather than storing the user's **password**, we can store a **hash**, or the result of a one-way function, instead. Then, when they enter their password, we perform the one-way function on the data they entered and compare it to the hash that's stored on disk. Since only the hash is stored, and the hashing algorithm can't be reversed to find the original password, hacker's can't compromise the authentication system by stealing this list of password hashes.

Hashes allow a user to prove that they know the password without the system having to know what the password actually is. Protecting passwords is the most common use for using hashing algorithms in computer security.

Public Key Encryption

While symmetric ciphers like secret key algorithms use the same key to encrypt and decrypt messages, public key encryption uses a different key to decrypt than was used to encrypt; so they are called **asymmetric algorithms**. In a public key encryption system, the encryption key is called the public key because it can be made public. The decryption key is called the **private key** because it must be kept private in order to remain secure.

The problem with secret key encryption is this: Both the sender and the recipient must have the same key in order to exchange encrypted messages over an insecure medium. If two parties decide to exchange private messages, or if two computers' network devices or programs must establish a secure channel, the two parties must decide on a common key. Either party may simply decide on a key, but that party will have no way to send it to the other without the risk of it being intercepted on its way. It's a chicken-and-egg problem: Without a secure channel, there is no way to establish a secure channel.

With public key encryption, the receiver can send a public encryption key to the sender. There is no need to keep the **public key** a secret because it can only be used to encode messages, not decode them. You can publish your public key to the world for anyone to use for encoding message they send to you.

password
A secret key that is remembered by humans.

hash
The result of applying a one-way function to a value.

asymmetrical algorithm
A mathematical function which has no reciprocal function.

private key
A secretly held key for an asymmetrical encryption algorithm that can only be used to decode messages or encode digital signatures.

public key
A publicly distributed key for an asymmetrical encryption algorithm, which can only be used to encode messages or decode digital signatures.

When the receiver gets a message that has been encoded with their public key, they can use their private key to decode the message. Revealing their public key to the world for encoding does not allow anyone else to decode their private messages.

Public key cryptography is a relatively new development in **cryptography**, one that solves many long-standing problems with cryptographic systems—especially the chicken-and-egg conundrum of how to exchange secret keys. In 1976, Witfield Diffie and Martin Hellman figured out a way out of the secure channel dilemma. They found that some one-way functions could be undone by using a different decryption key than was used for encryption. Their solution (called public key cryptography) takes advantage of a characteristic of prime and almost prime numbers: specifically, how hard it is to find the two factors of a large number that has only two factors, both of which are prime. Since Diffie and Hellman developed their system, some other public key ciphers have been introduced using even more difficult one-way functions.

One problem that plagues secure public key ciphers is that they are slow—much slower than symmetric ciphers. You can expect a good public key cipher to take 1,000 times as long to encrypt the same amount of data as a good symmetric cipher would take. This can be quite a drag on your computer's performance if you have a lot of data to transmit or receive.

Hybrid Cryptosystems

Although it is much slower than symmetric systems, the public key-private key system neatly solves the problem that bedevils symmetric cryptosystems—exchanging secret keys.

But there's no need to give up the speed of secret key cryptosystems just because secret keys can't be exchanged securely. **Hybrid cryptosystems** use public key encryption to exchange secret keys, and then use the secret keys to establish a communication channel. Nearly all modern cryptosystems work this way.

When two people (or devices) need to establish a secure channel for communication, one of them can generate a random secret key and then encrypt that secret key using the receiver's public key. The encrypted key is then sent to the receiver. Even if the key is intercepted, only the intended recipient can decrypt the message containing the secret key, using their private key.

Once both parties have the secret key, they can begin using a much faster secret key cryptosystem to exchange secret messages.

Authentication

Authentication is used to verify the identity of users in order to control access to resources, to prevent unauthorized users from gaining access to the system, and to record the activities of users in order to hold them accountable for their activities.

It's used to authenticate users logging on to computers, it's used to ensure that software you download from the Internet comes from a reputable source, and it's used to ensure that the person who sends a message is really who they say they are.

Password Authentication

Passwords are the oldest and simplest form of authentication—they've been used since time immemorial to prove that an individual should be given access to some resource. Technically, passwords are secret keys.

Password authentication is simple: by knowing a secret key, an individual proves that the individual who invented the secret trusted them with that secret key, and that the trust should bestowed upon them. This sort of password authentication proves only that access to a resource should be allowed—it does not prove identity.

To prove identity, a password must be unique to a specific person. In secure computer systems, this is accomplished by creating user accounts, which are assigned to individuals. The account contains information about who the owner is, and includes a unique account name and password.

When a user logs on to the system, they simply type in their account name to assert their identity, and then they provide the password associated with that user account to prove that they are allowed to use that account. If the entered password matches the stored password, the user is allowed access to the system.

Password authentication can fail in a number of ways:

- ◇ There's no way to control password distribution. If the account holder looses control of the password, it can be distributed to anyone. Once a password has been compromised, password authentication can no longer be used to prove identity.

- ◇ Passwords are often simple and easy to guess, and many systems limit passwords to lengths that lend themselves to **brute-force** guessing. This can lead to password compromise and is one of the most common ways that hackers gain access to systems.

- ◇ Naïve implementations may not protect the password in transit or may be compromised through simple techniques like **replay**.

brute-force attack
An attack where every possible combination of values is tried in sequence against a password system. Given an unlimited amount of time, these attacks will always succeed, but they are impractical against long passwords, which could require more time than the age of the universe to crack.

replay attack
An attack in which a secret value like a hash is captured and then reused at a later time to gain access to a system without ever decrypting or decoding the hash. Replay attacks only work against systems that don't uniquely encrypt hashes for each session.

5I

Despite the common failure of password based systems to actually prove identity and restrict access, they are the most common way to secure computers by a wide margin.

Password Hashing

In order to prevent hackers from capturing your password from your computer's hard disk or while it transits the network, passwords can be encrypted using a one-way function or hashing algorithm to keep the password from being revealed.

In most modern operating systems, the operating system does not compare your password to a stored password. Instead, it encrypts your password using a one-way cryptographic function, and then compares the result to the original result that was stored when you created your password. Since the hashing function is one-way, it cannot be reversed to decrypt your password.

However, password hashing is susceptible to brute-force indexed decryption. Using this technique, hackers create a "dictionary" of all possible passwords by encrypting every possible password (i.e., AAAAAA through ZZZZZZ in a system limited to six letters) using the same hashing function as the password system and storing the results in a database along with the original text. Then, by capturing your hash, they can look up the matching value in their database of hashed values and find the original password. Although compiling this sort of dictionary can take a long time for a single computer, it is the sort of problem that could be easily distributed over a network of computers (like the Internet) to speed up completion. Once finished, the hashing algorithm would be all but worthless for encrypting passwords and a new algorithm would be required to maintain password security.

Challenge/Response Authentication

One-way hashes are great for preventing password lists from being exploited, but they can't be used securely over a network. The problem is that a hacker might be wiretapping or "sniffing" the network connection between the two computers, and could intercept the hashed password and "replay" it later to gain access. This is actually a very common problem that can occur whether or not the password has been hashed. A large number of older TCP/IP protocols like FTP and telnet are susceptible to sniffing and replay attacks.

Challenge/response authentication defeats replay by encrypting the hashed password using secret key encryption. A challenge and response authentication session works like this:

1. The client requests a connection.

2. The server sends a random secret key to the client.

3. The client encrypts the random secret key using a hashed password and transmits the result to the server.

4. The server decrypts the secret using the stored hashed password and compares it to the original secret key to decide whether to accept the logon.

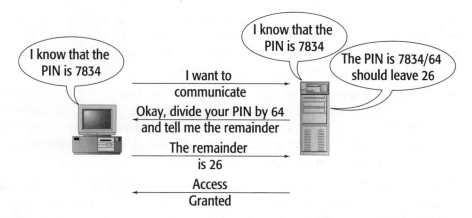

This system works because the password is never transmitted over the network, even in hashed form; only a random number and an encrypted random number are sent, and no amount of cryptographic work can be used to decrypt the encrypted random number because all possible results are equally likely.

Challenge and response authentication can also be used to defeat a brute-force indexed hash decryption as well—as long as the hacker's computer isn't the one you're trying to gain access to. If it is, the hacker can decrypt your hash because they sent you the secret key that you encrypted. By decrypting the secret key, they have your hash and can then compare it to their database of encrypted hashes. For this reason, it's imperative that you never log on to a hacker's system using your system's encrypted hash.

WARNING

Internet Explorer will automatically hand over an encrypted hash of your Windows logon account name and password to any website that asks for it—behind the scenes and without asking for your permission. This means that by attracting you to a website, hackers could steal your account name and password for your local system. This is one of the many esoteric security flaws that Microsoft has committed in the name of ease of use.

Session Authentication

Sessions are used to ensure that, once authentication has occurred, further communications between the parties can be trusted—in other words, that others cannot hijack the connection by forging packets. The authentication that occurs at the beginning of the session can be reliably carried forward throughout the remainder of the packet stream until both parties agree to end the session.

As you know, all modern networking systems are packet based. Packets transmitted from one computer to the next are reconstructed into a communication stream by putting them back in their original order using a special number embedded in each packet called a sequence number.

Sequence numbers are exactly that—a number that indicates which packet in the stream a specific packet represents. Sequence numbers could be simple serial numbers, like 1, 2, 3, 4, etc. Unfortunately, that would be too easy to predict, and a hacker could insert the fifth packet in a stream by simply inserting it into the communication with a sequence number of 5.

To prevent sequence number prediction, sequence numbers are not sequentially generated; they're generated using a special function called a **pseudorandom number generator** or PRNG, that can reliably create the same sequence of random numbers given a known **seed** number.

> **NOTE**
>
> Computers are very good at performing the same calculations reliably every time. But the property of reliability makes them terrible at generating random numbers. To generate truly random numbers, computers require some real-world external input. But computers can generate numbers that seem to be random—**pseudorandom numbers**.

Pseudorandom numbers have all of the same properties as random numbers, like even distribution in a set, no predictable recurrences, and so forth but they're not truly random because they use the same PRNG algorithm to generate numbers from the same starting number (or seed); hence the exact same series of pseudorandom numbers will be generated every time.

For example, consider the number pi. As we all know, it starts with 3.1415926… and goes on ad infinitum. There is no known sequence to the numbers in pi, and the numbers in the series seem to be completely random one to the next. So, if an algorithm can calculate a specific digit in pi (let's call the function pi, so that pi(473) would give you the 473rd number in pi), the number pi(n+1) is completely random compared to pi(n). We can generate seemingly random numbers by simply starting at pi(1) and sequencing through the algorithm. This is exactly

---

session
An authenticated stream of related packets.

Pseudorandom Number Generator (PRNG)
An algorithm that generates pseusdorandom numbers.

seed
The starting point for a specific set of pseudorandom numbers for a specific PRNG.

pseudorandom number
A member of a set of numbers which has all the same properties as a similarly sized set of truly random numbers, like even distribution in a set, no predictable reoccurrences, and incompressibility, but which occur in a predictable order from a given starting point (seed).

how pseudorandom number generators work. In fact, a number of them are based on calculating pi or the square root of 2 or other such irrational numbers. In this example, *n*, or the location in the series, is the seed.

NOTE

PRNGs are terrible for games, because games would play the exact same way each time given the same user input and the same starting number, but they're great for the specific purpose of generating session sequence numbers.

If a hacker does not know the seed number for a PRNG, the pseudorandom numbers in a sequence are, for all intents and purposes, completely random and unpredictable. But if a remote computer does know the seed, then the series of pseudorandom numbers is as predictable a sequence as 1, 2, and 3. This is how sessions pass authentication from one packet to the next. By starting the sequence with a known encrypted seed number, every packet following in the session with the correct sequence number is known to have a chain of authentication back to the securely transmitted and authenticated seed number.

Public Key Authentication

To use public **key** cryptography for authentication, the system administrator can install a user's public key on the system. For a user to gain access, the system sends a random number to the user, who then encrypts the number using their private key. This number is then sent to the remote system. If the system can decrypt the number using the stored public key and the result is the same random number that was originally provided, then the user has proven that she has the private key. This proves that the administrator installed the corresponding public key, and that the user should therefore be granted access to the system.

Public key authentication is often used when authentication should be performed automatically without user intervention. The systems involved can trade public keys and authentication information without the user interacting with the system. For this reason, public key–based authentication and its derivatives like **certificate**-based authentication are frequently used for machine authentication and for establishing anonymous encrypted sessions like SSL.

Certificate-Based Authentication

Certificates are simply **digital signatures** that have themselves been "signed" using the digital signature of some trusted authority, thus creating a "chain" of authentication.

key
A secret value used to encrypt information.

public key authentication
Authentication by means of a digital signature.

certificate
A digital signature that has been digitally signed by one or more trusted authorities.

digital signature
Any identity information encrypted with a private key and therefore decryptable—with a public key. Digital signatures are used to prove the validity of publicly available documents by proving that they were encrypted with a specific secretly held private key.

Digital signatures are used to prove that a specific piece of information came from a certain individual or other legal entity. Digital signatures do this by performing public key encryption in reverse—that is, the document is encrypted using the private key (which cannot be encrypted by any other key) and decrypted by anyone using the sender's public key.

Because everyone can have the sender's public key, the encrypted information cannot be considered secure or secret, but it can be trusted as authentic because only the person holding the original private key could possibly have created the digital signature.

Typically, a digital signature contains identity information that is easily recognizable, such as the signer's name, physical address, and other easily verifiable information, along with a hash of the entire document which can be used to prove that the signed document has not been modified. If a document has been modified, the hash inside the encrypted signature (which cannot be modified) would not match a new hashing of the document during the authentication process.

The signature is usually appended to the end of the document and appears as a series of hexadecimal or ASCII text. When a document has been hashed and has a digital signature attached to it, it is said to have been "digitally signed."

Certificates are useful when you want to allow wide access to a system by means of distributed authenticators. For example, the government could set up a system whereby public notaries are given digital certificates created by the government. Then, when a member of the public at large wanted a certificate that could be used to prove their identity, they could go to a notary public, prove their identity, and have that notary generate a certificate for them. Because that certificate contains a digital signature that can be proven to have come from a notary, which in turn contains a digital signature that can be proven to have come from a government body, then anyone who trusts the government body to verify identity can trust that the person using the certificate is who they say they are.

In a certificate hierarchy, the ultimate authority is called the **Root Certifying Authority** or **Root CA**. Users of the system simply have to trust that the Root CA is a legitimate body. Currently, the vast majority of "rooted" certificates come from a single company, VeriSign, or it's subsidiary, Thawte. Entrust is another large Root CA.

Certificates can be used for Authentication in the same way that digital signatures can, but authentication systems can be configured to allow access based on higher level certificates. For example, if your company received a single certificate from a Root CA, the system administrator could use it to generate unique certificates for each department. The department administrators could then generate unique certificates for each user. Then, when you needed to access a

Root Certifying Authority

An organization that exists simply to be trusted by participants in order to provide transitive trust. Root CAs certify the identities of all members, so that members who trust the Root CA can trust anyone that they've certified. Root CAs are analogous to Public Notaries.

56

resource, the resource server could use the certificate to verify your identity (or the identity of the department that signed your certificate or the company that you work for).If the resource server only cared that you worked for the company, the company signature in your certificate would be the only data that it checked.

Biometric Authentication

Biometric authentication uses physical sensors to detect patterns that uniquely identify a person, such as facial features, fingerprints, handprints, vocal characteristics, blood vessels in the eye, or DNA. These patterns are applied through a hashing algorithm to come up with a hash value that is invariant (in other words, a secret key) which can be matched to a stored value on a server.

Biometric scanning devices can range from simple to complex:

- ◇ Microphone (vocal characteristics)
- ◇ Optical scanner (fingerprint, handprint)
- ◇ Electrostatic grid (fingerprint, handprint)
- ◇ Digital Video Camera (facial features, retinal pattern)
- ◇ Di-Ribonucleic Acid Sequencer (DNA)

Currently, low cost (<$150) fingerprint scanners are popular choices for biometric authentication, but I think they will probably be supplanted by voiceprint recognition because most computers already contain the hardware necessary to perform voiceprint authentication. Voiceprint sensors can also be sensitive enough to fail when stress is detected in the user's voice (such as when they're being coerced into providing access to a system).

Usually, biometric authentication devices use a challenge/response mechanism to ensure that the hashed value never leaves the sensor, because it could be captured in transit and "replayed" to foil the authentication system. Because biometric "scans" are never exactly the same twice and must be hashed to generate the key, the system can store a copy of each authentication (or a separate type of hash that is unique) to record a "history" of logins, which can be compared to new attempts to ensure that they are unique and not replays.

An example of a replay attack against a biometric algorithm would be the recording and playback of a person's **pass phrase**. Without replay detection, there would be no way for the sensing algorithm to determine that a recording (and not the authorized user's actual voice) was being used to gain access to the system.

biometric authentication
Authentication by means of invariant and unique biological characteristics such as fingerprints or DNA.

pass phrase
A very long password consisting of multiple words.

Review Questions

1. What is the primary purpose of encryption?

2. Secret key encryption is said to be "symmetrical." Why?

3. What is a hash?

4. What is the most common use for hashing algorithms?

5. What is the difference between public key encryption and secret key encryption?

6. What long-standing security problem does public key encryption solve?

7. What is the major problem with public key encryption when compared to secret key encryption?

8. What is a hybrid cryptosystem?

9. What is authentication used for?

10. What hacking attack is challenge/response authentication used to prevent?

_____

11. How are sessions kept secure against hijacking?

_____

12. What is the difference between a random number and a pseudorandom number?

_____

13. What is a digital signature?

_____

14. What is the difference between a certificate and a digital signature?

_____

15. What sort of characteristics are typically used for biometric authentication?

_____

Terms to Know
❏ pass phrase
❏ password
❏ private key
❏ pseudorandom number
❏ Pseudorandom Number Generator (PRNG)
❏ public key
❏ public key authentication
❏ public key encryption
❏ replay attack
❏ Root Certifying Authority
❏ secret key
❏ secret key encryption
❏ seed
❏ session
❏ symmetrical algorithm

Chapter

4

Managing
Security

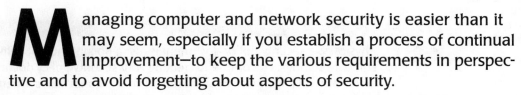

Managing computer and network security is easier than it may seem, especially if you establish a process of continual improvement—to keep the various requirements in perspective and to avoid forgetting about aspects of security.

Security management centers on the concept of a security policy, which is a document containing a set of rules that describes how security should be configured for all systems to defend against a complete set of known threats. The security policy creates a balance between security and usability. The executive management of your organization should determine where to draw the line between security concerns and ease of use. Just think of a security policy as the security rules for your organization, along with policies for continual enforcement and improvement.

In this chapter, you will learn about:

 Developing a security policy

 Implementing the security policy

 Updating the security policy in response to new threats

Developing a Security Policy

The first step in developing a security **policy** is to establish your network usability **requirements** by examining what things users must be able to do with the network. For example, the ability to send e-mail may be a requirement. Once you know what you are required to allow, you have a basis to determine which security measures need to be taken.

policy
A collection of rules.

requirements
A list of functions which are necessary in a system.

TIP

Physically, a security policy document is just a document, not software or software settings. I recommend creating your security policy document as an HTML web page that can be stored on your organization's intranet. This makes it easy to update and ensures that whenever someone reads it, they're reading the most recent version.

After you've got your requirements, make a list of features users may want but which are not expressly required. Add these to the list of requirements, but be sure to indicate that they can be eliminated if they conflict with a security requirement.

Finally, create a list of security requirements—things users should not be able to perform, protections that should be taken against anonymous access, and so forth.

The list of all of these requirements should simply be a series of sweeping statements, like:

- ◇ Users must be able to send and receive e-mail on the Internet. (use requirement)

- ◇ Users must be able to store documents on internal servers. (use requirement)

- ◇ Hackers should have no access to the interior of the network. (security requirement)

- ◇ There should be no way that users can accidentally circumvent file system permissions. (security requirement)

- ◇ Passwords should be impossible to guess and take at least a year to discover using an automated attack with currently available technology. (security requirement)

- ◇ Users should be able to determine exactly who should have access to the files they create. (security requirement)

Creating a Policy Requirements Outline

Once you have a list of sweeping statements about requirements and restrictions, examine each statement to determine how it can be implemented. For example, preventing hacker access could be implemented by not having an Internet connection or more practically, a strong firewall could help ensure that hackers will have no access to your network.

Create an outline, with the requirements as the major headings, and then break them down into methods that could be used to implement them. Include all possible ways that the requirement could be met that you can think of. For example, to prevent public access, you could implement a firewall or you could simply not have an internet connection. Don't eliminate possibilities at this point, even if you know that some of them will conflict with other requirements. The idea at this point is to get a complete set of options that will be reduced later.

Continue to analyze the methods that you write down, writing newer and more specific methods for each in turn, until you are left with a set of policies that can be implemented in outline format. Here is an example:

```
I. Hackers should have no access to the interior of the network

    A. Allow no Internet Connection

    B. Implement a firewall for Internet connections.

        1. Block all inbound access at the firewall.

        2. Block dangerous outbound requests:

            (a) Strip e-mail attachments

            (b) Block downloads via HTTP and FTP

    C. Allow no dial-up access.

    D. Require call-back security for dial-up access.
```

When you create this outline, be sure to include every possible method of implementing the security requirement. This will allow you to eliminate those methods that mutually exclude some other requirement, leaving you with the set that can be implemented.

Eliminate Conflicting Requirements

Once you have the complete set of use and security requirements and you've broken them down to specific steps that can be implemented, analyze the document and eliminate those security steps that conflict with network requirements.

63

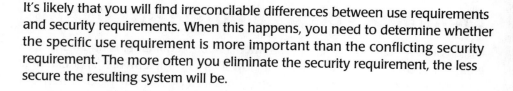

It's likely that you will find irreconcilable differences between use requirements and security requirements. When this happens, you need to determine whether the specific use requirement is more important than the conflicting security requirement. The more often you eliminate the security requirement, the less secure the resulting system will be.

Distilling the Security Policy

Once you've pared down the security requirements outline to include only those policies that will work in your organization, it's time to extract the individual rules into a simple list. Then, take that list and group the rules by the system that will implement them. For example, in the outline above, "Strip e-mail attachments" is one of the individual policy rules, and it would be grouped with other rules that pertain to e-mail handling. By extracting the individual rules out of the outline and then regrouping them by the systems in which they are implemented, you can create a coherent policy that you can easily deploy. This reorganization changes the security requirements outline, which is organized by requirements not by the **systems** that will implement those requirements, into a final security policy document that should be organized by functional groups.

Selecting Enforceable Policy Rules

Relying on humans to implement security policies rather than establishing automatic security limitations is analogous to painting lines on the road instead of building median barricades. A center double yellow line doesn't actually prevent people from driving over it; it just makes it a violation if they do. A central barricade between opposing lanes absolutely prevents anyone from driving over it, so further enforcement is not necessary. When you determine how to implement policy rules, remember to construct barricades (like file system permissions and firewall port blocking) rather than paint lines (like saying "Users may not check personal e-mail on work computers" or "Users should not send documents as e-mail attachments")—that way, you don't have to enforce the policy and your users won't be tempted to cheat.

Security configurations for computers are the barricades that you will set up. These configurations, when documented, are the security policies for the individual devices. **Firewalls** have a rule-base that describes their configuration. Windows servers allow you to control use by using **group policies** and **permissions**. Unix network services are individually configured for security based on files that are usually stored in the /etc directory. No matter how automated policies are managed by specific systems, they should be derived from your human-readable security policy, so that when new applications are added to the network, the

system

A collection of processing entities, such as computers, firewalls, domain controllers, network devices, e-mail systems, and humans.

firewall

A device that filters communications between a private network and a public network based on a company's security policy.

group policies

In Windows 2000, a collection of security options that are managed as a set and which can be applied to various collections of user accounts or computer systems.

permissions

A security mechanism that controls access to individual resources, like files, based on user identity.

way that they should be configured will be obvious. Most of the remainder of this book details how to implement these automated security policies.

Creating an Appropriate Use Policy

An **appropriate use policy** is the portion of your security policy that users will be relied upon to implement. An appropriate use policy is simply a document for users stating how computers may be used in your organization. It is that part of the security policy that remains after you've automated enforcement as much as you possibly can—it's the painted lines that you couldn't avoid using because systems could not be configured to implement the barrier automatically.

The computer appropriate use policy is a document for users that explains what rules have been placed into effect for the network automatically and what behaviors they should avoid.

NOTE

Your automated policy for firewall configuration, server security settings, backup tape rotation policy, and other such administrative rules need not be explained to end-users because they won't be responsible for implementing them.

The computer appropriate use policy can vary widely from one organization to the next depending on each company's security requirements and management edicts. For example, in some organizations, web browsing is encouraged, whereas in others, web use is forbidden altogether.

Users are the least reliable component of a security strategy, so you should only rely on them when there is no way to automate a particular component of a security policy. In the beginning, you may find that your entire security policy has to be implemented through rules for users because you haven't had time to configure devices for security. This is the natural starting point. Ultimately, the best computer appropriate use policy has no entries because all security rules have been automated. This is your goal as a security administrator: to take all the rules that humans have to enforce manually and make them automatic (and therefore uncircumventable) over time.

The following is a simple example of a single computer use rule:

Policy: Users shall not e-mail document attachments.

> **Justification:**   E-mailed documents represent a threat for numerous reasons. First, e-mail requests for a document can be forged. A hacker may forge an e-mail requesting a document, coercing a user to e-mail

appropriate use policy
A policy that explains how humans are allowed to use a system.

the document outside the company. Users may accidentally e-mail documents outside the organization in a mass reply or thinking that a specific user is internal to the company. Secondly, e-mailing a document nullifies the file system permissions for a document, making it highly likely that a document may be e-mailed to a user who should not have permission to see it. Once a document has been e-mailed, its security can no longer be managed by the system. Finally, attachments are a serious storage burden on the e-mail system and cause numerous document versioning problems. They increase the likelihood of malfunction of office and e-mail applications.

Remedy: Users shall e-mail links to documents stored on servers. This way, border firewalls will prevent documents from leaking outside the company, and the server can enforce permissions.

Enforcement: Currently, users are asked not to send document attachments. In the future, enforcement will be automatic and attachments will be stripped on the e-mail server and will not be forwarded from our e-mail system.

This example is straightforward and shows the structure you may want to use for individual rules. It's important to include a justification for rules; people are far more likely to agree and abide by a rule if they understand why it exists. Unjustified rules will seem like heavy-handed control-mongering on the part of the security staff. Once the software to implement this rule automatically has been activated, it can be removed from the acceptable use policy because humans will no longer be relied upon to enforce it.

NOTE

This specific example is also a good example of why a computer use policy must be tailored to your organization. While this rule is effective and appropriate for most businesses, it would have been difficult to produce this book without e-mailing attachments. The book production process is largely managed using e-mail attachments.

Security Policy Best Practices

So far, this chapter has introduced a lot of theory but very little practical policy information. This section shares some security best practices to get you started with your policy document.

Password Policies

It's difficult to talk about a security policy without bringing up **passwords**. Passwords are used to secure almost all security systems in one way or another, and because of their ubiquity, they form a fundamental part of a security policy. Hopefully, this won't be the case for much longer—password security is very flawed, because the theory is strong but the implementation is weak. In theory, a 14-character password could take so long to crack that the universe would end before a hacker would gain access by automated guessing. But in practice, I've cracked passwords on servers over the Internet in as little as eleven seconds.

Problems with Passwords

Passwords are the easiest way to gain unauthorized access to a system. Why? Because your network is protected by passwords that average only six characters in length and most are combinations of just 26 letters—this yields a mere 320 million possibilities. That may sound like a large number, but cracking software exists that can run through a 100 million passwords per day over the Internet. Since most passwords are common English words or names, they are limited to a field of about 50,000 possibilities. Any modern computer can check that number of passwords against a password file in a few hours. Try typing your personal password into a word processor. If it passes the spell-checker unchallenged, change it.

WARNING

A flaw in Windows 2000 allows hackers to use a freely downloadable tool to check passwords over the Internet at a rate of over 72,000 passwords *per minute* by exploiting the new (and rarely blocked) SMB over TCP/IP service on port 445. Never use Windows servers on the public Internet without blocking ports 135, 139, and 445 at a bare minimum.

Though most of your network users may have strong passwords, it only takes one user with a poorly chosen one for a hacker to gain access to your network.

NOTE

When guessing passwords, most hackers don't bother checking a large number of passwords against a single account—they check a large number of accounts against a few passwords. The more accounts you have on your system, the more likely it is that a hacker will find a valid account name/password combination.

password
A secret key or word that is used to prove someone's or something's identity.

Passwords are generally chosen out of the information people already have to remember anyway. This means that anyone familiar with a network account holder stands a reasonable chance of guessing his or her password. Also consider that most people don't change their password unless they are forced to, and then they typically rotate among two or three favorite passwords. This is a natural consequence of the fact that people simply can't be expected to frequently devise and remember a strong, unique new password.

Common sources of passwords include:

- Names of pets or close relatives
- Slang swear words (these are the easiest to guess)
- Birthdays or anniversaries
- Phone numbers and social security numbers
- Permutations: The name of the account, the name of the account holder, the company name, the word password, or any of the above spelled backwards.
- Simple sequences: "1234", "123456", "9876", "asdf", etc.

Most people also tend to use the same account names and passwords on all systems. For instance, a person may choose to use their network account name and password on an online service or on a membership website. That way they don't have to remember a different account name and password for every different service they use. This means that a security breach on a system you don't control can quite plausibly yield account names and passwords that work on your system.

Random passwords tend to be difficult for people to remember. Writing passwords down is the natural way for users to solve that problem—thus making their daytimer a codebook for network access.

One major hole in many network systems is the initial password problem: how does a network administrator create a number of new accounts and assign passwords that people can use immediately to all of them? Usually, by assigning a default password like "password" or the user account name itself as the password and then requiring that the user change the password the first time they log in. The problem with this approach is that out of 100 employees, typically only 98 of them actually log on and change it. For whatever reason, two of the users don't actually need accounts—because they don't have computers, or they're the janitor, or whatever. This leaves two percent of your accounts with easily hacked passwords just waiting for the right hacker to come along. The best way to handle initial passwords is for the administrator to assign a long and cryptic random password, and have the user report to the administrator in person to receive it.

Many membership-based websites don't take measures to encrypt the transmission of user account names and passwords while they are in transit over the internet, so if people reuse network information on these sites an interception can also provide valid account names and passwords that can be used to attack your network.

Lastly, there exists the slight possibility that a membership website may be set up with the covert purpose of gleaning account names and passwords from the public at large to provide targets of opportunity for hackers. The e-mail address you provide generally indicates another network on which that account name and password will work.

Effective Password Management

There are a variety of steps you can take to make passwords more effective. First, set the network password policy to force users to create long passwords. Eight characters is the bare minimum required to significantly lessen the odds of a brute-force password attack using currently available computing power.

Don't force frequent periodic password changes. This recommendation flies in the face of standard industry practice, but the policy of requiring users to change passwords often causes them to select very easily guessed passwords or to modify their simple passwords only slightly so they can keep reusing them. Rather than enforcing frequent password changes, require each user to memorize a highly cryptic password, and only change it when they suspect that it may have been compromised.

Mandate that all systems lock users out after no more than five incorrect password logon attempts and remain locked out until an administrator resets the account. This is the most effective way to thwart automated password guessing attacks.

WARNING

The built-in Windows administrator account cannot be locked out. For this reason, this is the account that hackers will always attempt to exploit. Rename the administrator account to prevent this problem, and create a disabled account named "Administrator" to foil attacks against it. You can then monitor access to the decoy account using a Windows 2000 audit policy, knowing that any attempt to use it is fraudulent.

Ask users to select and remember at least three passwords at the same time: A simple password for use on web-based subscription services, a stronger password for their own personal and financial use outside the company, and a highly cryptic password randomly created by the security manager and memorized by the user for use on the LAN. Tell users that any use of their LAN password outside the company is a violation of the computer acceptable use policy.

Consider disallowing users from changing their own passwords unless you can automatically enforce strong passwords. Have users include punctuation in their passwords to keep them from being exposed to brute-force dictionary hacks or password guessing.

TIP

Watch out for users with international keyboards—some keyboards cannot create all the punctuation characters an administrator might include in an assigned password.

Set up e-mail accounts using the employee's real name instead of the account name. Never use network account names on anything that goes outside your organization.

Set up a security/recycling policy that requires printouts to be thrown away in special security/ recycling containers, or set up a document shredding policy.

Make sure everyone knows that no one should ever ask for a user's password. If an administrator needs to log on as a user, the administrator can change the user's password, complete the administrative work, and then sit down with the user to change the password back to the user's chosen password. This way a user will know if an administrator has logged into their accounts.

Implement a secure method to assign initial passwords, for example by having employees report directly to the network administrator to have their password set.

Application Security

Some **applications** are a lot more dangerous to a system's security than others. In particular, any application that contains an **execution environment**, like **Java**, a web browser, or a **macro**-enabled office program represents special security challenges and should be specifically addressed in your security policy.

What is an execution environment? Quite simply, it's any system that interprets codes and carries out actions on the computer host outside the scope of the interpreting program. What makes that different than, say, codes in a word processing document is that word processing codes only affect the activity of the word processor—they merely indicate how text should be displayed according to a very limited set of possibilities. When the set of possibilities is as wide as a programming language, then you have an execution environment to be feared.

application
Software that allows users to perform their work, as opposed to software used to manage systems, entertain, or perform other utility functions. Applications are the reason that systems are implemented.

execution environment
A portion of an application that interprets codes and carries out actions on the computer host irrespective of the scope or security context of the application.

Java
A cross-platform execution environment developed by Sun Microsystems that allows the same program to be executed across many different operating systems. Java applets can be delivered automatically from web servers to browsers and executed within the web browser's security context.

macro
A script for an execution environment that is embedded within an application.

Office Documents

Viruses require an execution environment in order to propagate. A word processor document alone cannot spread viruses. But if you add a programming language to the word processing program, like say Visual Basic, you create an execution environment that can spread viruses.

Microsoft has virus-enabled all of their Office applications; Excel, Word, PowerPoint, Outlook, Access, Project, and Visio all contain Visual Basic and can all act as hosts for viruses. Outlook (and its feature-disabled cousin Outlook Express) is especially dangerous because it can automatically e-mail viruses to everyone you know.

Disable macro execution in all Office programs. Unless your company's work is the processing of documents (like my publisher's is, for example) there's little reason why you should rely on macros in Office. If you really think you need macros, you probably need an office automation system way beyond what Microsoft Office is really going to do for you anyway.

E-mail Security & Policy

E-mail is not secure. The best e-mail policy is simply to make certain that everyone knows that. If a user receives a strange request from someone, instruct them to phone the sender to verify the request and to make sure that it's not a forged e-mail.

E-mailing **attachments** is extremely dangerous. E-mail viruses and Trojan horses are spread primarily through e-mail attachments. Without attachments or executable environments embedded in mail programs, e-mail would not be a significant security threat.

attachment
A file inserted into to an e-mail.

NOTE

E-mailing attachments within the boundaries of a single facility is always the wrong way to work, anyway. It creates uncontrolled versions of documents, eliminates document permissions, and creates an extreme load on e-mail servers, local e-mail storage, and the network. Teach users to e-mail links to documents rather than the documents themselves to solve all of these problems.

Get rid of Microsoft Outlook and Outlook Express, if possible. These two programs are the platform for every automatic e-mail virus to date. No other e-mail software is written with as little security in mind as these two, and their ease-of-use translates to ease-of-misuse for most users. If you can't get rid of Outlook, set your servers up to strip inbound and outbound attachments. Attachments of particular concern are executables, such as `.exe`, `.cmd`, `.com`, `.bat`, `.scr`, `.js`, `.vb`, and `.pif`.

Web Browsing Security & Policy

There are four major web browser security problems:

1. The downloading of executable programs that are actually Trojan horses or viruses.

2. Connecting to executable content like **ActiveX** or Java controls that can exploit the local system (this is actually a subset of problem #1).

3. Bugs in web browsers can sometimes be exploited to gain access to a computer.

4. Web browsers may automate the transmission of your network password to a web server.

In theory, Java is supposed to be limited to a security **sandbox** environment that cannot reach the executing host. Unfortunately, this limitation is an artificial boundary that has been punched through many times by various exploits, all of which have been patched by Sun as they were found. But because the limitation is not inherent, more vulnerabilities will certainly be found.

NOTE

ActiveX is like Java minus any serious attempt to implement security. ActiveX controls are native computer programs designed to be plugged into the web browser and executed on demand—they are web browser plug-ins (modules) that download and execute automatically. There are no restrictions on the actions that an ActiveX control can take.

Microsoft's attempt at security for ActiveX controls is called **content signing**, where digital signatures affirm that the code hasn't been modified between the provider and you. It does not indicate that the code is secure or that the writers aren't modifying your computer settings or uploading information from your computer. The theory goes like this: If the ActiveX control is signed, if you trust the signing authority, if you trust the motivation of the code provider, and you trust that they don't have any bugs in their code, go ahead and download. In practice, that's far too extenuated to make any sense in the real world, and most people have no idea what it means anyway or how they would validate the signing authority even if they did know what it meant.

ActiveX
An execution environment for the Microsoft Internet Explorer web browser and applications that allow code to be delivered over the Internet and executed on the local machine.

sandbox
An execution environment that does not allow accesses outside itself, and so cannot be exploited to cause problem on the host system.

content signing
The process of embedding a hash in a document or executable code to prove that the content has not been modified, and to identify with certainty the author of the content.

These problems are relatively easy to mitigate with a content-inspecting firewall or proxy server. Configure your firewall or proxy to strip ActiveX, Java, and executable attachments (including those embedded in zip files). This will prevent users from accidentally downloading dangerous content. Avoid using services that rely on these inherently unsafe practices in order to operate.

The automatic password problem is a lot more sinister. Microsoft Internet Explorer will automatically transmit your network account name and a hash of your password to any server that is configured to require Windows Challenge and Response as its authentication method. This hash can be decrypted to reveal your actual network password. Be sure to configure Internet Explorer's security settings to prevent this, or use Netscape Navigator instead of Internet Explorer to decouple the web browser from the operating system.

Implementing Security Policy

Once you've completed your security policy document, it's time to translate it from human readable form into the various configurations that will actually implement the policy.

Implementation varies from one system to the next. A policy of "Strip e-mail attachments on all mail servers" is implemented far differently in UNIX Sendmail, Microsoft Exchange, or Lotus Notes. Your policies should not be written specifically to certain systems; they should be general statements that apply to any system that performs the specified function.

Implementation occurs when a security policy is applied to a specific system. But nothing in your policy will help you select which systems to use to implement the policy. A requirement that "Permissions can be used to block access to certain documents" does not stipulate Windows 2000, UNIX, or the Mac OS X systems—they can all perform this function. It does eliminate the choice of Windows 98, MS-DOS, or the original Mac OS, because they have no true permissions infrastructure. In order to select systems that match your security policy requirements, make a complete list of possible systems and eliminate those systems that cannot implement your security requirements. Select the systems that can implement your security requirements most easily from the remaining candidates.

Of course, this only works in the theoretical world where security requirements are defined before systems are built, rather than after hackers exploit systems in a major way and reveal the lack of security. When you are retrofitting security policy, be prepared for the fact that some of your systems and software may have to be replaced in order to achieve real security.

Applying Automated Policy

The method you'll use to apply automated policy differs for each system in your network. On firewalls, you'll use a web browser or an "enterprise manager" application. In Windows 2000, you'll modify group policy objects in the Active Directory. In Linux, you'll directly edit text files in the /etc directory. You may change the startup type of a service or remove operating system components that provide unnecessary services. You may block certain port ranges on your firewall, or allow only approved outbound connections.

There is no standardized way to apply an automated policy. A few attempts have been made at automating policy by various vendors, but the lack of consensus and protocol keeps that from happening.

So what is a security administrator to do? That's the hard part. You have to individually learn and understand the security interface for each type of system in your network. Typically, this will mean understanding the interface for every operating system in use in your network and each security-related device. This is the major reason why consolidating on a single operating system is a good idea.

Most modern operating systems have graphical user interfaces that combine security configuration management into some sort of unified view. In Windows 2000, this is called the group policy manager. In most firewalls, it's either a web-based user interface or a program that runs on an administrator's computer. The remainder of this book contains details for applying automated policy, but for the most part, the technical manuals for your various systems will teach you how to apply their specific security policies.

Human Security

After everything that can be automated has been automated, humans must implement any parts of the security policy that are left over. They are therefore an integral and necessary component of computer security.

People are the most likely breach in any security environment, including secure networks. Most breaches are completely accidental; few people actually set out to sabotage network security. In fact, most people never find out that they've compromised the network's security. Hackers routinely exploit weaknesses in network security caused by this lack of awareness among users.

For example, humans select memorable passwords by nature, and then write them down on post-it notes so they don't forget them. Employees are sometimes enticed to provide information for favors, money, or higher paying jobs. Traveling sales people can leave your office and head for the office of your competition with interesting tidbits of information to trade.

Of course it is not the intent of this chapter to leave you feeling that your co-workers and business associates cannot be trusted. The vast majority of them can, but it takes only one individual in your entire organization with access to your network to compromise its security. Unfortunately, this means that security restrictions must be applied to everyone because you don't know who is going to slip up in the future.

People cause security problems because they:

Don't understand security.   Security is not an instinct—it must be taught. You cannot simply tell people to choose strong passwords and expect to have an impenetrable fortress. You must teach security to every person who participates in a secure environment.

Underestimate the threat. Many people simply don't believe that much of a problem really exists. They've never met or known anyone affected by a hacker, and they've never seen a disgruntled worker cause serious problems. For them, security is an abstraction that simply isn't all that important. As a security manager, your job is to explain the threat clearly. This is getting easier, as most people have been affected by a computer virus at least once.

Fail to make security a work habit. Many people simply don't change easily. They have old habits—and old passwords. Habitual security is hard to force, so make it as simple for users as possible by implementing automated policies that don't rely on people to remember security; have the policies be enforced by the network and by the work environment.

Forget about security outside the work environment. Many people leave their work at work—and their security habits too. They may take an employee list home and throw it in their trash. They may brag to a recent acquaintance about the importance of their job. They may write down their password on a sticky note and leave it in their daytimer. These sorts of problems can only be dealt with by reminding people to leave work completely at work—don't talk about it except in vague references and don't transfer company materials between work and home. Remind them never to re-use their work password or account name on other systems, like membership websites.

Passively resist security measures. Many people see security as an abridgement of their personal liberty and freedoms or as an indication that they are not trusted. Remind them that they are free to live their lives as they please when they are not at work, but that as an employee they have a responsibility to safeguard the company's proprietary information. Explain that security policies by nature must deal with the lowest common denominator of trust, and that security should not be viewed as an insult to any single individual.

Human security is problematic because it is the only aspect of total network security not directly controlled by the information system staff. Unlike computers, your co-workers cannot simply be programmed with a strong security policy and let run. They must be taught, reminded, and encouraged.

Security managers are often given the responsibility to enforce security policy without being given the authority to enforce security on end users. You probably won't be able to fire anyone for a major security breach, you can't dock his or her pay, and you may not even be able to write an administrative letter of reprimand. Without some form of force, the concept enforcement is meaningless.

Fortunately, humans are gregarious creatures and respond well to group opinion. This means that for serious security breaches, you can use publicity both to embarrass the people at fault and to teach everyone else what not to do. Publicize security failures within the company as part of a **lessons learned** document,

lessons learned
A documented failure analysis that is disseminated to system users in order to prevent the same failure from recurring.

usually in the form of an e-mail message to everyone in the company. Whether or not you identify people by name is up to you and probably depends largely on company policy and the severity of the breach (and even if you don't name them, the buzz around the water cooler will). Each lesson learned should be appended to your security policy for further analysis so these breaches can be prevented in the future.

Teaching Security Principles

The best way to avoid security lapses due to human activity is to teach proactive security and to get every user to commit to taking security seriously.

Teaching security is not that difficult. Set up security seminars for groups of employees that are small enough to be interactive—up to about 25 at a time in my experience—and simply go through the computer acceptable use policy item by item. Let's face it: e-mailing (a link to) CAUP.DOC to every user in your system will encourage exactly nobody to actually read it. By holding a seminar, you will simply be reading it to them, with a darkened room, a projector, and donuts to mesmerize them into listening.

But you'll also have the opportunity to explain why the policies are important and which threats the company is worried about. You can provide anecdotes about hacker break-ins, what happened at companies that didn't implement policy, and so forth.

Understanding policy is the key to gaining the all-important "buy-in," or the acceptance of a personal responsibility to implement security policy. Without buy-in, users are likely to at best ignore and at worst circumvent an acceptable use policy.

At the end of the security training, present each user with a certificate of completion/contract that let's them agree in writing to abide by the company's acceptable use policy. By requiring their signature on a security contract, you will let users know exactly how serious security is to the organization.

Users should go through the security training seminar when they are hired and once per year thereafter, so they can learn about new threats, ask questions about restrictions they've run into, and otherwise stay in the security loop.

Updating the Security Policy

So, you've outlined your security requirements, derived a security policy, refined elements of policy, separated them into human security and automated policy, created an acceptable use policy, read it to the end-users, and applied the security settings required by policy for all of your systems.

Now you're done, right? Wrong. Now you start over.

Security administration is a perpetual cycle because new threats appear all the time. Every time you integrate a new device into your network, you need to consider its security ramifications and update your security policy. In short, you're never done.

The Security Cycle

Security administration is work that must be continually performed to keep a system as free from the loss or compromise of company data as is practicable. As a security administrator, it is your job to determine which security measures need to be taken and if those security measures have been properly executed. Although the task is daunting, it can be broken down into discreet steps that can be methodically executed. The cycle of security administration is as follows:

- ◇ Identify potential vulnerabilities.
- ◇ Evaluate vulnerabilities to determine how they can be effectively nullified.
- ◇ Determine which of the identified countermeasures you can effectively employ against the vulnerabilities.
- ◇ Employ countermeasures.
- ◇ Test countermeasures for effectiveness by simulating an attack.
- ◇ Monitor server logs and firewalls for evidence of security breaches.
- ◇ Investigate any indications of a breach to determine the breach progression and identify new potential vulnerabilities.
- ◇ Study public security sources for news of newly discovered security vulnerabilities.
- ◇ Repeat the cycle of security administration.

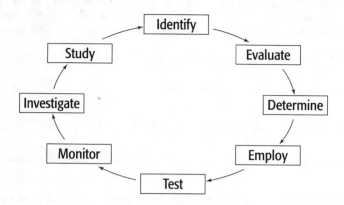

The cyclical nature of security cannot be stressed enough. Unlike a vault, which is static through time and suffers from only a few well-known vulnerabilities, computer networks are not static—they change constantly. Every new addition, be it software or hardware, must be evaluated in the context of security to determine if it will add a new vulnerability to the system. The methods used by hackers to gain access to a system must be continually researched, and system software must be updated as new security fixes are released. Network security is like walking against a treadmill—you have to keep moving just to stay in place because as time goes by, new vectors of attack will be discovered and your network will become less secure without any changes at all on your part.

Review Questions

1. What is the purpose of a security policy?

2. What is the first step in developing a security policy?

3. Why is it important to automate security policies as much as possible?

4. Why is an appropriate use policy important?

5. How often should users be required to change their passwords?

6. What is the minimum length of a password that could be considered to be "strong" in the context of today's computing power?

7. Why is the inconvenient policy of enforcing a password lockout after a few incorrect attempts important?

8. Why are execution environments dangerous?

9. Which is more secure: ActiveX or Java?

_____

_____

10. Why doesn't a digital signature mean that an ActiveX control is secure?

_____

_____

Chapter
5

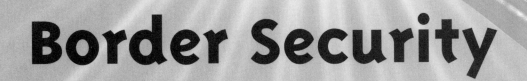

Border Security

Where does your network stop, and the Internet begin? That's like asking where one country stops and another starts. The line between them is merely a subjective boundary where one set of rules start and another set of rules stop. But like the border between China and Russia, where one country is built out and densely populated right to the edge, while the other is nothing but forest for hundreds of miles, the place where the force of these two sets of networking rules meet delineates a dramatic change in character of the networking landscape.

Firewalls, also called **border gateways**, are routers whose purpose is to give administrators fine-grain control over which traffic is passed to and from the Internet and which is rejected. Modern firewalls also perform on-the-fly modification of streams, authentication, and **tunneling** in order to further eliminate threats from the Internet.

Firewalls are the foundation of border security. The strength of your border security is equal to the strength of your firewalls and their proper configuration. Firewall security is by far the most important aspect of Internet security.

In this chapter, you will learn about:

 The principles of border security

 Understanding firewalls

 Fundamental firewall functions, such as packet filtering, Network Address Translation (NAT), and proxy services.

 Selecting a firewall that's right for your network

Principles of Border Security

Your network and the Internet both utilize TCP/IP as a connection methodology, and since you have at least some valid Internet addresses, your network is technically just part of the larger Internet. From a security standpoint, "your" network is actually defined as that place where you begin to enforce rules about how the network will be used. Outside those borders, it's no-man's land.

firewall
A gateway that connects a private network to a public network and enforces a security policy by allowing only those connections that match the device's security settings.

border gateway
A firewall.

tunneling
The process of encapsulating packets within IP packets for the purpose of transporting the interior packets through many public intermediate systems. When reassembled at the remote end, the interior packets will appear to have transited only one router on the private networks.

Like nations, you could simply have open borders and enforce security within every city. This would be analogous to having servers and clients placed directly on the Internet and requiring them to each handle their own security. This is exactly how the Internet worked originally. Prior to 1990, there were so few hacking attempts (CERT listed only six for 1988) that serious attempts at security would have been an unnecessary distraction.

TIP

This chapter serves as an introduction to border security. Border security is a vast topic that would easily fill a book. I recommend mine: *Firewalls 24seven, 2nd Ed.* (Sybex, 2002)

But today, enforcing security at every machine within your network would put a serious burden on your users and staff, and you would have no control over the use of bandwidth within your network—hacking attempts could reach inside your network and propagate there. (Universities began having this problem in the early nineties, as students began setting up their own web servers, which would become popular suddenly and begin consuming tremendous bandwidth.)

Border security theory requires these measures:

Control every crossing.   You can control all the data flowing between your network and the Internet by placing firewalls at every connection to your network. In this case, "every crossing" literally means every connection. Controlling every possible connection to the Internet is the most important measure you can take to control security on your network. A single connection into your network that isn't monitored by firewalls could allow an intrusion. Like a leaking dam, your security policy means nothing if it is not universally enforced. This means that wireless network access points, modems, and any other method of transmitting data must be taken into account (eliminated or placed behind a firewall) in order to truly secure your network.

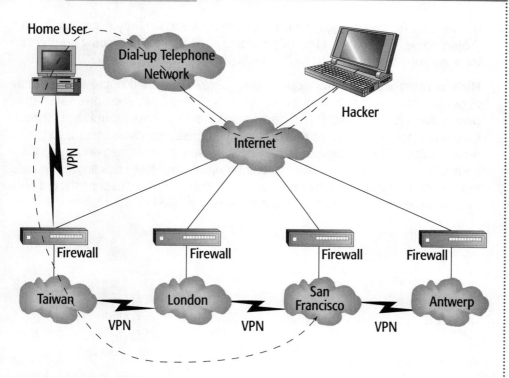

demilitarized zone
A security zone with a separate, more relaxed security policy that is used to partition public servers like e-mail and web servers away from the Internal network while providing them firewall protection.

Apply the same policy universally. If you want to control a specific type of traffic, you have to control it the same way at every crossing, because the net effect of your security policy is equal to the loosest policy on any single firewall; if you allow a protocol to pass on one firewall, you're allowing that protocol in, so blocking it on another firewall is essentially pointless.

If you need two different levels of security for different purposes, put a firewall behind the machines that require expanded Internet access, so that if they are breached, the remainder of your network is still firewalled. This configuration is called a **demilitarized zone** (DMZ). A DMZ is simply a separate interface to which you can apply a separate and more relaxed firewall policy.

Enterprise level firewalls, like Check Point FireWall-1, allow you to create a single policy and then apply it to all firewalls. Most other firewalls require vigilance on the part of security administrators to ensure that their policies are uniform across their pool of firewalls.

Deny by default. Early firewalls allowed all Internet traffic except that which was specifically blocked. This didn't work for long. To be secure, you must deny all traffic except that which you specifically want to allow. This is important for both incoming and outgoing data. The effect of accidentally downloading a Trojan horse is mitigated if the Trojan horse can't open an outgoing connection through your firewall.

Hide as much information as possible.   Firewalls should not reveal anything about the nature of the interior of the network—in fact, they shouldn't reveal their own existence, if possible. When hackers scan for networks using Ping scanners, they rely upon the victim to respond. No response means no victim, so your firewalls should be configured to hide their presence by not responding to these sorts of scans. This also means that technologies like SNMP should not be used to manage firewalls from the public side and that the administrator should only be able to reach the firewall from the private interface.

Understanding Firewalls

Firewalls keep your Internet connection as secure as possible by inspecting and then approving or rejecting each connection attempt made between your internal network and external networks like the Internet. Strong firewalls protect your network at all software layers—from the data link (such as Ethernet) layer up through the application layer (such as HTTP).

Firewalls sit on the borders of your network, connected directly to the circuits that provide access to other networks. For that reason, firewalls are frequently referred to as border security. The concept of border security is important— without it, every host on your network would have to perform the functions of a firewall themselves, needlessly consuming compute resources and increasing the amount of time required to connect, authenticate, and encrypt data in local area, high-speed networks. Firewalls allow you to centralize all network security services in machines that are optimized for and dedicated to the task. Inspecting traffic at the border gateways also has the benefit of preventing hacking traffic from consuming the bandwidth on your internal network.

By their nature, firewalls create bottlenecks between the internal and external networks because all traffic transiting between the internal network and the external must pass through a single point of control. This is a small price to pay for security. Since external leased-line connections are relatively slow compared to the speed of modern computers, the latency caused by firewalls can be completely transparent. For most users, relatively inexpensive firewall devices are more than sufficient to keep up with a standard T1 connection to the Internet. For businesses and ISPs whose Internet traffic is far higher, a new breed of extremely high-speed (and high-cost) firewalls have been developed that can keep up with even the most demanding private networks. Some countries actually censor the entire Internet using high-speed firewalls.

Fundamental Firewall Functions

There are three basic functions that modern firewalls perform:

◇ Packet filtering

◇ Network Address Translation

◇ Proxy service

proxy server
A server that hosts application proxies.

packet filter
A router that is capable of dropping packets that don't meet security requirements.

source routing
An often-abused TCP/IP troubleshooting mechanism that allows the sender of a packet to define a list of routers through which the packet must flow.

Nearly all firewalls use these basic methods to provide a security service. There are literally hundreds of firewall products on the market now, all vying for your security dollar. Most are very strong products that vary only in superficial details.

You could use devices or servers that perform only one of the above functions; for instance, you could have a router that performs packet filtering, and then have a **proxy server** in a separate machine. That way, the packet filter must either pass traffic through to the proxy server, or the proxy server must sit outside your network without the protection of packet filtering. Both scenarios are more dangerous than using a single firewall product that performs all the security functions in one place.

Many strong firewalls do not actually perform proxy services, but the strongest firewalls do. Proxy services strengthen the security of a firewall by inspecting information at the application layer—however, very few firewalls actually proxy any protocols other than HTTP and SMTP.

Packet Filtering

Packet filters implemented inside firewalls prevent suspicious traffic from reaching the destination network. Filtered routers protect all the machines on the destination network from suspicious traffic. Filters typically follow these rules:

◇ Dropping inbound connection attempts but allowing outbound connection attempts to pass.

◇ Eliminating TCP packets bound for ports that shouldn't be available to the Internet (such as the NetBIOS session port) but allowing packets that are required (such as SMTP) to pass. Most filters can specify exactly which server a specific sort of traffic should go to—for instance, SMTP traffic on port 25 should only go to the IP address of a mail server.

◇ Restricting inbound access to internal IP ranges.

Sophisticated filters examine the states of all connections that flow through them, looking for the telltale signs of hacking, such as **source routing**, ICMP redirection, and IP spoofing. Connections that exhibit these characteristics are dropped.

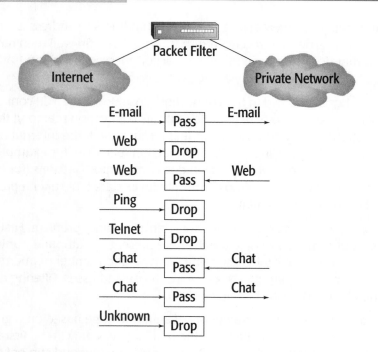

stateless packet filters
Packet filters that make pass/reject decisions based only on the information contained in each individual packet.

stateful inspection
A packet-filtering methodology that retains the state of a TCP connection and can pass or reject packets based on that state, rather than simply on information contained in the packet.

circuit-layer switch
A TCP proxy service. Circuit-layer switches terminate a TCP connection on one interface and regenerate it on the other. This allows the interior network to be hidden from the external network (similar to the way a network address translator works) and also completely regenerates the TCP/IP packets, so malformed packets are not passed through. Circuit-layer switches break the routed connection between networks, but they are not specific to higher-level protocols the way that application proxies are.

Internal clients are generally allowed to create connections to outside hosts, and external hosts are usually prevented from initiating connection attempts. When an internal host decides to initiate a TCP connection, it sends a TCP message to the IP address and port number of the public server (for example, www.microsoft.com:80 to connect to Microsoft's website). In the connection initiation message, it tells the remote server what its IP address is and on which port it is listening for a response (for example, 192.168.212.35:2050).

There are two types of packet filters:

   ◆ **Stateless packet filters**, which do not maintain the state of connections and make pass/drop decisions based purely upon information contained within each individual packet. Stateless packet filters are obsolete unless used along with NAT or proxy services because they cannot block the complete range of threatening data.

   ◆ **Stateful inspection** packet filters, which maintain tables of information about the connections flowing through them. They can pass or drop packets based on information contained in earlier packets in a connection stream.

All modern firewalls are either stateful inspectors or **circuit-layer switches** (TCP proxies). The external server sends data back by transmitting it to the port given by the internal client. Since your firewall inspects all the traffic exchanged between both hosts, it knows that the connection was initiated by an internal host attached to its internal interface, what that host's IP address is, and which port that host expects to receive return traffic on. The firewall then remembers to allow that host addressed in the connection message to return traffic to the internal host's IP address only at the port specified.

When the hosts involved in the connection close down the TCP connection, the firewall removes the entry in its state table (its connection memory) that allows the remote host to return traffic to the internal host. If the internal host stops responding before closing the TCP connection (because, for example, it has crashed) or if the protocol in question does not support sessions (for example, UDP), then the firewall will remove the entry in its state table after a programmed timeout of usually a few minutes.

Filtering does not completely solve the Internet security problem. First, the IP addresses of computers inside the filter are present in outbound traffic, which makes it somewhat easy to determine the type and number of Internet hosts inside a filter and to target attacks against those addresses. Filtering does not hide the identity of hosts behind the filter.

Filters cannot check all the fragments of an IP message based on higher-level protocols like TCP headers because the header exists only in the first fragment. Subsequent fragments have no TCP header information and can only be compared to IP level rules, which are usually relaxed to allow some traffic through the filter. This allows bugs in the destination IP stacks of computers on the network to be exploited, and could allow communications with a Trojan horse installed inside the network.

Finally, filters are not complex enough to check the legitimacy of the protocols inside the network-layer packets. For example, filters don't inspect the HTTP data contained in TCP packets to determine if it contains exploits that target the web browser or web server on your end of the connection. Most modern hacking attempts are based upon exploiting higher-level services because firewalls have nearly eliminated successful network-layer hacking (beyond the nuisance of denial-of-service attacks).

Network Address Translation (NAT)

Network Address Translation allows you to multiplex a single public IP address across an entire network. Many small companies rely upon the services of an upstream Internet service provider that may be reluctant to provide large blocks of addresses because their own range is relatively restricted. You may want to share a single dial-up or cable modem address without telling your ISP. These options are all possible using Network Address Translation.

Network Address Translation (NAT)

The process of rewriting the IP addresses of a packet stream as it flows through a router for the purpose of multiplexing a single IP address across a network of interior computers and for hiding internal hosts.

NAT was originally developed because it was difficult to get large blocks of public IP addresses, and networks frequently ran out of their assigned pool before they could request more addresses from InterNIC. InterNIC began conserving addresses when the Internet boom began because the pool of available addresses was quickly running out. By multiplexing a single public address to numerous interior hosts in a private IP range, a company could get by with as little as one single public IP address.

Fortuitously, Network Address Translation also solves the problem of hiding internal hosts. NAT is actually a network-layer proxy: On the Internet, it appears as if a single host makes requests on behalf of all internal hosts, thus hiding their identity from the public network.

NAT hides internal IP addresses by converting all internal host addresses to the public address of the firewall. The firewall then translates the address of the internal host, from its own address, using the TCP port number to keep track of which connections on the public side map to which hosts on the private side. To the Internet, all the traffic on your network appears to be coming from one extremely busy computer.

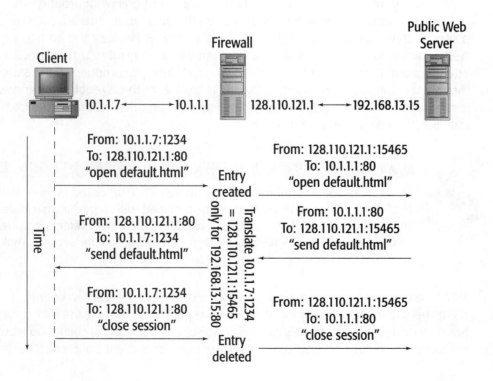

NAT effectively hides all TCP/IP-level information about your internal hosts from prying eyes on the Internet. Address translation also allows you to use any IP address range you want on your internal network, even if those addresses are already in use elsewhere on the Internet. This means you don't have to register a large block of addresses from InterNIC or reassign network numbers you were using before you connected your network to the Internet.

On the down side, NAT is implemented only at the TCP/IP level. This means that information hidden in the data payload of TCP/IP traffic could be transmitted to a higher-level service and used to exploit weaknesses in higher-level traffic or to communicate with a Trojan horse. You'll still have to use a higher-level service like a proxy to prevent higher-level service security breaches.

Finally, many protocols also include the host's IP address in the data payload, so when the address is rewritten while passing through NAT, the address in the payload becomes invalid. This occurs with active-mode FTP, H.323, IPSec, and nearly every other protocol that relies upon establishing a secondary communication stream between the client and the server. It is also not possible to connect to a host inside the private network, because there is no way to address hosts directly from the Internet. Most NAT implementations work around this problem for these protocols by "holding open the door" for the return path of protocols that they know will be coming back, like FTP. Because the host connection went out through the translator, it knows to expect a return connection attempt from these protocols and it knows which interior computer to translate the return channel for. So as long as a NAT is "aware" of these problem protocols, it can handle them. New protocols or applications can often be problematic to implement through NATs for this reason.

WARNING

Using an obsolete troubleshooting feature of TCP/IP called "source routing," where a list of IP addresses are provided with a packet that determines the route it should take, it's possible to connect directly through many early NAT implementations. If you are using NAT for security, make sure that the NAT device drops source-routed packets.

NAT is also a problem for network administrators who may want to connect to clients behind the NAT server for administrative purposes. Because the NAT server has only one IP address, there's no way to specify which internal client you want to reach. This keeps hackers from connecting to internal clients, but it also keeps legitimate users at bay as well. Fortunately, most modern NAT implementations allow you to create port-forwarding rules that allow internal hosts to be reached.

NOTE

Windows 2000 and XP, Linux, and many modern Unix operating systems provide this function as part of the operating system distribution. Windows NT does not.

Proxy Services

NAT solves many of the problems associated with direct Internet connections, but it still doesn't completely restrict the flow of packets through your firewall. It's possible for someone with a network monitor to watch traffic coming out of your firewall and determine that the firewall is translating addresses for other machines. It is then possible for a hacker to hijack TCP connections or to spoof connections back through the firewall.

Application-layer proxies prevent this. Application-layer proxies allow you to completely disconnect the flow of network-level protocols through your firewall and restrict traffic only to higher-level protocols like HTTP, FTP, and SMTP. When a connection is made through a proxy server, the proxy server receives the connection, extracts the high-level protocol (like HTTP), examines it and makes decisions on its content based on its security policy. The proxy server then creates a new TCP connection on the public interface to the ultimate destination and sends the high-level protocol out through the new connection. Because the network-layer protocol is completely regenerated, attacks that rely upon malformed TCP/IP packets are eliminated.

Proxies straddle two networks that are not connected by routers. When a client on the protected network makes a connection to a server on the public side, the proxy receives the connection request and then makes the connection on behalf of the protected client. The proxy then forwards the response from the public server onto the internal network. The graphic on the following page shows this process in detail.

NOTE

Proxies are a good example of how an intermediate system between you and another end system could potentially perform any sort of processing without your permission.

application-layer proxy
A service for a specific application-layer protocol like HTTP or SMTP that makes connections to the public Internet on behalf of internal private clients. Because application-layer proxies understand the specific protocol for which they proxy, they are able to detect and block malformed or maliciously modified streams.

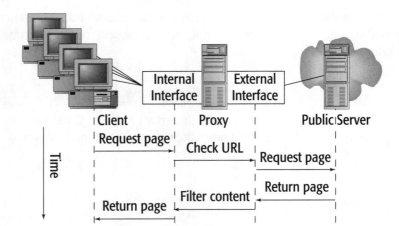

transparent
A proxy server that is capable of automatically proxying a protocol without the client's awareness.

Application proxies (like Microsoft Proxy Server) are unlike Network Address Translators and filters in that the Internet client application is (usually) set up to talk to the proxy. For instance, you tell Internet Explorer the address of your web proxy, and Internet Explorer sends all web requests to that server rather than resolving the IP address and establishing a connection directly. Some modern firewalls support transparent proxying, where they appear to be routers but actually perform application-layer protocol proxying rather than forwarding packets.

Application proxies don't have to run on firewalls; any server can perform the role of a proxy, either inside or outside of your network. Without a firewall, you still don't have any real security, so you need both. At least some sort of packet filter must be in place to protect the proxy server from network-layer denial-of-service attacks (like the infamous "ping of death"). And, if the proxy doesn't run on the firewall, you'll have to open a channel through your firewall in one way or another. Ideally, your firewall should perform the proxy function. This keeps packets from the public side from being forwarded through your firewall.

Some firewall proxies are more sophisticated than others. Because they have the functionality of an IP filter and network address translator, they can simply block outbound connection attempts (on port 80 in the case of HTTP) to remote hosts rather than having the client software configured to address the proxy service specifically. The firewall proxy then connects to the remote server and requests data on behalf of the blocked client. The retrieved data is returned to the requesting client using the firewall's NAT functionality to look just like the actual remote server. Proxies that operate in this manner are said to be **transparent**.

Security proxies are even capable of performing application-level filtering for specific content. For instance, some firewall HTTP proxies look for tags in HTML pages that refer to Java or ActiveX embedded applets and then strip them out. This prevents the applet from executing on your client computers and eliminates the risk that a user will accidentally download a Trojan horse. This sort of filtering is extremely important because filtering, proxying, and masquerading can't prevent your network from being compromised if your users are lured into downloading a Trojan horse embedded in an ActiveX applet.

You may have noticed that as we've climbed through the networking layers, the security services have gotten more specific. For instance, filtering is specific to IP and then to TCP and UDP. Applications that use IP with other protocols like Banyan Vines must use special high-cost or unusually robust firewalls.

Proxies are extremely specific because they can only work for a specific application. For instance, you must have a proxy software module for HTTP, another proxy module for FTP, and another module for Telnet. As these protocols evolve (HTTP is particularly fast moving), the proxy module for that protocol will have to be updated.

Many protocols exist that are either proprietary or rare enough that no security proxies exist. Proxies don't exist for proprietary application protocols like Lotus Notes, so those protocols must either be sent through a network-layer filter or proxied by a generic TCP proxy that regenerates the packet and simply transfers the payload. SOCKS is a specific form of generic proxy that is sometimes called a circuit-level gateway. Although generic proxying cannot prevent attacks from the content of a protocol, it is still more secure than filtered routing because the network-layer packets are completely regenerated and thus scrubbed of malformations that might not be detected by the firewall.

Whenever possible, use proxy servers for all application protocols. Consider disallowing application protocols for which you do not have proxy servers. Use high-level proxies capable of stripping executable content like ActiveX and Java from web pages.

Firewall Privacy Services

Firewall Privacy Services are used to allow appropriate connections through the firewall, either from remote users or from firewalls at other sites belonging to the same company. These services are:

   ◇ Encrypted Authentication
   ◇ Virtual Private Networking

With many firewalls, these services are extra-cost options that must be enabled, but some manufacturers include these services at no additional cost. As with basic firewalling functions, these services could be performed by other devices on your network, but they are more secure when combined into a border router.

You don't have to incorporate these functions on your firewall—you could use a VPN device and a firewall in parallel, each performing its separate function. But then you have a situation where the VPN device itself is not firewalled and could be exploited (this was a serious problem with a widely deployed brand of VPN device) and where extra routers are required to properly route outbound traffic through either the VPN or the firewall. By combining VPN and firewall functions on a single device, these problems are eliminated.

Virtual Private Network
An encrypted tunnel.

Authentication

Authentication allows users on the public network to prove their identity to the firewall in order to gain access to the private network.

Essentially, authentication allows users to "log in" to the firewall itself, which will then allow the sessions from their computer to pass through it. For example, you might use this feature to allow remote salespeople to log into their e-mail accounts. Rather than leaving the IMAP, POP3, or MAPI ports open to the public, the firewall will only open these ports to those IP addresses that have successfully passed an authentication challenge. This keeps hackers from trying to run attacks against those ports, and you're not relying solely on the often-insecure login features of the application itself.

Often, authentication is combined with a VPN, but there's nothing that inherently restricts encrypted authentication from working with alone.

Virtual Private Networks

Virtual Private Networking establishes a secure connection between two private networks over a public medium like the Internet. This allows physically separated networks to use the Internet rather than leased-line connections to communicate as though they were directly connected. VPNs are also called encrypted tunnels.

NOTE

VPNs are extremely important to TCP/IP security, and are the exclusive topic of Chapter 6.

Other Border Services

While not specifically related to TCP/IP security, some security-related services are easily performed on border firewalls. These services are:

- ❖ Virus scanning
- ❖ Content filtering

There's no limit to the number of services that could be performed on a border firewall—but increasing the amount of software on any computing device increases the odds that a bug will make the software vulnerable to attack. For that reason, firewalls should only run software that is required to enact your security policy.

Virus Scanning

Virus scanning means searching inbound data streams for the signatures of viruses. Keeping up with current virus signatures requires a subscription to the virus update service provided by the firewall vendor.

> **NOTE**
>
> Chapter 8 discusses virus-scanning options in detail.

Content Blocking

Content blocking allows you to block internal users from accessing certain types of content by category, such as pornography, websites relating to hate groups, pornography, hacking sites, and pornography. Keeping up with the current list of blocked sites for a specific category also requires a subscription.

In my experience, content blocking doesn't work. There are so many new sites of these types cropping up that blocking vendors can't keep track of them. Users often feel like any site that isn't blocked is fair game, so content filtering frequently turns into a childish game of escalation between users and the IT staff. For example, you can't keep legitimate web users from using Google, but its Google Images search feature could easily be used to browse for unblocked pornography. Filters often "over block" by simply blocking on keywords, which leads to the blocking of legitimate sites that mention, for example, breast cancer or the holocaust.

virus scanning
Searching a file or communication stream for the identifying signature of a virus. A virus signature is simply a series of bytes that is deemed to be unique to the virus.

content blocking
A security measure that blocks access to websites based on keywords contained in the content.

A more realistic and manageable approach is to simply tell users that their website visits are logged on the firewall, and that they will be asked to justify browsing any suspicious sites. This will keep them from doing anything that violates your policy, allow broad access to legitimate sites, and won't require content-blocking subscriptions. You can often set up logs to include the amount of time a user spent on a specific website, so you can watch for inordinately long periods of random surfing, and eliminate "false hits" where a pop-up window in a justifiable site opens up a web page on the seedy side of the Internet.

Selecting a Firewall

There are hundreds of firewalls on the market, running on numerous different platforms. Selecting a firewall that matches your security requirements could take quite a bit of time.

Fortunately for you, the firewall market has shaken out a lot of competitors lately. Among the remaining firewalls, you need only seriously consider the following, which are among the strongest in the field and which remain reasonably inexpensive. They are listed here in order of ease-of use (easiest to hardest) and security (increasingly strong) order:

SonicWALL Firewalls   The easiest to use and least expensive device-based firewalls. They do not include proxy-level filtering, but can forward traffic to a proxy. Very similar to Firewall-1 in security and configuration, with a web interface.

WatchGuard Firebox Series   Strong security in a low-priced device-based firewall. These are the only true devices (no hard disk drive) that actually proxy the protocols. Based on Linux and FWTK underneath, with an administrative application that runs only in Windows.

Symantec VelociRaptor Security Device   A device (with hard disks) version of the strong Raptor security proxy. These are Sun RaQ computers preconfigured with Raptor Firewall.

NAI Gauntlet Firewall   The strongest firewall available, derived from the original TIS FWTK firewall software commissioned by the Defense Advanced Research Projects Agency. Also available in a "deviceified" version based on the Sun Sparc Ultra platform.

There's no reason to select a firewall just because it runs on the same operating system as the rest of your network. Most firewalls that run on operating systems are significantly less secure than device-based firewalls, because they rely on the operating system to withstand denial-of-service attacks at the lower layers and because other nonsecure services may be running on the operating system.

NOTE

The majority of firewalls are configured by creating a specific policy called a rule base, which typically lists pass/fail rules for specific protocols and ports. Typically, these rules are searched in top-down order, and the final order in the rule base is a "deny all" rule.

Once you've selected a firewall, configuration depends entirely upon the firewall you've selected. You need to make yourself an expert on that specific firewall. This isn't particularly difficult anymore, and there's little reason to worry about learning other firewalls once you've selected one.

Review Questions

1. Firewalls are derived from what type of network component?

   _____

2. What is the most important border security measure?

   _____

3. Why is it important that every firewall on your network have the same security policy applied?

   _____

4. What is a demilitarized zone?

   _____

5. Why is it important to deny by default rather than simply blocking dangerous protocols?

   _____

6. What fundamental firewall function was developed first?

   _____

7. Why was Network Address Translation originally developed?

   _____

8. Why can't hackers attack computers inside a Network Address Translator directly?

_____

9. How do proxies block malformed TCP/IP packet attacks?

_____

Chapter
6

Virtual
Private Networks

Virtual Private Networks provide secure remote access to individuals and businesses outside your network. VPNs are a cost-effective way to extend your LAN over the Internet to remote networks and remote client computers. VPNs use the Internet to route LAN traffic from one private network to another by encapsulating and encrypting unrestricted LAN traffic inside a standard TCP/IP connection between two VPN-enabled devices. The packets are unreadable by intermediary Internet computers because they are encrypted and they can encapsulate (or carry) any kind of LAN communications, including file and print access, LAN e-mail, and client/server database access. Think of a VPN as a private tunnel through the internet between firewalls within which any traffic can be passed securely.

Pure VPN systems do not protect your network—they merely transport data. You still need a firewall and other Internet security services to keep your network safe. However, most modern VPN systems are combined with firewalls in a single device.

In this chapter, you will learn about:

 The primary VPN mechanisms

 Characteristics of VPNs

 Common VPN implementations

 VPN Best practices

Chapter 6

Virtual Private Networking Explained

Virtual Private Networks solve the problem of direct Internet access to servers through a combination of the following fundamental components:

- IP **encapsulation**
- Cryptographic authentication
- Data payload encryption

All three components must exist in order to have a true VPN. Although cryptographic authentication and data payload encryption may seem like the same thing at first, they are actually entirely different functions and may exist independently of each other. For example, **Secure Socket Layer (SSL)** performs data payload encryption without cryptographic authentication of the remote user, and the standard Windows logon performs cryptographic authentication without performing data payload encryption.

IP Encapsulation

When you plan to connect your separated LANs over the Internet, you need to find a way to protect the data traffic that travels between those LANs. Ideally, the computers in each LAN should be unaware that there is anything special about communicating with the computers in the other LANs. Computers outside your virtual network should not be able to snoop on the traffic exchanged between the LANs or be able to insert their own data into the communications stream. Essentially, you need a private and protected tunnel through the public Internet.

An IP packet can contain any kind of information: program files, spreadsheet data, audio streams, or even other IP packets. When an IP packet contains another IP packet, it is called IP encapsulation, IP over IP, or IP/IP. Encapsulation is the process of embedding packets within other packets at the same network layer for the purpose of transporting them between the networks where they will be used. For example, you may want to connect two Novell networks that use IPX together over the Internet, so you could encapsulate the IPX packets within IP packets to transport them. The end router would remove IP packet and drop the IPX packet into the remote network.

Why encapsulate IP within IP? Because doing so makes it possible to refer to a host within another network when the route does not exist. For example, you can't route data to a computer inside the 10.0.0.0 domain because the Internet

Virtual Private Networks

A packet stream that is encrypted, encapsulated, and transmitted over a non-secure network like the Internet.

encapsulation

The insertion of a complete network layer packet within another network layer packet. The encapsulated protocol may or may not be the same as the encapsulating protocol, and may or may not be encrypted.

Secure Socket Layer (SSL)

A public key encryption technology that uses certificates to establish encrypted links without exchanging authentication information. SSL is used to provide encryption for public services or services that otherwise do not require identification of the parties involved but where privacy is important. SSL does not perform encapsulation.

backbone is configured to drop packets in this range. So connecting your branch office in Chicago (10.1.0.0 network) to your Headquarters in San Diego (10.2.0.0 network) cannot be accomplished over the Internet. However, you can encapsulate data exchanged between the two networks over the Internet by connecting to the routers (which have valid public IP addresses) and configuring the destination router to remove the encapsulated traffic and forward it to the interior of your network. This is called clear-channel tunneling.

NOTE

When the 10.0.0.0/8 and the 192.168.0.0/16 private network blocks were assigned, routing rules were created to ensure that they could not be routed over the Internet backbone. This provides a modicum of security and prevents conflicts with other networks using the same address block.

IP encapsulation can make it appear to computers inside the private network that distant networks are actually adjacent—separated from each other by a single router. But they are actually separated by many Internet routers and gateways that may not even use the same address space, because both internal networks are using address translation.

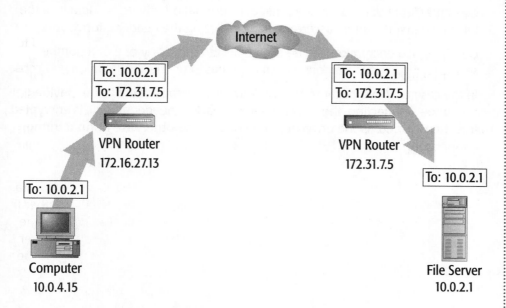

The tunnel endpoint—be it a router, firewall, VPN appliance, or a server running a tunneling protocol—will receive the public IP packet, remove the internal packet contained within it, decrypt it (assuming that it's encrypted—it doesn't have to be), and then apply its routing rules to send the embedded packet on its way in the internal network.

Cryptographic Authentication

Cryptographic authentication is used to securely validate the identity of the remote user so the system can determine what level of security is appropriate for that user. VPNs use cryptographic authentication to determine whether or not the user can participate in the encrypted tunnel and may also use the authentication to exchange the secret or public key used for payload encryption.

Many different forms of cryptographic authentication exist, and the types used by VPNs vary from vendor to vendor. In order for two devices from different vendors to be compatible, they must support the same authentication and payload encryption algorithms and implement them in the same way. Your best bet for determining compatibility is to perform a web search.

Data Payload Encryption

Data payload encryption is used to obfuscate the contents of the encapsulated data without relying on encapsulating an entire packet within another packet. In that manner, data payload encryption is exactly like normal IP networking except that the data payload has been encrypted. Payload encryption obfuscates the data but does not keep header information private, so details of the internal network can be ascertained by analyzing the header information.

Data payload encryption can be accomplished using any one of a number of secure cryptographic methods, which differ based on the VPN solution you chose.

In the case of VPNs, because the "real" traffic is encapsulated as the payload of the tunnel connection, the entire private IP packet, header and all, is encrypted. It is then carried as the encrypted payload of the otherwise normal tunnel connection.

local area networks (LAN)
High-speed (short distance) networks existing (usually) within a single building. Computers on the same local area network can directly address one another using data link–layer protocols like Ethernet or Token Ring, and do not require routing in order to reach other computers on the same LAN.

wide area networks (WAN)
Networks that span long distances using digital telephony trunks like dedicated leased lines, frame relay, satellite, or alternative access technologies to link local area networks.

dedicated leased lines
Digital telephone trunk lines leased from a telephone company and used to transmit digitized voice or data.

Characteristics of VPNs

When you consider establishing a VPN for your company, you should understand the advantages and disadvantages of VPNs when compared with traditional **local area networks (LANs)** and **wide area networks (WANs)**.

VPNS are cheaper than WANS.   A single dedicated leased line between two major cities costs many thousands of dollars per month, depending on the amount of bandwidth you need and how far the circuit must travel. A company's dedicated connection to an ISP is usually made with a leased line of this sort, but the circuit is much shorter—usually only a few miles—and an IP connection is usually already in place and budgeted for. With a VPN, only one leased line to an ISP is required and it can be used for both Internet and VPN traffic. ISPs can be selected for proximity to your operation to reduce cost.

VPNs are easier to establish.   It typically takes at least two months to get a traditional WAN established using **dedicated leased lines** or **frame relay**, and a lot of coordination with the various telecommunications companies is usually involved. In contrast, you can establish a VPN wherever an existing Internet connection exists, over any mix of circuits, and using whatever technology is most cost effective in each locale.

VPNs are slower than LANs.   You will not get the same performance out of your VPN that you would with computers that share the same LAN. Typical LANs transfer data at 10 or 100Mbps while the Internet limits VPNs to the slowest of the links that connect the source computer to the destination computer. Of course, WANs are no different; if you linked the same LANs directly via **T1 leased lines**, you would still have a 1.5Mbps (each way) bandwidth limit. Furthermore, you will find that Internet congestion between your VPN endpoints may put a serious drag on your network. The best way to take care of this problem is to use the same national or global ISP to connect your systems. This way, all your data will travel over their private network, thus avoiding the congested **commercial Internet exchange** network access points.

VPNs are less reliable than WANs.   Unexpected surges in Internet activity can reduce the bandwidth available to users of your VPN. Internet outages are more common than Telco circuit outages, and (recently) hacking and Internet worm activity has begun to eat up a considerable amount of bandwidth on the Internet, creating weather-like random effects. How susceptible your VPN is to these problems depends largely on the number of ISPs between your systems.

VPNs are less secure than isolated LANs or WANs.   Before a hacker can attack your network, there must be a way for the hacker to reach it. VPNs require Internet connections, whereas WANs don't, but most networks are connected to the Internet anyway. A VPN is marginally more vulnerable to network intrusion than a LAN or WAN that is connected to the Internet, because the VPN protocol's service port is one more vector for the hacker to try to attack.

frame relay
A data link–layer packet-switching protocol that emulates a traditional point-to-point leased line. Frame Relay allows the telephone companies to create a permanent virtual circuit between any two points on their digital networks by programming routes into their frame relay routers.

T1 leased lines
The traditional designator for the most common type of digital leased line. T1 lines operate at 1.544Mbps (as a single channel, or 1.536Mbps when multiplexed into 24 channels) over two pairs of category 2 twisted-pair wiring.

commercial Internet exchange (CIX)
One of an increasing number of regional datacenters where the various tier-1 ISPs interconnect their private networks via TCP/IP to form the nexus of the Internet.

Common VPN Implementations

Although theoretically any cryptographically strong algorithm can be used with some form of IP encapsulation to create a VPN, a few market leading implementations have arisen—either because they are easy to splice together from existing separate tools, because they are the agreed upon standards of numerous small vendors, or because a large vendor implemented them and incorporated them for free into ubiquitous products like operating systems. The common VPN implementations are:

- IPSec Tunnel Mode
- L2TP
- PPTP
- PPP/SSL or PPP/SSH

Each of these common implementations is detailed in the following sections.

IPSec

IPSec is the IETF's standard suite for secure IP communications that relies on encryption to ensure the authenticity and privacy of IP communications. IPSec provides mechanisms that can be used to do the following:

- Authenticate individual IP packets and guarantee that they are unmodified
- Encrypt the payload (data) of individual IP packets between two end systems
- Encapsulate a TCP or UDP socket between two end systems (hosts) inside an encrypted IP link (tunnel) established between intermediate systems (routers) to provide virtual private networking

IPSec performs these three functions using two independent mechanisms: Authenticated Headers (AH) to provide authenticity and Encapsulating Security Payload (ESP) to encrypt the data portion of an IP Packet. These two mechanisms may be used together or independently.

Authenticated Headers work by computing a checksum of all of the TCP/IP header information and encrypting the checksum with the public key of the receiver. The receiver then decrypts the checksum using its secret key and then checks the header against the decrypted checksum. If the computed checksum is different than the header checksum, it means that either the decryption failed because the key was wrong or the header was modified in transit. In either case, the packet is dropped.

NOTE

Because NAT changes header information, IPSec Authenticated Headers cannot be reliably passed through a network address translator (although some NATs can perform translation automatically for a single internal host). ESP can still be used to encrypt the payload, but support for ESP without AH varies among implementations of IPSec. These variations account for the incompatibilities between some vendor's IPSec VPN implementations.

With Encapsulating Security Payload, the transmitter encrypts the payload of an IP packet using the public key of the receiver. The receiver then decrypts the payload upon receipt and acts accordingly.

IPSec can operate in one of two modes: transport mode, which works exactly like regular IP except that the headers are authenticated (AH) and the contents are encrypted (ESP), or tunnel mode where complete IP packets are encapsulated inside AH/ESP packets to provide a secure tunnel. Transport mode is used for providing secure or authenticated communication over public IP ranges between any Internet-connected hosts for any purpose, while tunnel mode is used to create VPNs.

Internet Key Exchange

IPSec uses the concept of the **Security Associations (SA)** to create named combinations of keys, identifiers of cryptographic algorithms, and rules to protect information for a specific function. The policy (rule) may indicate a specific user, host IP address, or network address to be authenticated or it may specify the route for information to take.

In early IPSec systems, public keys for each SA were manually installed via file transfer or by actually typing them in. For each SA, each machine's public key had to be installed on the reciprocal machine. As the number of security associations a host required increased, the burden of manually keying machines became seriously problematic—IPSec was used primarily only for point-to-point systems because of this.

The **Internet Key Exchange (IKE)** protocol obviates the necessity to manually key systems. IKE uses private key security to validate the remote firewall's authority to create an IPSec connection and to securely exchange public keys. IKE is also capable of negotiating a compatible set of encryption protocols with a destination host, so that administrators don't have to know exactly which encryption protocols are supported on the destination host. Once the public keys are exchanged and the encryption protocols are negotiated, a security association is automatically created on both hosts and normal IPSec communications can

Security Associations (SA)
A set of cryptographic keys and protocol identifiers programmed into a VPN endpoint to allow communication with a reciprocal VPN endpoint. IKE allows security associations to be negotiated on-the-fly between two devices if they both know the same secret key.

Internet Key Exchange (IKE)
An protocol that allows the exchange of IPSec Security Associations based on trust established by knowledge of a private key.

be established. With IKE, each computer that needs to communicate via IPSec needs only to be keyed with a single private key. That key can be used to create an IPSec connection to any other IPSec host that has the same private key.

L2TP

Layer 2 Tunneling Protocol (L2TP) is an extension to the **Point-to-Point Protocol (PPP)** that allows the separation of the data link–layer endpoint and the physical-layer network access point. This means that, for example, you could outsource a **dial-up modem bank** to your phone company and have them forward the data in the modem conversation to you, so that your own routers can extract it and determine what to do with it. You save the cost of expensive telephone banks while retaining the ability to connect directly to dial-up users.

Like PPP, L2TP includes a mechanism for secure authentication using a number of different authentication mechanisms that can be negotiated amongst the connecting computers. L2TP is a tunneling protocol–its purpose is to embed higher layer packets into a protocol that can be transported between locations. Unlike pure IPSec tunneling, L2TP can support any interior protocol, including **IPX**, **AppleTalk**, or **NetBEUI**, so it can be used to create links over the Internet for protocols that are not Internet compatible. L2TP packets can also be encrypted using IPSec.

L2TP is also not a transport protocol–it can be transported over any data link–layer protocol (ATM, Ethernet, etc.) or network-layer protocol (IP, IPX, etc.). LT2P is essentially an "any-to-any" shim that allows you to move any protocol over any other protocol in a manner that can be negotiated between compatible endpoints.

You may have noticed that L2TP supports the three requisite functions to create a VPN: authentication, encryption, and tunneling. Microsoft and Cisco both recommend it as their primary method for creating VPNs. It is not yet supported by most firewall vendors, however.

PPTP

PPTP was Microsoft's first attempt at secure remote access for network users. Essentially, PPTP creates an encrypted PPP session between two TCP/IP hosts. Unlike L2TP, PPTP operates only over TCP/IP–L2TP can operate over any packet transport, including Frame Relay and **Asynchronous Transfer Mode (ATM)**. PPTP does not use IPSec to encrypt packets–rather it uses a hash of the user's Windows NT password to create a private key between the client and the remote server. This (in the 128-bit encrypted version) is salted with a random number to increase the encryption strength.

Layer 2 Tunneling Protocol (L2TP)

An industry standard protocol for separating the data link layer transmission of packets from the flow control, session, authentication, compression, and encryption protocols. L2TP is typically used for remote access applications and is the successor to PPP.

Point-to-Point Protocol (PPP)

A protocol originally developed to allow modem links to carry different types of network-layer protocols like TCP/IP, IPX, NetBEUI, and AppleTalk. PPP includes authentication and protocol negotiation, as well as control signals between the two points, but does not allow for addressing since only two participants are involved in the communication.

dial-up modem bank

A collection of modems connected to a high-speed network that are dedicated to the task of answering calls from the modems of end users, thereby connecting them to the network.

NOTE

L2TP is the successor to PPTP—it is more generalized in that it works over any packet transport, and its encryption strength is far stronger thanks to IPSec encryption. PPTP should be used for legacy compatibility, but new installations should favor L2TP for secure remote access.

Open-source developers for Unix implementations including Linux and the various **open source** BSD derivatives have implemented PPTP to support inexpensive encrypted tunnels with Windows clients. Both client-side and server-side implementations are available that interoperate well with Microsoft's implementation of PPTP. So while IPSec is still the future of VPNs, PPTP is a pragmatic "here now" solution to cross-platform VPN interoperability.

PPP/SSL or PPP/SSH

PPP (Point to Point Protocol) over Secure Socket Layer (SSL) or **Secure Shell (SSH)** are two common methods that Unix and open-source operating system administrators employ to create VPNs "on the fly." Both methods, which might be considered "hacks" in the Windows world, employ a clever combination of an existing encrypted transport (SSL or SSH) and an existing tunnel provider, PPP.

PPP

Point-to-Point Protocol was originally designed to support multiprotocol transport over serial lines. Originally, the dial-up access world was clearly split into operating system–specific camps. Windows, which supported only NetBIOS connections over modem links, Macintosh, which supported only AppleTalk connections, Unix, which supported only Serial Line IP (SLIP) connections, and NetWare which supported only IPX connections to NetWare servers. PPP was developed originally to abstract the protocol away from the connection so that a serial line connection could be established that would then be able to carry any network-layer protocol. So, essentially, PPP creates a data link–layer connection between endpoints over which a network-layer protocol can be transported—or, in other words, a tunnel.

Because of its flexibility, PPP can be used to create a connection between any two IP systems, and then transport IP over the PPP connection. This is an easy way to create IP/IP tunnels without specific operating system support for tunneling. But PPP performs no encryption, so while tunneling is useful, it's not secure.

Internetwork Packet Exchange (IPX)
IPX is the routable LAN protocol developed by Novell for their NetWare server operating system. IPX is very similar to TCP/IP, but it uses the data link–layer Media Access Control (MAC) address for unique addressing rather than a user-configured address, and is therefore easier to configure. IPX routes broadcasts around the entire network, and is therefore unsuitable in larger networks.

AppleTalk
The proprietary file and resource sharing mechanism for Apple Macintosh computers. Recent versions of the Mac OS are also compatible with the Windows (SMB) file sharing protocol.

NetBEUI
Microsoft's original networking protocol that allows for file and resource sharing but which is not routable and is therefore limited to operation on a single LAN. As with any protocol, NetBEUI can be encapsulated within a routable protocol to bridge distant networks.

SSL

Secure Socket Layer is a public key encryption protocol developed by Netscape to support secure web browsing. SSL does not perform authentication—its only purpose is to encrypt the contents of a connection between a client and a public server. So SSL performs an essentially "pure" public key exchange—when a client connects to the SSL port on a server, the server transmits an encryption key which the client uses to encrypt its data stream. The client does the same thing, so a bi-directional secure stream can be established. This stream is used to exchange a pair of randomly generated secret keys so that high-speed encryption algorithms can be used.

SSH

SSH is the Unix secure shell, which was originally designed to shore up the serious security flaws in Telnet. Telnet allowed users to connect to a Unix host and establish a remote text console from which the host could be operated. Because Telnet hails from those early days when hackers did not have access to the Internet, it performs no encryption and only simple unencrypted password challenges. SSH shores this up by performing secure authenticated logons using perfect forward secrecy and then by encrypting the communication session between the client and the host. Like most Unix applications, SSH can accept redirection to and from other running applications by correctly constructing "pipes" on the Unix command prompt. Unlike SSL, SSH uses secret key encryption so both parties must know the secret key in advance to establish a connection.

Securing PPP

Given the PPP command built into most modern implementations of Unix and either SSH or SSL, it's a simple task to construct a command that can direct the establishment of an encrypted tunnel and pipe its input and output streams to the PPP command. This, in essence, creates a virtual network adapter on each host system that is connected via PPP to the remote host, which is in turn encrypted by either SSH or SSL.

The security of a system like this is based mostly on the security of the underlying cryptosystem—SSL or SSH. If the administrator has done his homework and knows for certain the identity of the hosts involved in the connection, these connection methods can be as secure as PPTP or L2TP.

Asynchronous Transfer Mode (ATM)

A packet-switched data link–layer framing protocol used for high-speed digital circuits that is compatible across a wide range of physical circuit speeds. ATM is typically used for inter-city and metropolitan area circuits.

open source

Software produced by a free association of programmers who have all agreed to make their work available at no cost along with the original source code. Actual licensing terms vary, but generally there are stipulations that prevent the code from being incorporated into otherwise copyrighted software.

Secure Shell

A secure version of Telnet that includes public key-based authentication and encryption.

NOTE

Although the implementation differs in unimportant ways, PPTP is essentially PPP over SSL and provides basically equivalent security.

VPN Best Practices

Virtual Private Networks are convenient, but they can also create gaping security holes in your network. The following practices will help you avoid trouble.

Use a real firewall.   As with every other security component, the best way to ensure you have comprehensive security is to combine security functions on a single machine. Firewalls make ideal VPN endpoints because they can route translated packets between private systems. If your VPN solution weren't combined with your NAT solution, you'd have to open some route through your firewall for the VPN software or the NAT software, either of which could create a vector for attack.

Real firewalls are also most likely to use provably secure encryption and authentication methods, and their vendors are more likely to have implemented the protocol correctly. Ideally, you'd be able to find an open-source firewall whose source code you (and everyone else) could inspect for discernable problems.

Secure the base operating system.   No VPN solution provides effective security if the operating system of the machine is not secure. Presumably, the firewall will protect the base operating system from attack, which is another reason why you should combine your VPN solution with your firewall.

Implementing any sort of VPN endpoint on a server without also implementing strong filtering is asking for trouble—without a secure base operating system, the VPN can be easily hacked to gain access to your network from anywhere.

Use a single ISP.   Using a single ISP to connect all the hosts acting as tunnel endpoints will increase both the speed and security of your tunnel, because ISPs will keep as much traffic as they possibly can on their own networks. This means that your traffic is less exposed to the Internet as a whole and that the routes your ISP uses will avoid congestion points in the Internet. When you use multiple ISPs, they will most likely connect through the commercial Internet exchange network access points—the most congested spots on the Internet. This practically guarantees that your VPN tunnel will be slow, often uselessly slow for some protocols.

Choose an ISP that can also provide dial-up service to your remote users who need it. Alternatively, you may choose a local ISP that is downstream from your national ISP, because they are also on the national ISP's network and many national ISPs don't provide dial-up service.

Use packet filtering to reject unknown hosts.   You should always use packet filtering to reject connection attempts from every computer except those you've specifically set up to connect to your network remotely. If you are creating a simple network-to-network VPN, this is easy—simply cross-filter on the foreign server's IP address and you'll be highly secure. If you're providing VPN access to remote users whose IP address changes dynamically, you'll have to filter on the network address of the ISP's dial-up TCP/IP domain. Although this method is less secure, it's still considerably more secure than allowing the entire Internet to attempt to authenticate with your firewall.

Use public key encryption and secure authentication.   Public key authentication is considerably more secure than the simple, shared secret authentication used in some VPN implementations—especially those that use your network account name and password to create your secret key the way PPTP does. Select VPN solutions that use strong public key encryption to perform authentication and to exchange the secret keys used for bulk stream encryption.

Microsoft's implementation of PPTP is an example of a very insecure authentication method. PPTP relies upon the Windows NT account name and password to generate the authentication hash. This means that anyone with access to a valid name and password (like a malicious website that one of your users has visited that may have initiated a surreptitious password exchange with Internet Explorer) can authenticate with your PPTP server.

Compress before you encrypt.   You can get more data through your connection by stream compressing the data before you put it through your VPN. Compression works by removing redundancy. Since encryption salts your data with non-redundant random data, properly encrypted data cannot be compressed. This means that if you want to use compression, you must compress before you encrypt. Any VPN solution that includes compression will automatically take care of that function for you.

Secure remote hosts.   Make sure the remote access users who connect to your VPN using VPN client software are properly secured. Hacking Windows home computers from the Internet is depressingly easy, and can become a vector directly into your network if that home computer is running a VPN tunnel to it. Consider the case of a home user with more than one computer using a proxy product like WinGate to share his Internet connection who also has a VPN tunnel established over the Internet to your network. Any hacker on the planet could then proxy through the WinGate server directly into your private network. This configuration is far more common than it should be.

The new breed of Internet worms like Code Red, Nimda, and their derivatives are running rampant on the cable modem and DSL networks of home users right now. Here they find a garden of unpatched default installations of IIS, Microsoft's notoriously insecure web server. These clients are suddenly the Typhoid Marys of the corporate world, propagating worms to the interior of corporate networks through their VPN connections.

Alert users to the risks of running a proxy or web server (or any other unnecessary service) software on their home machines. Purchase personal firewall software to protect each of your home users; remember that when they're attached to your network, a weakness in their home computer security is a weakness in your network security.

Prefer compatible IPSec with IKE VPNs.   To achieve the maximum flexibility in firewalls and remote access software, choose IPSec with IKE VPN solutions that have been tested to work correctly with each other. IPSec with IKE is the closest thing to a standard encryption protocol there is, and although compatibility problems abound among various implementations, it is better than being locked into a proprietary encryption protocol that in turn locks you into a specific firewall vendor.

Review Questions

1. What are the three fundamental methods implemented by VPNs to securely transport data?

   _____

2. What is encapsulation?

   _____

3. Why are VPNs easier to establish than WANs?

   _____

4. What is the difference between IPSec transport mode and IPSec tunnel mode?

   _____

5. What functions does IKE perform?

   _____

6. What common sense measure can you take to ensure the reliability and speed of a VPN?

   _____

7. What is the most common protocol used among VPN vendors?

   _____

8. What's the primary difference between L2TP and PPP?

_____

9. What encryption algorithm is specified for L2TP?

_____

Terms to Know
- ❏ local area networks (LAN)
- ❏ NetBEUI
- ❏ open source
- ❏ Point-to-Point Protocol (PPP)
- ❏ Secure Shell
- ❏ Secure Socket Layer (SSL)
- ❏ Security Associations (SA)
- ❏ T1 leased lines
- ❏ Virtual Private Networks
- ❏ wide area networks (WAN)

Chapter

7

Securing Remote and Home Users

Just as a web browser can connect from a home computer to any web server on the planet, so can any network-enabled computer connect to any other type of server over the Internet. This means that home users can technically connect from their home computers directly to servers at work, just as if they were there (except slower). In the security-naïve early days of the Internet, many users did just this.

Since the Internet is simply a big network, there are no inherent restrictions on any type of use. Users from home could technically have direct access to files on a file server, could print to a network printer at the office, and could connect a database client directly to a database server.

But the requirement that the company's information technology assets be secured against hackers also secures them against remote home users. The firewalls that drop hackers' connection attempts will also drop remote users' attempts to connect to the network.

By establishing a VPN, you can both secure the transmission and enforce strong authentication, thus ensuring that remote home users will have access while hackers will not.

But VPNs are just the beginning of the real security problem.

In this chapter, you will learn about:

 The two major problems with remote access

 How to protect remote machines

 How to protect your network against remote users

The Remote Security Problem

There are two major problems with allowing legitimate remote users to access your network:

- ◇ Hackers can easily exploit home computers and use those computers' VPN connections to penetrate your network.
- ◇ Thieves can steal laptops containing VPN software and keys and use them to connect to your network.

The next two sections explain these problems in detail.

Virtual Private Security Holes

Many companies use VPNs to allow authorized users to securely transit fire-walls—the practice has become increasingly common in the last two years due to the convenience and efficiency it allows.

But this seriously undermines your network security policy. The problem is that hackers can quite easily exploit home computers that have not themselves been secured. And if that home computer has a VPN connection to your network, hackers can relay through the home computer and through the firewall via the virtual private tunnel. Most businesses do not attempt to enforce any sort of security requirements for remote home users, because they don't own the equipment and they can't really prevent users from circumventing security measures on their own computers.

This means that, in effect, every remote VPN connection you allow into your network is a potential vector for hackers to exploit.

Laptops

Laptops are an extraordinary convenience, especially for users who travel extensively. But they suffer from two very serious security problems.

Firstly, laptops are the Typhoid Marys of the computer world. They connect to networks all over the place, within your organization, the organizations of your business partners, Internet cafes, hotels, and home networks. Any viruses in these locations can easily jump to laptops, hibernate there, and then infect your network when the laptop is again attached to it. My company has a client whose network was infected by the Nimda worm because a third-party consultant brought his infected laptop to their company and attached it to the network.

Secondly, an amazing number of laptops are stolen every year. We all know that airports, hotels, taxis, and rental cars are obvious places from which a laptop may be stolen, but according to the FBI, 75% of all computer theft is perpetrated by employees or contractors of the business that experiences the loss. In 2000, nearly 400,000 laptops were stolen in the United States. Generally, 1 out of every 14 laptops will be stolen within 12 months of purchase, and 65% of companies that use laptops have reported that at least one of their laptops has been stolen. The FBI reports that 57% of corporate crimes (of all sorts) are eventually traced back to a stolen laptop that contained proprietary secrets or provided both the means and the information necessary to remotely penetrate the corporate network. Between the time that I wrote this chapter and reviewed it, a client of mine had four laptops, a projector, and a flat panel stolen by employees of its cleaning company.

While losing the hardware is an expensive inconvenience, losing the data can often be devastating. Loss of work done is bad enough, but the loss of proprietary secrets can potentially ruin a company.

But worse than all of that is losing control of security keys and VPN software when a laptop is stolen that could allow the thief to directly access your network. Many people never consider that "one-click" convenience to attach to the VPN using stored keys means that their laptop is essentially a portal into the network for anyone. Keep in mind that passwords in Windows 2000 and NTFS file system permissions are really just user-grade security efforts that any Windows administrator or competent hacker could easily defeat.

Protecting Remote Machines

Protecting remote machines from exploitation is actually pretty easy, but it requires diligence and constant monitoring. Diligence because you must protect every remote computer that you allow to connect to your machine. Just one unprotected machine connecting to your network allows a potential vector in, and with the contemporary threat of automated Internet worms, it's likely that every computer that can be exploited will be exploited—it's just a matter of time.

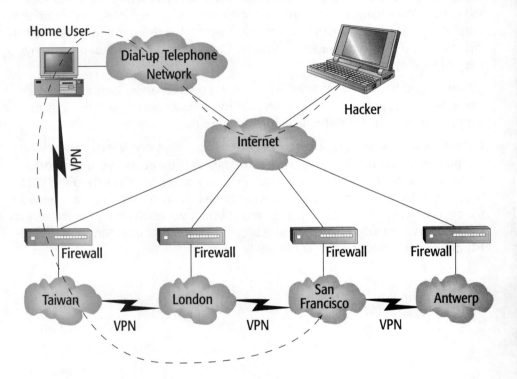

Monitoring is required to discover when a remote machine has become unprotected for some reason. The easiest way to monitor remote networks is to use the same tools that hackers use to find them: port scanners. By setting up a scriptable port scanner to constantly check for ports that a hacker might exploit across the entire range of remote computers, you can discover and close those ports. For machines that do not have fixed IP addresses, a clever administrator could create a script that receives the VPN client's public IP address, scans it, and then drops the VPN connection if the machine might be exploitable.

Due Diligence

A perfect example of the necessity for constant diligence is my own failure to protect my laptop. Even though I completely understand the risks of unprotected Internet access, I once forgot to enable a software firewall on my laptop when I was connected to an unprotected Internet connection. Frankly, I was so used to working behind a firewall that I forgot that the Internet connection at my ISP's co-location facility was open to the Internet. During just the 15 minutes that I was using this connection, before I remembered that it was not secure, my computer had already been scanned and was in the process of uploading the Code Red worm when I stopped it and enabled its software firewall. It was only the unusual activity of the hard disk light that alerted me to the fact that something was going on. So I've since mandated that firewalling software should be left enabled by default on all laptops at my firm, except when the laptops are being used for network sniffing and ping scanning (which the firewall software will interfere with).

personal firewall applications
Software programs that protect an individual computer from intrusion by filtering all communications that enter through network connections.

VPN software client
A software application for individual computers that creates VPN connections to VPN servers or devices.

VPN Connections

You need to provide the same sort of firewall protection for remote users that you provide to your network in order to properly secure a computer that will be connecting to your network via VPN.

There are two methods you can use: provide an actual firewall for home users, or provide software firewall applications.

Software Firewall Applications

Software-based PC **personal firewall applications** like Symantec's Norton Personal Firewall and ZoneAlarm are excellent ways to prevent direct intrusion into a client computer. But they can cause problems for users, since they get in the way of file sharing and can cause other similar problems for users who want to use networking at home.

VPN software clients, which are required to connect to the company network and must operate on the same computer as the software firewall filters, are notoriously hard to use and glitchy. They are usually difficult to set up, and they frequently cause problems for the host operating system because the software tends to require very specific versions of certain operating system files. It's likely that upgrading to a new service pack will cause problems for these programs, and it's certain that upgrading to a new operating system will. They also tend not to play well with software firewall filters because the filters block the protocols that the VPN software requires to establish the connection.

The only way to figure out exactly what's going to work and what isn't, is for you to take the VPN software client software that allows remote users to connect to your company firewall and test it with various software firewall applications that you are considering to protect remote users. Firewall applications vary widely in both software quality and feature set. Many of them aren't as secure as they seem, and some cause serious problems for the computers that they are installed upon. Testing is crucial to uncovering these problems before the software is deployed to end users.

Firewall Devices for Home Users

A vastly better (but more expensive) solution is to simply use a real device-based firewall for every home user. This device category is becoming very broad, with entries from firewall vendors like SonicWALL and WatchGuard below the $500 mark, that include VPN connectivity. These devices are true firewalls and support features like NAT, VPN, and sophisticated filter setup. When you connect these firewalls to a home user's broadband Internet connection, you are ensuring their security with the same level of protection that you use to ensure your company's security.

But $500 can be expensive when multiplied by every remote user you need to support. Fortunately, devices called **NAT routers** made by companies like Linksys, NETGEAR, and D-Link can provide very strong firewall security for less than $100. These devices were originally devised as a way to share a single broadband Internet connection. Because they are NAT devices, they automatically block all inbound connections since there's no route to the interior private network. Because they are devices in general, they don't require any software setup on the protected computers and won't interfere with file sharing for interior machines. The latest versions of these devices support IPSec passthrough for a single connection, which allows remote users to use VPN software from a machine protected by the NAT device. Most of these devices contain an embedded web server for administration, so you just point your web browser to their LAN address to manage them.

Linksys has just released a version of its very popular NAT router for well under $200 that includes a full IPSec client, so it can be directly connected to your company LAN to provide all the computers in a home office or even a small branch office with a true VPN connection. My company has used these devices

NAT routers

Small routers that provide (typically) just the network address translation function of a firewall. Originally used to share a single IP connection for home users, they have recently become more important for home computer security since they are natural firewalls. These devices are frequently marketed as "cable-DSL routers."

to connect to various high-end firewalls with great success. The competitors are certain to follow suit shortly.

When you consider that VPN client software typically runs $70 per client, and a firewall application costs $40 per client, paying for a VPN-enabled NAT router that requires less administration, causes fewer problems, and is highly reliable makes sense.

Data Protection and Reliability

The laptops of traveling users can't be secured with NAT routers very conveniently, especially if the laptop users frequently use modem connections. For these users, there's little choice but to use VPN clients and software firewall applications.

To mitigate the loss of control over information when a laptop is stolen, use encryption software like ScramDisk (my personal favorite), Windows 2000 Encrypting File Service, or any of a number of other encryption services. Most of these services work by creating a single large encrypted volume that is mounted like a normal hard disk drive once you enter the key phrases. The Encrypting File Service encrypts individual files and directories based on a key stored in the registry, which could theoretically be retrieved unless you use Microsoft's Syskey utility for encrypting the Security Accounts Manager portion of the registry and configure it to request a password at boot time. In any case, any reasonable type of encryption will prevent most hackers and thieves from retrieving anything of value from your computer.

WARNING

You must configure Syskey to ask for a password during the boot process in order for it to remain secure, as its default mode (with a key stored in the registry) is only one iteration of obscurity beyond the SAM itself, and it has already been cracked.

To prevent files from being lost when a laptop is damaged by dropping it, store your documents on a **flash memory** device like a PCMCIA card, CardFlash, Smart Media, Memory Stick, Secure Digital or MultiMedia Card, or USB Flash memory fob. These devices are solid state and impervious to normal failure and most accidental damage. An easy way to achieve true data protection is to encrypt the contents of the flash device, so that if the memory card is lost or stolen it won't compromise your information.

flash memory
A trade name for Electrically Erasable Programmable Read-Only Memory (EEPROM) that can be erased using the same voltage levels with which it can be programmed. Flash memory is non-volatile permanent storage that is exceptionally reliable, and is now used in almost every computing device on the market to store upgradeable boot loaders or operating systems. Flash memory is also used to make a wide variety of convenient memory storage for cameras, PDAs, and laptops in various form factors.

My company uses USB keychain flash memory to store secure information. Our laptops have the encryption software, and the file containing the encrypted disk is stored on the USB keychain, which is kept with each user's car keys. This way, encrypted data isn't lost when the laptops are stolen or broken, and the keychains don't suffer from hard disk failure because they're solid state. Also, the USB interface is ubiquitous (unlike PCMCIA, CardFlash, Memory Stick, or Smart Media memory solutions) and can be mounted on any computer with the encryption software. The encryption software we use performs steganography, so our encrypted disk stores are actually large sound files that remain playable with encrypted data in them, thus fooling anyone who happens to find the keychain into thinking that it's just a dongle with a song on it.

Backups and Archiving

Laptops almost never get backed up, because it's exceptionally difficult to attach a tape drive to them, and most other forms of removable media are too inconvenient to bother with.

I break with tradition on this problem and recommend that you don't bother trying to enforce a backup policy for laptops. Rather, it is most effective for users to simply keep their working documents on removable flash memory in the laptop, which isn't going to fail when the hard disk fails.

This doesn't protect against theft or accidental loss, however. To protect against those problems, teach users to remove the flash memory whenever they aren't actually using the laptop and store it somewhere safe and not along with the laptop. I recommend using USB keychain–style flash memory for this purpose, because people never forget to remove their keychain from the laptop when they're done and they're good about keeping track of their keys.

Protecting against Remote Users

Despite all of these security precautions, it remains impossible for you to truly control what happens to computers that are outside of your network. A coworker's child may download a Trojan horse in a video game demo, which connects back to a hacker and then allows that hacker access to your VPN. No firewall device or personal firewall application can prevent these sorts of problems because home users will circumvent the highly restrictive policies that would be required to mitigate this type of problem.

So you have to ask yourself if allowing VPN access from home users is necessary and wise considering your security posture. You may very well be better off allowing controlled access for specific protocols through your firewall than providing the wide open unencumbered access that a VPN provides. While hackers could attempt to exploit your open protocols, securing a single known open protocol is far easier than securing against the wide range of exploits that could be perpetrated through a VPN.

If users really only need a single protocol to perform their work, and that protocol doesn't suffer from known exploits, and the protocol provides strong authentication, it's a good candidate for simply passing through your firewall.

An example of a protocol that could be reliably used in this manner is **Windows Terminal Services**. Terminal servers provide a broad range of services to users very efficiently and are commonly used to provide low-bandwidth users with access to a network's data.

As long as passwords aren't easily guessed, exposing Terminal Services to the Internet is a lot more secure than opening up VPN connections to your network. Viruses cannot automatically transit through a Terminal Services connection because there's no file services connection. A hacker who has exploited a home user's computer doesn't have any more access to the terminal server than he would have from his own home, because he would still need the account name and password for the remote network in order to log in.

Once remote users have logged into Terminal Services, they will have just as much access to applications and ability to perform work as they would have if they were in the building. The relative richness of the protocol is what makes it a good candidate to simply replace VPN accessibility for remote users.

Other protocols that could be candidates for opening to the Internet are **Secure Shell (SSH)** (for text-based applications on Unix machines) and secure web-enabled applications (as long as proper web server security measures have been implemented).

Windows Terminal Services
A service of Windows that implements the Remote Data Protocol (RDP), which intercepts video calls to the operating system and repackages them for transmission to a remote user (as well as receiving keystrokes and mouse pointer data from the remote user), thus enabling a low-bandwidth remotely controlled desktop environment in which any applications can be run.

secure shell (SSH)
A secure encrypted version of the classic Telnet application. SSH uses public key cryptography to authenticate SSH connections, and private key encryption with changing keys to secure data while in transit.

Review Questions

1. Why are VPN connections potentially dangerous?

   _____

2. What threats are presented to network security by laptop users?

   _____

3. Why are laptops the most likely source of virus infection in a protected network?

   _____

4. What percentage of corporate crimes has the FBI traced back to stolen laptops?

   _____

5. What software should be used to protect laptops from hackers?

   _____

6. What is the best way to protect home computers from hackers?

   _____

7. How should you reduce the risk posed by lost information when a laptop is stolen?

   _____

8. What is the best way to prevent the loss of data from a damaged or stolen laptop?

_____

9. Are VPNs always the most secure way to provide remote access to secure networks?

_____

Chapter
8

Virus Protection

Computer viruses are **self-replicating** malicious programs that attach themselves to normal programs without the user's awareness or consent. They are one of the most feared causes of data loss—but, as it turns out, they have more of a reputation than they deserve. More than 90% of viruses are completely harmless aside from the computing resources that they waste by propagating. You are much more likely to lose data due to a hardware failure or by human error than due to a virus infection.

Despite the fact that most viruses are harmless, some viruses cause all sorts of unexpected behavior like system crashes, strange pop-up messages, and the deletion of important files. Some extremely clever worms copy themselves using the Internet and can absorb so much bandwidth that they interfere with the proper operation of your Internet connections. Even completely benign viruses that have no apparent ill affects expand the size of executable files and macro-enabled documents like barnacles encrusting a ship's hull.

In this chapter, you will learn about:

 How viruses operate in your network

 How viruses propagate

 Common types of virus attacks

 How to protect your network from viruses

Understanding Viruses

self-replicating
Having the ability to create copies of itself.

executable code
Information that represents computer instructions. Lists of code called programs are executed by a microprocessor in order to perform a function.

data
Information that represents some real world information, like a novel, a picture, a sound, or a bank account. Data is processed by code to create answers that are themselves represented by data and can be further processed.

macro
A list of instructions stored as data that is interpreted by a scripting host.

execution environments
Any environment that interprets data as actions and performs those actions. An execution environment might be a microprocessor, a virtual machine, or an application that interprets a script or macro.

To combat viruses effectively, you need to understand how they propagate and what defenses are available.

Computers store two entirely different types of information: **executable code** and **data**. Code specifies how the computer should operate, while data provides the information on which the operation is performed. For example, in the equation 1+1=2, the 1, 1, and 2 are the data and the + and = are code. The difference between code and data is crucial to virus defense because only code is susceptible to virus infection. Viruses can corrupt data but cannot propagate using pure data, because data does not provide an execution environment for viruses to run in.

But it's not always clear what is data and what is code. Is a Word document code or data? It's mostly data, but because Word documents can contains **macros** that Word interprets in order to perform complex operations, it can also contain code. The same goes for any macro-enabled application that stores a mixture of code and data in a single document. Applications that look at data and then perform wide-ranging operations based on that data are called **execution environments**, **interpreters,** or **scripting hosts**.

You could consider any use of data to be interpretation, but for viruses to propagate the execution environment needs to be complicated enough to allow for self-replication. This is a very high-level function that is typically only available when a scripting host running an interpreted computer language is built into an application.

What does all this really mean? Simple. You don't have to worry about viruses in pictures, audio files, online movies, and other programs that merely edit or display content, but you do need to worry about programs that use content to control the program's behavior. If the control mechanisms are complex enough to allow self-replication to occur, the application could host viruses.

> ### NOTE
> When you search the Web, you'll often see the term "virii" used as the plural for virus. Since "virus" comes from Greek and not Latin, its correct plural is "viruses," not "virii." But most hackers don't know that, so they use the term "virii" for the plural.

Virus Operation

Viruses have two separate and distinct functions:

- ◆ Propagation code is required for viruses to copy themselves. Without a **propagation engine**, viruses would just be normal programs.
- ◆ Attack code is included in viruses that have some specific malicious activity to perform, such as erasing data, installing a Trojan horse for further direct attacks, or displaying a message on the screen.

Benign viruses only have propagation code, and exist (usually) because hackers are testing a propagation engine and want to determine how far it will spread. Since the virus doesn't do anything, it's likely nobody will discover it, so the virus protection industry won't capture its signature and prevent its movement.

Malignant viruses include attack code that performs some annoying or damaging act, like deleting files, changing file names, and so forth. Many malignant viruses are not immediately triggered, but lie dormant waiting for a date or an event to occur before executing so that they can propagate before they damage their host.

A Brief History of Viruses

Believe it or not, viruses were invented by accident. Two men who owned a computer store in Pakistan devised a clever on-screen advertisement for their store. They wrote the advertisement so that it would propagate by copying itself to whatever program was loaded until it reached the boot sector, at which point it would flash its advertisement on the screen and copy itself to subsequently loaded files.

This advertisement eventually infected a hacker's computer. The hackers immediately understood the virus's potential to propagate mischief, and thus the Pakistani Brain virus was invented. That same virus engine was modified to become the infamous Stoned virus, as well as the Friday the 13th virus, and a host of others. Each of these viruses relied upon the sharing of programs via floppy disk in order to propagate.

The panic caused by these viruses spawned the virus protection industry. At first, it appeared that the virus makers would forever have the edge, because in the early days of the computer industry, software piracy was somewhat the norm—an environment in which viruses flourished. A lack of understanding and an ignorance of the damage caused by viruses led to a hysteria that was never really justified by the actual threat—oddly parallel to epidemics of biological viruses, which served only to strengthen the analogy between the two.

interpreter
A programming language application that loads scripts as data and then interprets commands step-by-step rather than by compiling them to machine language.

scripting hosts
Execution environments that can be called from applications in order to execute scripts contained in the application's data.

propagation engine
The code used by a virus to self-replicate.

benign viruses
Viruses that do not destroy data. Benign viruses may display a simple message or may simply propagate without performing any other function.

malignant viruses
Viruses that contain attack code that performs some malicious act.

But as anti-virus software became better and protection manufacturers became savvier, the tide began to turn. And once businesses became more willing to treat anti-virus software like a true tool and purchase it, the virus epidemic subsided. With the widespread use of permissions-based operating systems like derivatives of Windows NT and Unix, it's no longer possible for viruses to propagate "up the chain" to the operating system where they can be spread to other applications. In these environments, they sit dormant and can't spread. Since virus protection manufacturers now have far more development manpower than hackers, it's unlikely that old-fashioned executable computer viruses will ever again reach epidemic proportions.

But when new methods of virus propagation appear, it takes virus protection manufacturers days to detect and respond to the new threat. This gives time for the virus to spread without inhibition. So viruses that can spread quickly—by using the Internet and automatic methods like exploiting e-mail programs with scripting hosts (Microsoft Outlook)—can span the globe before the virus scanners are updated. Further complicating the problem is the fact that many users never update their virus protection software, so new types of viruses are not detected.

Understanding Virus Propagation

When you launch a program on any computer, you are directing an existing running program to launch it for you. In Windows, this program is (usually) Windows Explorer. It could technically be many other programs, like the command prompt or Internet Explorer (if you download the program and choose to open it from its current location). On a Macintosh it's usually the Finder, and in Unix it's the command shell or the X windows manager. The important concept is that every program is started by another program in an unbroken chain all the way back to the initial bootstrap code stored permanently in the computer's motherboard.

So how do viruses wedge themselves into this process? How do they know which programs to infect that will spread them and which will simply cause them to lie dormant? Usually, they don't. Viruses only know the program that was running when they were first executed (like Internet Explorer) and the program that started that program. When a virus is first executed, it attaches itself to the beginning of the current program. The next time that program is run, it takes the information about the program that started the current program to determine what file it should infect next, and attaches itself to the beginning of that program. In this way, the virus propagates one step closer to the beginning of the chain each time the programs in the startup chain are launched.

Viruses also attach themselves to each program that the current program launches. In most cases this is nothing—most applications can't launch other programs. But some do, and when those applications are found, the virus automatically spreads. The graphic that follows shows how a virus attached to Internet Explorer can propagate back to the program that launched it (Word), then back to Windows Explorer, and from there to other applications.

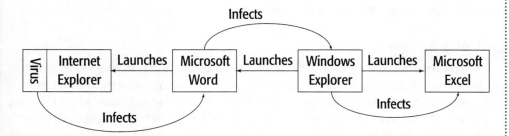

> **NOTE**
>
> It's important to note that viruses require human activity—booting a floppy, executing a program, or clicking on an attachment—in order to activate and spread. Viruses that can spread without human activity are referred to as **worms**.

Common Types of Virus Attacks

Types of viruses are defined mostly by the propagation method they use. In many cases, an entire class of viruses is composed of permutations of just a single virus, so they're nearly equivalent. Viruses are categorized by their ultimate target, as described in the following sections.

Boot Sector Viruses

Boot sector viruses were the original viruses, and they spread by the only common means of sharing information in the early days of computers—on floppy disks. Twenty years ago, networks were uncommon. Most data was shared by copying it to floppy disks. It was common at that time to boot floppy disks for special purposes like playing games or simply because the floppy had been left in the drive when the computer was turned off. Boot sector viruses would copy themselves to the boot sector of the host when the floppy was booted, and then subsequently infect every floppy that was inserted into the computer.

Thanks to the proliferation of networks, these viruses are practically extinct.

worms
Viruses that spread over a network automatically without human intervention.

boot sector
The first executable code stored on a disk, which is used to load the operating system.

135

Executable Viruses

Executable viruses infect the startup code for programs, and propagate back to the **shell** or desktop application of the computer in order to infect all programs launched from it.

Because of the native immunity to this activity in modern permissions-based operating systems, these viruses have become rare, except in places where older operating systems are common.

shell
A command-line interface to an operating system.

macro virus
Viruses that exist in the interpreted code embedded in Office documents. These viruses are not capable of escaping the confines of their interpreted environment, so they cannot infect executables.

Macro Viruses

Macro viruses are written in a higher-level language, such as the Visual Basic scripting language built into Microsoft Office, so they are related to other interpreted language viruses like those that can infest Java applications. Macro viruses attach themselves to document templates and can spread to other documents that are saved after opening the infected one. They spread like wildfire through corporate networks where users share documents indiscriminately.

Luckily, most Office document macro viruses are relatively harmless, and Microsoft has worked to close the security holes in the Office macro languages (the most common macro viruses are specific to Word and Excel). The latest version of Office ships with immunity enabled by default, so macro viruses will become obsolete when this software becomes widespread.

E-mail Viruses

Unfortunately, the same application language has been built into Microsoft Outlook, the e-mail software that comes with Office (and it's free with the operating system sibling, Outlook Express). Viruses written for Outlook can automatically read your list of contacts from the Address Book or Contacts folder and mail themselves to everyone you know, thus propagating extremely rapidly. Currently, Outlook e-mail viruses are by far the fastest spreading and largest threat in the virus world.

E-mail viruses are rarely completely automatic (although there are some susceptibilities in Outlook that could allow this to happen). They almost always rely upon the recipient to click on the embedded attachment to execute it, and then immediately propagate by scanning that user's address book and e-mailing itself to everyone that the user knows. Once they've propagated, they perform their attack code.

The latest versions of Outlook are automatically immune to most of these attacks, but since these attacks rely upon human psychology to activate the virus, it's likely that they will never completely go away.

Worms

Worms are viruses that spread automatically, irrespective of human behavior, by exploiting bugs in applications that are connected to the Internet. Code Red and Nimda are two recent and very widespread worms that illustrate exactly what happens with these types of viruses: From an infected machine, the virus scans the network searching for targets. It then contacts the target, initiates a benign exchange, exploits a bug in the receiver's server software to gain control of the server momentarily, and uploads itself to the target. Once the target is infected, the process starts again on it.

Worms are basically impossible for end users to prevent, and they typically exploit newly found bugs that are either un-patched or not widely patched in a vendor's code. When they attack extremely common systems like Windows or Linux, they spread very quickly and can cause enormous damage before they're stopped.

The only defense against worms is to avoid systems that are routinely compromised, like Microsoft Internet Information Server, and to stay up to date on patches and security fixes for all your public servers. Run only those services you intend to provide on public servers—don't just install everything for the sake of convenience when you set up a public server. Use firewalls to prevent worms from reaching the interior of your network from the Internet, and keep your virus-scanning software updated. But even with all these precautions, you can only be protected against worms that the vendors know about, and it's quite likely that a worm will infest your public servers at some point, so keep good backups as well.

Virus Protection

There are three ways to keep computers virus free:

◆ Prevention

◆ Natural Immunity

◆ Protection

Each method is an important part of total defense, and you should implement policies to encourage all of them. Of course, the best way to prevent viruses is to avoid risky behavior and programs altogether.

Prevention

There was a time when you could avoid viruses by never pirating software and avoiding free downloadable software from the Internet. Unfortunately, with the advent of e-mail viruses, you now also must ensure that you don't know anybody who does this either, which is basically impossible.

Macro viruses took the corporate world by storm because virus-scanning software wasn't prepared for them. When they first appeared, scanning software only checked executable code, not documents, and people were used to indiscriminately trading documents. Although these viruses could only infect Office documents, they wreaked havoc because the primary job of many corporate computers is to run Office applications.

Prevention today means the following:

◆ Being very selective about software you install from the Internet.

◆ Never clicking on e-mail attachments that you didn't ask for.

◆ Configuring programs like Outlook to automatically quarantine executable attachments according to the instructions at the www.Microsoft.com/security website.

◆ Disabling macro execution in Office applications unless you absolutely need it.

◆ Configuring your computer's BIOS to lock the boot sector, except when you are re-installing your operating system.

These measures will go a very long way in preventing you from getting a virus. In the two decades since viruses first appeared, no computer of mine has been infected or spread a virus to others, and I've never run virus software to protect them (although after catching an attempted worm infection in progress, I now run a personal firewall on my laptop to prevent Nimda infections).

Natural Immunity

Due to its inherent security, versions of Windows based on the NT kernel (Windows NT, Windows 2000, and Windows XP—hereafter referred to as NT to distinguish them from those based on the Windows 95 platform) are immune to executable file viruses as long as you use the NTFS file system and are not logged in as the administrator when you install software. However, NT cannot prevent the spread of viruses that infect non-executable files—like Office documents that normal users must have Write access to.

For a virus to spread to the program that loaded it, the user loading the program must have Write access to the executable file doing the loading. As soon as you hit an actual system file, the NT kernel will pop up with an Access Denied message, usually aborting the executable load. You may not know what's happening (and you may blame the operating system) but virus propagation is stopped cold by the NT kernel's inherent security.

However, users who store files on your NT-based server but run them on their Windows 95/98/Me-based computers have no such protection. Just because a virus can't spread to your server doesn't mean your server can't host it. Client operating systems see a server as just a big shared hard disk, so any executable files containing viruses they copy to your server will still contain viruses. You won't be able to run them on the server, but other users will be able to load them on other client computers running Windows 95/98/Me, MS-DOS, Apple Macintosh, or other simpler client operating systems. This is somewhat analogous to a carrier organism that is itself immune to the effects of a virus but is still contagious to other organisms.

Active Protection

Virus scanners provide the only way to actually recover from a virus infestation. Virus software works by scanning through every executable file looking for the **signatures** (unique code sequences) of viruses. The process is much like spell-checking a Word document—the scanner reads through the file looking for any virus signature in its dictionary of viruses. When a virus is found, the file is examined and the virus is removed from the file. After scanning all your mass storage devices, all viruses will be removed from your system.

Many viruses cause corruption to files beyond simply attaching to them, and frequently virus scanners can remove the virus but cannot fix the specific corruption that the virus caused. In this case, check the virus vendor's website for a special program that can repair the corruption caused by a specific virus. Some viruses also cause such widespread damage that special virus removal

virus scanner
Software that scans every executable file on a computer searching for virus signatures.

signature
A short sequence of codes known to be unique to a specific virus, which indicates that virus's presence in a system.

programs are required to completely eradicate them. If this is the case, your virus scanner should tell you that it was unable to remove a virus.

Most modern virus-protection software also comes with **inoculators** that check software as it is loaded and interrupts the load process if a virus is found. This can be very convenient, because it keeps infestation from happening in the first place.

Unfortunately, viruses tend to bounce around in network environments. Eliminating a network virus infestation is difficult because people often reintroduce viruses from machines that aren't yet clean. The only way to prevent this is to either disconnect all computers from the network and disallow their re-attachment until they've been cleaned, or to use enterprise virus-scanning software that can be centrally deployed and simultaneously scan all computers on the network.

inoculator

Anti-virus software that scans data files and executables at the moment they are invoked and which block them from being loaded if they contain a virus. Inoculators can prevent viruses from spreading.

Implementing Virus Protection

Although it used to be possible to avoid viruses by avoiding software downloads and avoiding clicking on e-mail attachments, it's no longer feasible to think that every user will always do the right thing in the face of the rampant virus propagation going on now. Especially with e-mail viruses and Internet worms (which you can receive irrespective of how you behave), you can no longer guarantee that you'll remain virus free no matter what you do.

You must implement virus scanners in order to protect your computer and your network from virus attack. But purchasing software once is not sufficient for staying up to date with the virus threat, because new viruses crop up every day. All major virus protection vendors offer subscription services that allow you to update your virus definitions on a regular basis. Whether or not this process can be performed automatically depends on the vendor, as does the administrative difficulty of setting up automatic updating.

TIP

Frequent (daily) automatic updates are a mandatory part of anti-virus defense, so don't even consider virus scanners that don't have a good automatic update service.

Virus scanners can be effectively implemented in the following places:

- On each client computer
- On servers
- On e-mail gateways
- On firewalls

Larger enterprises use virus scanners in all of these places, whereas most small businesses tend to go with virus protection installed on individual computers. Using all of these methods is overkill, but which methods you choose will depend largely on how you and your users work.

Client Virus Protection

Client-based virus protection is the traditional method of protecting computers from viruses. Virus scanners are installed like applications, and once installed they begin protecting your computer from viruses. There are two primary types, which are combined in most current packages.

Virus scanners   The original type of virus protection. In the days of MS-DOS and Windows 3.1, these programs ran during the boot process to scan for viruses and disinfected your computer each time you booted it. They did not protect you from contracting or spreading viruses, but they would make sure that it would not affect you for long.

Inoculators   A newer methodology that wedges itself into the operating system to intercept attempts to run programs or open files. Before the file can be run or opened, the inoculator scans the file silently in the background to ensure that it does not contain a known virus. If it does, the inoculator pops up, informs you of the problem, disinfects the file, and then allows you to proceed to use the file. Innoculators cannot find dormant viruses in unused files that may have been on your computer before you installed the scanner or in files that are mounted on removable media like zip disks or floppy drives.

Both types are required for total virus defense on a computer, and all modern virus applications include both.

The dark side of client-side virus protection software is the set of problems it can cause. Besides the obvious problems of buggy virus software, all virus software puts a serious load on your computer. Inoculators that scan files that are being copied can make transporting large amounts of data between computers extremely time intensive. Virus scanners will also interfere with most operating system upgrade programs and numerous setup programs for system services. To prevent these problems, you will probably have to disable the virus inoculators before installing many software applications on your computer.

Another problem with client-side virus protection is ubiquity: all the clients have to be running virus protection for it to remain effective. Machines that slip through the cracks can become infected and can transmit viruses to shared files, causing additional load and recurring corruption for users that do have virus applications.

Client-side virus scanners are good enough to keep most smaller businesses virus free. Even if dormant viruses exist on the server, they will be found and cleaned when they are eventually opened, and if the files are never again opened, the virus is irrelevant.

Server-Based Virus Protection

Server-based virus protection is basically the same as client-side protection, but it runs on servers. In the server environment, the emphasis is on virus scanning rather than inoculation because files are not opened on the server, they're merely copied to and from it. Scanning the network streams flowing into and out of a busy server would create far too much load, so server-based virus protection invariably relies upon scanning files on disk to protect against viruses. Servers themselves are naturally immune to viruses as long as administrators don't run applications indiscriminately on the servers while they are logged in with administrative privileges.

Server-side scanners are normally run periodically to search for viruses, either nightly (the preferred method) prior to the daily backup, or weekly, as configured by the administrator.

Server-based virus protection does not disinfect clients, so it alone is not sufficient for total virus protection. It is effective in eliminating the "ping-pong" effect where some clients that don't have virus protection continually cause problems for clients that do.

E-mail Gateway Virus Protection

E-mail gateway virus protection is a new but important method of controlling viruses. Since nearly all modern virus infections are transmitted by e-mail attachments, scanning for viruses on the e-mail gateway is an effective way to stop the vast majority of virus infestations before they start. Scanning the e-mail gateway can also prevent widespread transmission of a virus throughout a company that can occur even if most (but not all) of the clients have virus protection software running.

E-mail gateway virus protection works by scanning every e-mail as it is sent or received by the gateway. Because e-mail gateways tend to have a lot more computing power than they actually need, and because e-mail is not instantaneous anyway, scanning mail messages is a very transparent way to eliminate viruses without the negative impact of client-side virus scanning.

Modern e-mail scanners are even capable of unzipping compressed attachments and scanning their interior contents to make sure viruses can't slip through disguised by a compression algorithm.

Like all forms of server-based virus protection, e-mail gateway virus protection does not disinfect clients, so it alone is not sufficient for total virus protection. However, since the vast majority of viruses now come through e-mail, you can be reasonably secure with just e-mail gateway virus protection, a firewall to block worms, and prudent downloading practices.

TIP

Rather than installing client-side virus protection for computers behind a virus-scanned e-mail server, I just use Trend Micro's free and always-up-to-date web-based virus scanner to spot check computers if I think they might be infected. Check it out at housecall.antivirus.com.

Firewall-Based Virus Protection

Some modern firewalls include a virus-scanning function that actually scans all inbound communication streams for viruses and terminates the session if a virus signature is found. This can prevent infection via e-mail and Internet downloads.

Like all forms of server-based virus protection, e-mail gateway virus protection does not disinfect clients, so it alone is not sufficient for total virus protection.

WARNING

Unlike e-mail gateway–based virus scanners, firewall scanners cannot unzip compressed files to check their contents for viruses. Since most downloaded programs are compressed, these scanners won't catch embedded viruses in them either.

Enterprise Virus Protection

Enterprise virus protection is simply a term for applications that include all or most of the previously discussed functions, and include management software to automate the deployment of client's virus protection software and the updating of this software.

A typical enterprise virus scanner is deployed on all clients, servers, and e-mail gateways, and is managed from a central server that downloads definition updates and then pushes the updates to each client. The best ones can even remotely deploy the virus-scanning software automatically on machines that it detects do not already have it.

TIP

Symantec's Norton AntiVirus for Enterprises is (in my opinion) the best enterprise virus scanner available. It works well, causes few problems, automatically deploys and updates, and is relatively inexpensive.

Review Questions

1. Where do viruses come from?

   _____

2. Can data contain a virus?

   _____

3. Do all viruses cause problems?

   _____

4. What is a worm?

   _____

5. Are all applications susceptible to macro viruses?

   _____

6. What is the only family of e-mail clients that are susceptible to e-mail viruses?

   _____

7. If you run NT kernel–based operating systems, do you still need anti-virus protection?

   _____

8. What two types of anti-virus methods are required for total virus defense?

   _____

9. How often should you update your virus definitions?

   _____

10. Where is anti-virus software typically installed?

    _____

Terms to Know

- ❑ benign viruses
- ❑ boot sector
- ❑ data
- ❑ executable code
- ❑ execution environments
- ❑ inoculator
- ❑ interpreter
- ❑ macro
- ❑ macro virus
- ❑ malignant viruses
- ❑ propagation engine
- ❑ scripting hosts
- ❑ self-replicating
- ❑ shell
- ❑ signature
- ❑ virus scanner
- ❑ worms

Chapter

9

Creating Fault Tolerance

Security means more than just keeping hackers out of your computers. It really means keeping your data safe from loss of any kind, including accidental loss due to user error, bugs in software, and hardware failure.

Systems that can tolerate hardware and software failure without losing data are said to be fault tolerant. The term is usually applied to systems that can remain functional when hardware or software errors occur, but the concept of fault tolerance can include data backup and archiving systems that keep redundant copies of information to ensure that the information isn't lost if the hardware it is stored upon fails.

Fault tolerance theory is simple: Duplicate every component that could be subject to failure. From this simple theory springs very complex solutions, like backup systems that duplicate all the data stored in an enterprise, clustered servers that can take over for one another automatically, redundant disk arrays that can tolerate the failure of a disk in the pack without going offline, and network protocols that can automatically reroute traffic to an entirely different city in the event that an Internet circuit fails.

In this chapter, you will learn about:

 The most common causes of data loss

 Improving fault tolerance

 Backing up your network

 Testing the fault tolerance of your system

Causes for Loss

To correctly plan for **fault tolerance**, you should consider what types of loss are likely to occur. Different types of loss require different fault tolerance measures, and not all types of loss are likely to occur to all clients.

fault tolerance
The ability of a system to withstand failure and remain operational.

At the end of each of these sections, there will be a tip box that lists the fault tolerance measures that can effectively mitigate these causes for loss. To create an effective fault tolerance policy, rank the following causes for loss in the order that you think they're likely to occur in your system. Then list the effective remedy measures for those causes for loss in the same order, and implement those remedies in top-down order until you exhaust your budget.

NOTE

The solutions mentioned in this section are covered in the second half of this chapter.

Human Error

User error is the most common reason for loss. Everyone has accidentally lost information by deleting a file or overwriting it with something else. Users frequently play with configuration settings without really understanding what those settings do, which can cause problems as well. Believe it or not, most computer downtime in businesses is caused by the activities of the computer maintenance staff. Deploying patches without testing them first can cause servers to fail, performing maintenance during working hours can cause bugs to manifest and servers to crash. Leading edge solutions are far more likely to have undiscovered problems, and routinely selecting them over more mature solutions means that your systems will be less stable.

TIP

A good archiving policy provides the means to recover from human error easily. Use permissions to prevent users' mistakes from causing widespread damage.

Routine Failure Events

Routine failure events are the second most likely causes for loss. Routine failures fall into a few categories that are each handled differently.

Hardware Failure

Hardware failure is the second most common reason for loss and is highly likely to occur in servers and client computers. Hardware failure is considerably less likely to occur in devices that do not contain moving parts.

The primary rule of disk management is: Stay in the mass market—don't get esoteric. Unusual solutions are harder to maintain, are more likely to have buggy drivers, and are usually more complex than they are worth.

Every hard disk will eventually fail. This bears repeating: Every hard disk will eventually fail. They run constantly in servers at high speed, and they generate the very heat that destroys their spindle lubricant. These two conditions combine to ensure that hard disks wear out through normal use within about 10 years.

NOTE

Early in the computer industry, the **Mean Time Between Failure (MTBF)** of a hard disk drive was an important selling point.

The real problem with disk failure is that hard disks are the only component in computers that can't be simply swapped out because they are individually customized with your data. To tolerate the failure of your data, you must have a copy of it elsewhere. That elsewhere can be another hard disk in the same computer or in another computer, on tape, or on **removable media**.

Some options don't work well—any backup medium that's smaller than the source medium will require more effort than it's worth to swap the media. Usually this means you must either use another hard disk of equivalent or greater size or tape, which can be quite capacious.

TIP

Solutions for hardware failure include implementing RAID-1 or RAID-5 and strong backup and archiving policies. Keeping spare parts handy and purchasing all of your equipment from the same sources makes it easier and faster to repair hardware when problems occur.

Mean Time Between Failures (MTBF)
The average life expectancy of electronic equipment. Most hard disks have an MTBF of about five years.

removable media
Computer storage media that can be removed from the drive, such as floppy disks, flash cards, and tape.

Software Failures

Software problems cause a surprising amount of data loss. Software sometimes cause serious problems that can cause servers to fail because of misconfiguration or incompatibility between applications installed on the same server.

TIP

The solution to software failure is to perform rigorous deployment testing before deploying software on production servers. Test software compatibility without risking downtime by using servers that are configured the same way as production servers but which are not used to provide your working environment.

Power Failure

Unexpected power failures have become relatively rare in the United States, as advances in power delivery have made transmission systems themselves very fault tolerant. Unfortunately, poor planning has created a situation in many parts of the world where demand for power very nearly exceeds capacity. Last year in California, rolling blackouts struck, causing the most reliable power transmission systems in the world to fail despite their fault tolerance systems.

TIP

The solution to power failure problems is to use uninterruptible power supplies and, when necessary, emergency power generators.

Data Circuit Failure

Circuit failures are rare, but they do happen, and when they do, networks can become cut off from their users. Circuit failure is especially critical to public websites that depend upon access for their revenue, but they are also problematic for branch offices that rely on services at their headquarters site.

TIP

The solution to circuit failure is to have multiple redundant circuits from different ISPs and to configure your routers to balance across the circuits and route around them in the event of failure.

circuit

In the context of information technology, a circuit is a data network connection between two points, usually different facilities. The term circuit traditionally applies to high capacity telephone trunk lines.

Crimes

As a group, crimes are the third most likely cause for loss of data in a network. As the level of hacking activity on the Internet increases, this category is currently increasing dramatically as a cause for loss and may soon surpass routine failures as the second most likely cause for loss in a network.

Hacking

If hackers gain access to your systems, especially if they are able to gain administrative privilege, they can wreak serious havoc, sabotaging anything they please. Even simple attacks can cause the denials of service similar to those caused by a circuit failure.

That said, most hacking does not significantly damage systems, because most hackers are not motivated to maliciously destroy data. Most hackers are either joyriding to simply gain access to systems or looking to steal information. Like common criminals, they don't want to get caught, so they usually don't do anything to make their presence known.

However, younger naïve hackers, those with a chip on their shoulder, or ideological hackers with an agenda may cause extreme damage to your systems in order to cause you as many problems as possible.

TIP

The solutions to hacking problems are presented throughout this book. Strong border security, the use of permissions to restrict access to individual accounts, and **offline** backups can eliminate this problem.

Theft

We all know that laptops are routinely stolen, but servers and data center equipment aren't immune to theft either. Expensive servers are worth about ten percent of their retail value on the black market, so your $15,000 server can pay a thief's rent for a month. If you've got a data center full of servers that someone could back a truck into, you could be a target for theft.

Who would know about your expensive systems? According to the FBI, most computer thefts are inside jobs either perpetrated or facilitated by employees and contractors; like cleaning crews and other service providers. Typically, an employee or contractor acts as a "spotter," identifying high value systems and providing copies of keys or security codes and instructions for how to find

offline
Data that is not immediately available to running systems, such as data stored on tape.

valuable systems. Then, while the inside accomplice is performing some public activity that provides a strong alibi, the employee's criminal associates will perpetrate the theft of equipment.

TIP

The solution to physical theft of equipment is strong physical security and offsite backups. Measures like live security guards or video surveillance can eliminate equipment theft as a serous concern. Offsite backups allow for quick restoration in the event of a burglary.

Sabotage

Sadly, sabotage by system users is rather common. Sabotage can be as subtle as one user sabotaging another by deleting files for some personal reason or as blatant as an employee deliberately physically destroying a computer.

Disgruntled employees can cause a tremendous amount of damage—more so than any other form of loss—because employees know where valuable data is stored and they usually have the access to get to the data.

TIP

The solution to sabotage is strong physical security to restrict access and provide evidence, proper permissions to restrict access, auditing to provide evidence and proof of activity, and offsite backups to restore information in the worst case. If employees know that there's no way for them to get away with acts of sabotage, they are far less likely to attempt it.

Terrorism

Acts of war or terrorism are exceptionally rare, but they should be planned for if you expect your business to survive through them. Because the specific events might take any form, they should be planned for like you would for earthquakes.

TIP

Solutions to acts of war and terrorism are offsite distant backups (preferably in another country) and offsite distant clustering, if you expect to be able to continue business operations through these types of events.

Environmental Events

Environmental events are the least likely events to occur, but they can be devastating because they usually take people by surprise.

Fire

Fires are rare, but they are a potential problem at most sites. Fires destroy everything, including computers and onsite backups. Being electrical equipment, it's possible that computers might even start fires; failing power supplies in computers can start small fires.

Fires create a situation where the cure is just as bad as the illness. Computers that may have survived a fire are certain to be ruined by water damage when the fire is put out. Sprinkler or chemical fire suppression systems can destroy computers and may be triggered by small fires that would not have seriously damaged a computer on its own.

TIP

The solution to fire damage for computers is sophisticated early fire detection and high-technology gas-based fire suppression systems. Offsite backups are also necessary to restore data in the event that computers are completely destroyed. For continuity of business, distant offsite clustering is required.

Flooding

Flooding, while relatively rare, is a surprisingly common source of failures. It only takes a small amount of water to destroy a running computer. Leaky roofs can allow rain to drip into a computer, HVAC units or other in-ceiling plumbing may leak onto a computer, a flooding bathroom in a floor above a server room may drain down into machines. Finally, minor fires may set off sprinkler systems that can destroy computers even though the fire itself is not a threat.

A source of water damage that most people fail to consider is the condensation caused by taking computers out of cool air-conditioned offices outside to high temperature humid air. This can cause just enough condensation in electrical equipment to short out power supplies or circuit cards, and this is why most electrical equipment has maximum operating humidity specifications.

TIP

The solution to flooding is offsite backups, and for continuity of business, offsite clustering. In the case of flooding, clustering can often be performed in the same building as long as the clustered servers are on a different floor.

Earthquake

We all know that earthquakes can potentially destroy an entire facility. While earthquakes of this magnitude are very rare, they're much more common in certain parts of the world than others. Consult your local government for statistics on the likelihood of damage-causing earthquakes.

TIP

Those in areas where earthquakes are common should employ multi-city fault tolerance measures, where backups and clustered solutions exist in different cities. You can easily weather more moderate earthquakes by using rack-mounted computers in racks that are properly secured to walls.

Fault Tolerance Measures

The following fault tolerance measures are the typical measures used to mitigate the causes of loss listed in the first section of this chapter. Some of these measures are detailed here, while others that are covered in other chapters are merely mentioned here along with a reference to their respective chapters.

Backups

Backups are the most common specific form of fault tolerance and are sometimes naively considered to be a cure-all for all types of loss. Backups are simply a snapshot copy of the data on a machine at a specific time, usually when users are not using the system. Traditionally, backups are performed to a tape device, but as disks have become less expensive, they have begun to replace tape as backup devices.

Backup Methods

Traditional backup works like this: Every night, you insert a fresh tape into your server. The next morning when you arrive at work, you remove the tape, mark the date, and store it in your tape vault. At larger companies, you'll never use that tape again—it's a permanent record of your network on that date. In smaller companies, that's the same tape you use every Wednesday, and you only keep tapes made over the weekend or perhaps you reuse them once a month.

Nearly all operating systems, including all Microsoft operating systems and all versions of Unix, support a backup methodology called **archive marking**, which is implemented through a single bit flag attached to every file as an attribute. The archive bit is set every time a file is written to and is only cleared by archive software. This allows the system to retain a memory of which files have changed since the last backup.

Windows and Unix both come with simple tape backup solutions that are capable of performing full and incremental system backups to tape or disk (except Windows NT prior to Windows 2000, which can only backup to tape) on a regularly scheduled basis. In Windows, the tool is called NTBACKUP.EXE, and in UNIX the tool is called "tar" (Tape Archive). (Tar is also commonly used to distribute software in the Unix environment.) Both applications work similarly; they create a single large backup file out of the set of backed up directories and files, and write it to tape or to a file on disk.

archive marking
A method used by operating systems to indicate when a file has been changed and should thus be included in an incremental backup.

With effort, you can do anything you need with the built-in backup tools for these operating systems. But larger sites will prefer to automate backup procedures with enterprise backup software that can automatically backup multiple servers to a central archive server.

TIP

You can script your own custom backup methodology using file copy programs like `tar` (Unix) and XCOPY (Windows) to backup files as well. Both programs can be configured to respect archive marking.

Most backup software offers a variety of backup options:

Full Backup   Archives every file on the computer and clears all the archive bits so that all future writes will be marked for archiving.

Copy Backup   Archives every file on the computer without modifying the archive bit flags. Copy operations proceed faster and can archive read-only files since the file does not have to be opened for write operations to reset the archive bit flag.

Incremental Backup   Archives every file that has its archive bit set (meaning it has changed since the last backup) and resets the bit so that the next incremental backup will not re-archive the file.

Differential Backup   Archives every file that has its archive bit set, but it does not reset the bit; therefore, every differential backup tape includes the complete set of files since the last full system backup.

Periodic Backup   Archives all files that have been written to since a certain date.

Because software vendors have begun to realize how badly traditional solutions perform for restoration, a new type of tape backup called image backup has become available. In an image backup, a complete sector copy of the disk is written to tape, including all the information necessary to reconstruct the drive's partitions. Because the backup occurs below the file level, image archives are capable of archiving open files.

Restoration is where an image backup shines. The image backup software will create a set of boot floppies for emergency restoration. By inserting the emergency restore boot floppy and an image tape, the computer will boot a proprietary restore program that simply copies the image on the tape back to disk. One reboot later and you're looking at your old familiar computer.

Image backup is not for archiving—file access is not as good as traditional backup software, and in many cases is not available at all. But there's no reason you can't use different software for archiving and backup.

Tape Hardware

Tape devices range from simple single cartridge units to sophisticated robotic tape changers. Tape auto-changers are devices that use some mechanical method to change tapes among a library of installed cartridges. When one tape is filled to capacity, the next tape in the changer is installed, and the archive operation proceeds. With auto-changers, literally any amount of data can be archived. They suffer from the problem that the archive operation takes as long as there are cartridges to be used, because the operation is sequential, and the mechanical devices used to change tapes are (as are all moving devices) subject to failure. Auto-changers frequently can take more time to perform an archive than is allotted because of the volume of information involved and their sequential nature.

Redundant Arrays of Independent Tapes (RAIT) is the latest development in archiving technology. This technology, also called TapeRAID, is an adaptation of disk RAID technology. RAIT uses as many tape devices in parallel as your backup problem requires. RAIT is usually cheaper and always faster than tape auto-changers because auto-changers are low-volume devices that are always expensive, and individual tape units are relatively inexpensive. They are faster because the archival operation operates simultaneously. It takes only the time that a single tape archive takes, no matter how many devices are involved.

Problems with Tape Backup

The problem with using tape for archiving and backup is that it is not reliable—in fact, it's highly unreliable. You may find this shocking, but two-thirds of attempts to completely restore a system from tape fail. That's an awfully high number, especially considering how many people rely upon tape as their sole medium of backup.

Humans are the major cause of backup failure. Humans have to change that tape every day. This means that in any organization that doesn't have a dedicated tape archivist, the overburdened IS team is bound to forget. And if you've tried to train a non-IS employee to change the tape, you probably feel lucky if it happens at all.

One of two things will occur when the backup software detects that the tape has not been changed. Poorly designed or configured software will refuse to run the backup in a misguided attempt to protect the data already on the tape. Better-configured software will simply overwrite the tape assuming that a more recent backup is better than no backup at all. So in many cases, the same tape may sit in a server (wearing out) for days or weeks on end, while business goes by and everyone forgets about the backup software.

NOTE

An individual tape cartridge is only reliable for between 10 and 100 uses—and unless you verify your backups, you won't know when it has become unreliable. Be certain that your tape rotation policy only re-uses tapes ten times (or the manufacturer recommended amount) before they are discarded.

It is a combination of tape wear, truculent backup software, and this human failure component that contribute to the high failure rate of tape restorations.

A typical restore operation is very problematic. Assuming the worst—you lost your storage system completely—here's what you have to look forward to: After installing new hard disks, you must reinstall Windows or Unix from scratch. Then you must reinstall your tape backup software. Once you've finished these tasks (after a frantic search for the BackupExec or ARCserve installation code that is required to reinstall the tape software and a panicked call to their tech support to beg forgiveness, mercy, and a new code number), you're ready to completely overwrite the installation effort with a full restoration from tape. You now get to sit in front of your server providing all the base system tapes, then the Monday incremental tape, the Tuesday incremental tape, and so forth until you hit the current day of the week—the whole time cursing your decision to use daily incremental backups. Once you're completely finished, and assuming that all six tapes involved worked flawlessly, you're ready to reboot your server—an entire work day after you began the restore operation.

Backup Best Practices

Backup is a critical security component of any network. Allocate a large enough budget to do it correctly.

Use tape devices and media large enough to perform an entire backup onto a single tape. In the event that this is not possible, use RAIT software to allow the simultaneous unattended backup of the entire system.

Always set your tape backup software to overwrite media that may have been left in the machine, without having to ask you to change or overwrite.

Choose image backup software rather than file-based backup software. Restorations are far easier and faster with this software.

Turn off disk-based catalogs. They take up far more space than they're worth, and they're never available when the computer has crashed. Use media-based catalogs that are stored on tape.

Perform a full-system backup every day. Differential, incremental, and daily backups that don't create a complete image cause headaches and complications during a restoration operation and increase the likelihood of failure by adding more components to the process. If your backup system is too slow to backup your entire data set in the allotted time, get a new one that is capable of handling all your data in this time frame.

Use software with an open-file backup feature to backup opened files or force them closed if you perform your backup at night. Use the Windows "force system logoff" user policy to shut down user connections at night and force all files to close just prior to the backup.

If you reuse tapes, mark them each time they've been written to. Discard tapes after their 10th backup. Saving a few dollars on media isn't worth the potential for loss.

If you haven't implemented online archiving, pull out a full system backup once a week (or once a month at the longest) and store it permanently. You never know when a deleted file will be needed again.

Test your backups with full system restores to test servers at least once per quarter. This will help you identify practices that will make restoration difficult in an emergency.

Don't bother backing up workstations. Rather, get users comfortable with the idea that no files stored locally on their computers will be backed up—if it's important, put it on a network file server. This reduces the complexity of your backup problem considerably. Workstations should contain operating system and application files only, all of which can be restored from the original software CD-ROMs.

Use enterprise-based backup software that is capable of transmitting backup data over the network to a central backup server. Watch for network capacity, though, because that much data can often overwhelm a network. Schedule each server's transmission so it doesn't conflict when running over the same shared media as other servers do. You should put your archive server on your backbone or at the central point of your network.

You don't have to spend a lot of money on esoteric archive servers, even for large environments. When you consider that a good 80GB DLT drive is going to cost $2,000, adding another $1,000 for a motherboard, hard disk, RAM, network adapter, and a copy of your operating system isn't all that big of a deal. The software you have to install is likely to cost more than all the hardware combined anyway. So feel free to have six or eight computers dedicated to large backup problems. They can all run simultaneously to backup different portions of your network without investing in expensive RAIT software or auto-loading tape devices. You'll save money and have a more standard solution that you can fix.

Uninterruptible Power Supplies (UPS) and Power Generators

Uninterruptible power supplies (UPS) are battery systems that provide emergency power when power mains fail. UPSs also condition poorly regulated power, which increases the life of the computer's internal power supply and decreases the probability of the power supply causing a fire.

Use uninterruptible power supplies to shut systems down gracefully in the event of a power failure. UPSs are not really designed to run through long power outages, so if power is not restored within a few minutes, you need to shut your servers down and wait out the power failure. UPSs are very common and can be purchased either with computers or in retail channels anywhere. Installing them is as simple as plugging them into the power mains, plugging computers into them, connecting them to computers using serial cables so they can trigger a shutdown, and installing the UPS monitoring software on your computers.

It's only really necessary to use UPSs on computers that store data. If you've set up your network to store data only on servers, you won't need UPSs on all your workstations. Remember to put UPSs on hubs and routers if servers will need to communicate with one another during the power failure event.

If the system must be operational during a power failure, you need emergency power generators, which are extremely expensive. Emergency power generators are machines based on truck engines that are designed to generate power. They are started within a few minutes after the main power failure, while computers are still running on their UPS systems. Once the power generators are delivering power, the UPS systems go back to their normal condition because they're receiving power from the generators. When main power is restored, the generators shut down again.

Once you have UPSs and power generators in place, it's imperative that you test your power failure solution before a power event actually occurs. After working hours, throw the circuit breakers in your facility to simulate a power event and ensure that all the servers shut down correctly. When power is restored, you can usually configure servers to either restart automatically or remain off until they are manually started, as you prefer.

Redundant Array of Independent Disks (RAID)

Redundant Array of Independent Disks (RAID) technology allows you to add extra disks to a computer to compensate for the potential failure of a disk. RAID automatically spreads data across the extra disks, and can automatically recover it in the event that a disk fails. With hot-swappable disks, the failed drive can be replaced without shutting the system down.

RAID works in a number of different ways referred to as RAID levels. They are as follows:

RAID Level 0: Striping

Disk striping allows you to create a single volume that is spread across multiple disks. RAID-0 is not a form of fault tolerance because the failure of any single disk causes the volume to fail. RAID-0 is used to increase disk performance in engineering and scientific workstations, but it is not appropriate for use in a server.

RAID Level 1: Mirroring

Mirrors are exact copies of the data on one disk made onto another disk. Disk mirroring is considered a fault tolerant strategy, because in the event of a single disk failure, the data can be read and written to the still-working mirror partition. Mirroring also can be used to double the read speed of a partition, since data can be read from both disks at the same time.

RAID-1 requires two disks, and both disks should be exactly the same model. Using disks of different models is possible, but will likely cause speed synchronization problems that can dramatically affect disk performance.

Mirroring can be implemented in hardware with a simple and inexpensive RAID-1 controller, or can be implemented in software in Windows NT Server, Windows 2000 Server (all versions), and most popular versions of Unix including Linux and BSD. Implementing software mirroring in Unix is easily performed during the initial operating system installation. In Windows, mirroring is implemented using the disk manager at any time after the completion of the operating system installation. Both software and hardware mirroring are highly reliable and should be implemented on any server as a minimum protective measure against disk failure.

RAID
A family of related technologies that allows multiple disks to be combined into a volume. With all RAID versions except 0, the volume can tolerate the failure of at least one hard disk and remain fully functional.

RAID Level 5: Striping with Parity

RAID-5 allows you to create disk sets or **disk packs** of multiple drives that appear to be a single disk to the operating system. A single additional disk provides the space required for parity information (which is distributed across all disks) that can be used to recreate the data on any one disk in the set in the event that a single disk fails. (RAID-4 is a simpler form of RAID-5 that puts all parity information on the extra disk rather than distributing it across all drives, but it is now obsolete.)

The parity information, which is equal to the size of one drive member of the set, is spread across all disks and contains the mathematical sum of information contained in the other stripes. The loss of any disk can be tolerated because its information can be recreated from the information stored on the other disks and in the parity stripe.

For example, if you have six 20GB disks, you could create a RAID-5 pack that provides 100GB of storage ($5 \times 20 + 20$GB for parity information). RAID-5 works by using simple algebra: In the equation $A \times B \times C \times D \times E = F$, you can calculate the value of any missing variable (failed disk) if you know the result (parity information). RAID-5 automatically detects the failed disk and recreates its data from the parity information on demand so that the drive set can remain **online**.

Windows NT Server, Windows 2000 Server, and Linux support RAID level 5 in software, but software RAID-5 is not particularly reliable because detecting disk failure isn't necessarily easy for the operating system. Windows is not capable of booting from a software RAID-5 partition; Linux is.

Serious fault tolerance requires the use of hardware-based RAID-5, which is considerably more reliable and which allows booting from a RAID-5 partition. RAID-5 controllers can be purchased as an option in any built-to-purpose server. Configuration of RAID-5 packs must be performed prior to the installation of the operating system and is performed through the RAID-5 adapter's **BIOS** configuration menu during the boot process.

RAID 0+1: Striping with Mirroring

RAID 0+1 (also referred to as RAID-10) is a simple combination of RAID-0 striping and RAID-1 mirroring. RAID-10 allows you to create two identical RAID-0 stripe sets and then mirror across them.

For example, if you had a stripe set of three 20GB disks to create a 60GB volume, RAID-10 allows you to mirror that stripe set to an identical set of three 20GB disks. Your total storage remains 60GB. In theory, a RAID-10 set could withstand the failure of half of the disks (one of the sets) but in practice, you would replace the disks as they failed individually anyway.

disk packs
Multiple identical hard disk drives configured to store a single volume in a RAID set.

online
Data that is immediately available to running systems because it is stored on active disks.

BIOS (Basic Input/Output System)
The low-level program built into the computer's motherboard that is used to configure hardware and load the operating system.

162

Using the same six disks, RAID-5 would allow 100GB of storage with equal fault tolerance. However, hardware RAID-5 controllers are expensive because a microprocessor must be used to recalculate the parity information. RAID-10 controllers are cheap because, like mirroring, no calculation is required for redundancy.

Permissions

Permissions become a fault tolerance measure when they are used to prevent user error or sabotage. Judicious use of permissions can prevent users from accidentally deleting files and can prevent malicious users from destroying system files that could disable the computer.

Implementing permissions is covered in Chapters 10 and 11, and for further reading, I'd recommend *Mastering Windows 2000*, by Mark Minasi (Sybex, 2001) and *Linux Network Servers 24seven*, by Craig Hunt (Sybex, 2001).

Border Security

Border security is an extremely important measure for preventing hacking. Border security is covered in Chapter 5, and you can read more detail in my book *Firewalls 24seven* (Sybex, 2002).

Auditing

Auditing is the process of logging how users access files during their routine operations for the purpose of monitoring for improper access and to be used as evidence in case a crime is committed. Windows has strong support for auditing, and auditing measures can be implemented in Unix.

Implementing auditing is covered in Chapters 10 and 11.

Offsite Storage

Offsite storage is the process of removing data to another location on a regular basis so that if something disastrous occurs at the original facility, the backups or archives are not destroyed along with the online systems.

There are two ways to implement offsite storage: Physically moving backup media such as tapes to another location on a regular basis, or transmitting data to another facility via a network of data circuits.

You can outsource a tape pickup or storage service from companies like Iron Mountain or Archos. These companies will stop by your facility periodically to pick up tapes that are then stored in their secure bunkers and can be retrieved at any time with one day's notice. Outsourcing is far more reliable than relying on employees to take tapes offsite.

Of the two methods, transmitting data automatically over network links is far more reliable, because it can be automated so that it doesn't rely on unreliable human activity. Establishing automated offsite backups or archiving is as simple as copying a backup file across the network to a store located at another facility. You must ensure that you have enough bandwidth to complete the operation before the next operation queues up, so testing is imperative. You can use sophisticated file synchronization software to reduce the amount of data transmitted to changes only, which will allow you to use slower circuits to move data.

Archiving

Archiving is the process of retaining a copy of every file that is created by users on the system, and in many cases, every version of every file. The difference between backup and archiving is that archiving only copies user files, whereas backup copies everything. Archiving cannot be used to restore entire systems, but systems can be rebuilt from original sources and an archive copy.

Archiving and backup are not the same thing. Archiving refers to the permanent storage of information for future reference, whereas backup refers to the storage of information for the sole purpose of restoration in the event of a failure. The effective difference is that you can reuse backup tapes but not archive tapes.

Backup and archiving are most effectively approached separately—solutions that do both will do neither well. For example, image backup software is better for backups and restoration in an emergency, and file-based backup software is better for archiving permanently on cheap tape or CD-R media. There is no reason to choose one or the other when you can have both.

Archiving is designed to respond to human error more than machine failure, which is covered more effectively by backup. Archiving allows you to solve the "I deleted a file four months ago, and I realize that I need back" or "I accidentally overwrote this file four days ago with bad data. Can we get the old version back?" Because archiving permanently keeps copies of files and is usually implemented to keep all daily versions of files, you can easily recover from these sorts of problems. Trying to find individual files on tapes when you don't know the exact date is a long and tedious process akin to searching for a needle in a haystack.

Archives can be kept on online stores on special archive servers, which also run the archiving software and search other servers and computers for changed files. Archiving can be implemented by using various **file synchronization** packages, but software written specifically to do it is uncommon.

---

archiving

The process of retaining a copy of every version of files created by users for the purpose of restoring individual files in case of human error.

---

file synchronization

The process of comparing files in different locations and transmitting the differences between them to ensure that both copies remain the same. Synchronization is only easy if you can guarantee that the two files won't change on both ends at the same time. If they can, then decisions must be made about which version to keep, and it may not be possible to automate the decision-making process depending upon the nature of the information.

Deployment Testing

Deployment testing is the process of installing software and simulating normal use in order to discover problems with the software or compatibility before they affect production systems. Implementing deployment testing is as simple as maintaining a test server upon which you can create clones of existing servers, by restoring a backup tape to it and then performing an installation of the new software.

Despite how simple it is to perform software deployment testing, it's actually rarely performed in smaller to medium-sized environments, which is unfortunate because it could eliminate a major source of downtime.

Circuit Redundancy

Circuit redundancy is implemented by contracting for data circuits from separate Internet service providers, and then using sophisticated routing protocols like the Interior Gateway Routing Protocol (IGRP) or the Exterior Gateway Routing Protocol (EGRP), both of which are capable of detecting circuit failure and routing data around it. They can also be configured to load-balance traffic between multiple circuits so that while online, you can increase your available bandwidth. Proper circuit redundancy requires a complex router configuration, so you will probably need to bring in consultants who specialize in routing unless you have routing experts on staff.

Physical Security

Physical security is the set of security measures that don't apply to computers specifically, like locks on doors, security guards, and video surveillance.

Without physical security there is no security. This simply means that network security and software constructs can't keep your data secure if your server is stolen.

Centralization is axiomatic to security, and physical security is no exception. It's far easier to keep server and compute resources physically secure if they are located in the same room, or are clustered in rooms on each floor or in each building. Distributing servers throughout your organization is a great way to increase overall bandwidth, but you need to be sure you can adequately protect workgroup servers from penetration before you decide to use a distributed architecture.

Physical security relies upon locks. The benefits of a strong lock are obvious and don't need to be discussed in detail, but there are some subtle differences between locking devices that are not immediately apparent. Key locks may have unprotected copies floating around. Combinations are copied every time they're told to someone. Choose biometric sensors like handprint scanners if you can afford them, because they prove identity rather than simple possession of a device or code in order to allow access.

A secure space has secure lock mechanisms on each door, locks that can't simply be removed from the door, doors that can't be removed from outside the space, and no available access except doors. A secure space doesn't have glass windows, a drop ceiling adjoining other rooms, flimsy walls, or ventilation ducts large enough to crawl through.

Alarm systems add to the functionality of electronic locks by integrating them into a system capable of detecting unauthorized entry and alerting a monitoring agency. Most alarm systems are enabled and disabled with a keypad based on a **combination**—avoid these. Combinations are no more secure for alarm systems than they are for locks, and since most companies outsource their alarm monitoring, they're even less secure since at least one other agency has access to your codes. Good alarm systems can automatically call the police, integrate with fire alarms, and page responsible employees when alarms go off. Alarm systems add considerably to the security of a facility.

Finally, if you think that crime is a serious consideration for your business, security guards are a very effective deterrent to direct intrusion attempts. Businesses with security guards are far less likely to suffer from an insider-assisted theft than businesses that are unguarded.

Clustered Servers

Clustering is the running of a single application on multiple machines at one time. This allows you to apply the resources of many machines to one problem, and when properly implemented, it is an excellent way to handle large problems like enterprise databases, commercial websites, and serious scientific applications.

There are actually two different technologies that fall in the clustering definition: fail-over clustering and load balancing.

Fail-over Clustering

Fail-over clustering, also called server replication, is the process of maintaining a running spare for a server that can take over automatically in the event that the primary server fails. Typically, these solutions use disk systems that can be switched from one machine to another automatically or they mirror changes to the disk from the primary server to the secondary server, so that if something happens to the primary server, the secondary server can take over immediately.

combination
A numeric code used to open a physical lock.

fail-over clustering
A fault tolerance method where a server can assume the services of a failed server.

Fail-over clustering does not allow multiple servers to handle the same service at the same time; rather, responsibility for clients is switched amongst members of the cluster when a failure event occurs.

These solutions are not without their problems—information stored in RAM on the servers is not maintained, so while the server can switch over, open network sessions will be dropped unless they are **stateless protocols** like HTTP. This would happen anyway if the primary server failed and was not replicated, and sessions can usually be automatically re-established on the new server for file sharing protocols without difficulty. But fail-over clustering must be specifically supported by application services like SQL servers and messaging servers, because those applications maintain responsibility for moving data amongst the members of the cluster.

NOTE

Fail-over clustering is the form implemented natively by Windows 2000 Advanced Server.

Load-Balancing

There is another form of clustering that works quite well for certain problems: load balancing. **Load balancing** is quite simple; it allows multiple machines to respond to the same IP address and balances the client load among that group. For problems such as a web service, this makes all the servers appear to be one server that can handle a massive number of simultaneous connections. Both Windows and Unix support this type of clustering.

Load balancing doesn't work for problems such as file service, database, or e-mail, because there's no standard way to replicate data stored on one server to all the rest of the servers. For example, if on your first session you stored a file to the cluster (meaning one of the machines in the cluster) and then connected to the cluster at a later date, there's only a small chance that you would connect again to the machine that had your file. Stateless clustering works only with applications that don't maintain any data transmitted by the client—you can think of them as "output only" applications. Examples of this sort of application are web and FTP services.

There is a solution to even that problem, though—all the clustered machines can transmit their stored data to a single back-end storage or database server. This puts all the information in one place, where any user can find it, no matter which clustered server they're attached to. Unfortunately, it also means that the cluster is no faster than the single machine used to store everything.

stateless protocol
Protocols which do not maintain any information about the client session on the server side. Stateless protocols can be easily clustered across multiple machines without fear of data loss or side effects because it does not matter which server the client connects to from one instance to the next.

Load balancing
A clustering mechanism where individual client sessions are connected to any one of a number of identically configured servers, so that the entire load of client sessions is spread evenly among the pool of servers.

Stateless clustering works well in the one environment it was designed for: web service for large commercial sites. The amount of user information to store for a website is usually miniscule compared to the massive amount of data transmitted to each user. Because some websites need to handle millions of simultaneous sessions, this method lets designers put the client-handling load on frontline web servers and maintain the database load on back-end database servers.

Simple Server Redundancy

High availability and clustering solutions are all expensive—the software to implement them is likely to cost as much as the server you put it on. There are easy ways to implement fault tolerance, but they change depending on what you're doing and exactly what level of fault tolerance you need. I'll present a few ideas here to get you thinking about your fault tolerance problems.

Vendors traditionally calculate the cost of downtime using this method:

Employees × Average Pay rate × Down Hours = Downtime Costs

Sounds reasonably complete, but it's based on the assumption that employees in your organization become worthless the moment their computers go down. Sometimes that's the case, but often it's not. I'm not advocating downtime, I'm merely saying that the assumptions used to cost downtime are flawed, and that short periods of downtime aren't nearly as expensive as data loss or the opportunity cost of lost business if your business relies on computers to transact.

If you can tolerate 15 minutes of downtime, a whole array of less expensive options emerges. For example, manually swapping an entire server doesn't take long, especially if the hard disks are on removable cartridges. For an event that might occur once a year, this really isn't all that bad.

The following inexpensive methods can achieve different measures of fault tolerance for specific applications.

The DNS service can assign more than one IP address to a single domain name. If there's no response from the first address, the client can check, in order, each of the next addresses until it gets a response (however, depending on the client-side address caching mechanism, it may take a few minutes for the client to make another DNS attempt). This means that for web service, you can simply put up an array of web servers, each with their own IP address, and trust that users will be able to get through to one of them. With web service, it rarely matters which server clients attach to as long as they're all serving the same data, you have fault tolerance.

Another way to solve the load-balancing problem is with firewalls. Many firewalls can be configured to load balance a single IP address across a group of identical machines, so you can have three web servers that all respond to a single address behind one of these firewalls.

Fault tolerance for standard file service can be achieved by simply cross-copying files among two or more servers. By doubling the amount of disk space in each server, you can maintain a complete copy of all the data on another machine by periodically running a script to copy files from one machine to another, or using a mechanism like the Windows File Replication Service. In the event that a machine has crashed, users can simply remap the drive letter they use for the primary machine to the machine with the share to which you have backed everything up. By using the archive bit to determine which files should be copied, you can update only those files that have changed, and you can make the update period fairly frequent—say, once per hour.

There is a time lag based on the periodicity of your copy operation, so this method may not work in every situation. Since it's not completely automatic (users have to recognize the problem and manually remap a drive letter), it's not appropriate for every environment. You reduce the automation problem by providing a desktop icon that users can click to run a batch file that will remap the drive.

Fault tolerance doesn't mean you have to spend a boatload of money on expensive hardware and esoteric software. It means that you must think about the problem and come up with the simplest workable solution. Sometimes that means expensive hardware and esoteric software, but not always.

Review Questions

1. What are the four major causes for loss, in order of likelihood?

   _____

2. What is the best way to recover from the effects of human error?

   _____

3. What is the most likely component to fail in a computer?

   _____

4. What is the most difficult component to replace in a computer?

   _____

5. What is the easiest way to avoid software bugs and compatibility problems?

   _____

6. How can you recover from a circuit failure when you have no control over the ISPs repair actions?

   _____

7. What are the best ways to mitigate the effects of hacking?

   _____

8. What is the most common form of fault tolerance?

   _____

9. What is the difference between an incremental backup and a differential backup?

   _____

10. What causes the majority of failures in a tape backup solution?

_____

11. Why is RAID-0 not appropriate as a form of fault tolerance?

_____

12. RAID-10 is a combination of which two technologies?

_____

13. If you create a RAID-5 pack out of five 36GB disks, how much storage will be available?

_____

14. What are the two methods used to perform offsite storage?

_____

15. What is the difference between backup and archiving?

_____

16. What are the two common types of clustering?

_____

Chapter

10

Windows Security

This chapter will provide you with all the information you need to understand the major Windows security mechanisms in the Windows NT/2000/XP family, along with some management advice and practical walkthroughs.

But no single chapter, and perhaps not even a single book, could cover the wide array of Windows security mechanisms in complete detail. Once you've read this chapter and used the information presented herein to design a security architecture for your network, consult the Internet RFCs upon which most of these standards are based for technical details of their operation. Microsoft's Resource Kits and Training Kits are the authoritative source for the Microsoft implementation of these mechanisms and should be consulted for configuration-specific information.

In the meantime, in this chapter, you will learn about:

 The elements of Windows local security

 Establishing permissions in Windows

 Managing NTFS File System

 Using the Encrypting File System

 Windows Network Security features, including Active Directory, Kerberos, group policies, and share security

Windows Local Security

Windows security is based on user authentication. Before you can use a Windows computer, you must supply a username and a password. The **logon prompt** (provided by the WinLogon process) identifies you to the computer, which then provides access to resources you are allowed to use and denies access to things you aren't. This combination of a user identity and password is called a **user account**.

logon prompt
The interface through which users identify themselves to the computer.

user account
The association between a user account name, a password, and a security identifier.

Security Group
A construct containing a SID that is used to create permissions for an object. User accounts are associated with security groups and inherit their permissions from them.

process
A running program.

> **NOTE**
>
> Windows 95/98/Me has no significant security mechanisms to speak of, and these systems are not in themselves secure, so no information in this chapter applies to them.

It is possible for a computer to be set up to automatically log on for you, using stored credentials or an account that has an empty password (as is the case by default in Windows XP Home), but an account is still logged on, and the security that applies to that account is used to manage permissions for that user session.

Windows also provides **Security Groups**. When a user account is a member of a security group, the permissions that apply to the security group also apply to the user account. For example, if a user is a member of the "Financial" security group, then the permissions of the Financial security group are applied to the user account. User accounts may be members of any number of security group accounts, and they accumulate the sum of the permissions allowed for all of those groups.

> **NOTE**
>
> Allowing multiple people to log in using a single account invalidates the concept of accountability that is central to Windows security. Even when a group of people do the same job, each user should have an individual account so that when one user violates security, you can track the violation back to a specific user rather than a group of people. If you want to control security for a group of people, use security groups rather than shared accounts.

User and group accounts are only valid for the Windows computer on which they are created. These accounts are local to the computer. The only exception to this rule is computers that are members of a domain and therefore trust the user accounts created in the Active Directory on a domain controller. Domain security is discussed in the next section. Computers that are members of a domain trust both their own local accounts and Active Directory accounts (Windows 2000) or the PDC's accounts (Windows NT).

WARNING

The most common Windows security flaw I see is administrators who strongly secure domain accounts yet forget about the local administrator account on workstations and member servers. These passwords are rarely changed from the installation default, which is frequently left blank or set to something simple during the operating system installation! Always set very strong local administrative account passwords.

Each Windows computer has its own list of local user and group accounts. The WinLogon **process** (which logs you on and sets up your computing environment) passes your credentials to the **Local Security Authority (LSA)** when you log in. The LSA determines whether you are attempting to log on using a local account or a domain account.

If you're using a local account, the LSA invokes the **Security Accounts Manager (SAM)**, which is the Windows operating system component that controls local account information. The SAM will refer to the database (stored in the **registry**) and return the information to the WinLogon process.

If you are logging in with a domain account, the Local Security Authority will query the NetLogon process on the domain controller and return the validated logon information (the Security Identifier) to the WinLogon process so that an access token can be created.

Irrespective of the source of authentication, access is allowed only to the local computer by the computer's Local Security Authority (LSA). When you access other computers on the network, the local computer's LSA establishes your credentials automatically with the LSA on the foreign computer, effecting a logon for each computer you contact. To gain access to a foreign computer, that computer must trust the credentials provided by your computer.

Security Identifiers

Security principles like user accounts and **computer accounts** are represented in the system as **Security Identifiers (SIDs)**. The SID is a serial number that uniquely identifies the security principle to all the computers in the domain, much the way that a Social Security number uniquely identifies national citizens. When you create an account using the User Manager (Windows NT) or the Local Users and Groups Snap-in (Windows 2000/XP), a new SID is always created, even if you use the same account name and password as a deleted account. The SID will remain with the account for as long as the account exists. You may change any other aspect of the account, including the username and password, but you

Local Security Authority (LSA)
The process that controls access to secured objects in Windows.

Security Accounts Manager (SAM)
The process that controls access to the user account database in the registry.

registry
A hierarchical database local to each Windows computer used for storing configuration information.

security principle
A user, computer, or security group account.

computer accounts
Security Identifiers that uniquely identify computers in a domain and authenticate their participation in the domain.

Security Identifier (SID)
A unique serial number used to identify user, computer, and security group accounts.

cannot change the SID under normal circumstances—if you did, you would create a new account.

Security Group accounts also have SIDs, which are unique identifiers that are created when the group is created. The same rules that apply to account SIDs also apply to group SIDs.

Logging In

When you log in, you identify yourself to the computer. The process of logging in is managed by the WinLogon mechanism of the Local Security Authority.

The LSA is a part of the kernel through which all access to secured objects is routed. When you request access to a file, the request is passed through the LSA for authentication before it is passed to the file system. The LSA is the gatekeeper of local security in Windows NT–based operating systems.

The WinLogon process checks your username and password (or smartcard, if so configured) to determine if you should be allowed to access the computer. If the name supplied in the logon box is the local computer name, the WinLogon process checks the account against the local SAM stored in the registry. Otherwise, the WinLogon process contacts a domain controller for the domain name specified and uses Kerberos (Windows 2000/XP) or **NTLM** (Windows NT) authentication to authenticate the user, depending upon the client operating system.

If the account name is valid and the password's hash matches the stored hash (thus indicating that the password is correct), the WinLogon process will create an **access token** for you. The access token is composed of the account SID, the SIDs of the groups the account belongs to, and a **Locally Unique Identifier (LUID)**, which indicates a specific logon session (to differentiate between two simultaneously logged in sessions).

> **NOTE**
>
> An access token is created each time you log onto Windows. This is why you must log off and then log back on again after making changes to your user account—you need a new access token that will reflect the changes you have made.

The WinLogon process then launches the program that is configured in the registry as the shell, usually Windows Explorer, and passes your access token to it. Windows Explorer then provides the access token to the LSA whenever it needs access to a secured object, like a file.

New Technology LAN Manager (NTLM)

The network authentication protocol used prior to Kerberos in Windows NT. NTLM is a much simpler authentication protocol that does not support transitive trusts and stores domain user accounts in the SAM of the Primary domain controller.

---

access token

A combination of security identifiers that represents the user account and the security groups that it belongs to. Access tokens are passed from the initial logon to all user-mode programs executed subsequently.

Locally Unique Identifier (LUID)

An identifier that is created for each logged-on instance of a user account to differentiate it from other logon sessions.

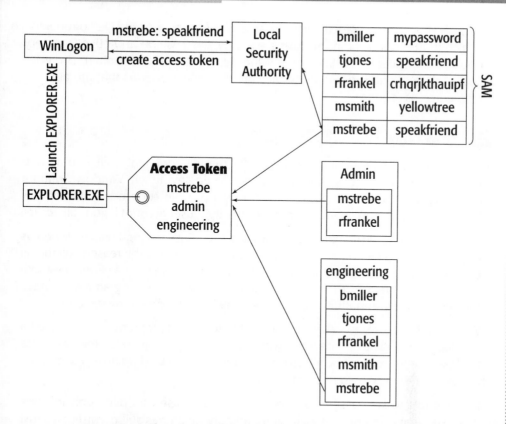

Windows Explorer
The shell program in Windows from which most user-mode programs are launched.

When Explorer launches another program, it passes the access token to it as well, so it can provide credentials to the LSA when it subsequently accesses secured objects.

Resource Access

Whenever a program is started in Windows, the program that launches it (usually **Windows Explorer**) provides it with an access token based on its own access token. This way, every program has an access token that will always match the identity of the person who originally logged in, which then it can provide to the system in order to gain access to secured resources. The forwarded access token is a copy of the one originally passed to Windows Explorer by the WinLogon process.

The WinLogon process was started from a user-generated interrupt (the Ctrl+Alt+Del keyboard interrupt) and is special in that it does not inherit an access token from its parent process; rather, it can create new access tokens by querying either the local Security Accounts Manager or the NetLogon Service (which in turn queries the **Directory Services Agent (DSA)** on an Active Directory domain controller or the SAM on a Windows NT domain controller). The Win-Logon process and the Run As service are the only processes that are able to create access tokens.

Directory Services Agent (DSA)
The service that communicates between the Local Security Authority and the Active Directory in order to authenticate domain users.

permission
An Access Control Entry in an object's Discretionary Access Control List.

objects
Data structures in a computer environment, such as files, directories, printers, shares, and so forth.

Mandatory Logons

The foundation of Windows security is the mandatory login. Unlike some networking systems, there is no way for a user to do anything in Windows without a user account name and password. Although you can choose to automatically log in with credentials provided from the registry, a user account logon still occurs.

Although it's not the friendliest of keystrokes, there's a very good reason Windows requires the Ctrl+Alt+Del keystroke to log in, and it's one of the reasons Windows is considered secure. Because the computer handles the Ctrl+Alt+Del keystroke as a hardware interrupt, there's literally no way to for a clever programmer to make the keystroke do something else without rewriting the operating system.

Without this feature, a hacker would be able to write a program that displayed a fake login screen and collected passwords from unsuspecting users. However, since the fake screen wouldn't be able to include the Ctrl+Alt+Del keystroke, users familiar with Windows would not be fooled.

It is possible to set passwords to be blank. In this case, you need only indicate your user name in order to login. A mandatory logon has still occurred; it's just not very secure because no password is required. This is the method used by default in Windows XP Home. Users merely click on an icon representing their identity and are not required to enter a password, unless they configure the operating system to require it. Microsoft seems committed to sacrificing security for the sake of user convenience.

Through this method, every program that is started after a user has logged on will have the access token that represents the user. Because programs must always provide that token to access resources, there is no way to circumvent Windows 2000 resource security.

Since the access token is passed to new programs when the programs are started, there is no further need to access the SAM database locally or the Active Directory on a domain controller for authentication once a user has logged on.

Objects and Permissions

In order for a user to perform an action on a secured entity like a file or directory, the user must have permission to do so. In this case, a **permission** is an access control entry that links the action to be performed to the security identifier of the user account attempting the operation. If the link exists, the operating system executes the action; otherwise, it will deny access and display an error message.

Windows maintains security for various types of **objects** including (but not limited to) directories, files, printers, processes, and network shares. Each object exposes services that the object allows to be performed upon it, for example: open, close, read, write, delete, start, stop, print, and so on.

The security information for an object is contained in the object's **Security Descriptor**. The security descriptor has four parts: owner, group, **Discretionary Access Control List (DACL)**, and **System Access Control List (SACL)**. Windows uses these parts of the security descriptor for the following purposes:

Owner   This part contains the SID of the user account that has ownership of the object. The object's **owner** may always change the settings in the DACL (the permissions) of the object, irrespective of whether or not the owner has permission to access the file.

Group   This part is used by the POSIX subsystem of Windows. Files and directories in Unix operating systems can belong to a group as well as to an individual user account. This part contains the SID of the group of this object for the purposes of POSIX compatibility. Windows does not use this field for any other purpose. Don't be confused by the name: Windows security groups cannot be owners of a resource. Group security and permissions are managed through the DACL, not through this field.

Discretionary Access Control List   The DACL contains a list of user accounts and group accounts that have permission to access the object's services. The DACL has as many access control entries as there are user or group accounts that have been specifically given access to the object.

System Access Control List   The SACL also contains **Access Control Entries (ACEs)**, but these ACEs are used for auditing rather than for permitting or denying access to the object's services. The SACL has as many ACEs as there are user or group accounts that are specifically being audited.

Access to a resource will be allowed if an access token contains any SID that matches a permission in the DACL that corresponds to the type of access requested. For example, if an individual account is allowed Read access, and the

---

Security Descriptor
Information stored with each object that specifies the owner and contains the Access Control List.

Discretionary Access Control List (DACL)
The Access Control List that is used to allow or deny access to an object.

System Access Control List (SACL)
An Access Control List used to determine how to audit objects.

owner
The user account that created an object or was otherwise assigned ownership. The owner of an object has the right to change its permissions irrespective of user account's permissions.

Access Control Entry (ACE)
An entry in an Access Control List that joins a security identifier to a type of allowed or denied access.

user account is a member of a group account that is allowed Write access, then the access token for that logged-on user will contain both SIDs and the LSA will allow Read and Write access to the object because the DACL contains an entry that matches each type of access. Deny ACEs still override any accumulation of permission.

deny ACE
An Access Control Entry that specifically denies permissions, in order to override other permissions that might allow access to the account.

For example, if user mstrebe wants to access a file called address.txt, then the system (actually a component called the Security Reference Monitor) will compare the access token of his running the WINWORD.EXE program to the DACL associated with address.txt. If address.txt has any SID in common with the access token for WINWORD.EXE that allows Read access, then he can open the file, otherwise access is denied.

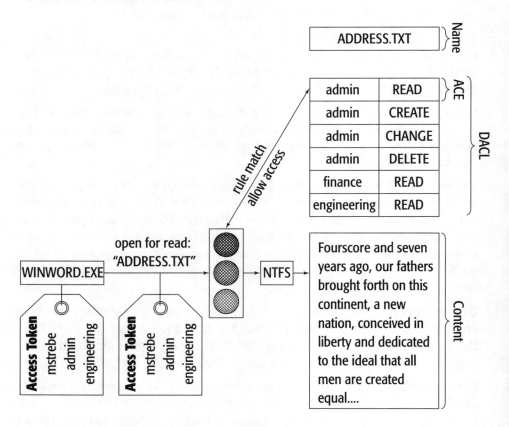

A special type of ACE, called a **deny ACE**, indicates that all access to the object will be denied to the account identified by the SID. A deny ACE overrides all other ACEs. Windows implements the No Access permission using the deny ACE.

The access control entries in the SACL are formed the same way as the ACEs in the DACL (they are composed of a SID and an access mask), but the access mask, in this case, identifies those services of the object for which the account will be audited.

Not every object has a security descriptor. The FAT file system, for example, does not record security information, so file and directory objects stored on a FAT volume lack owners, DACLs, and SACLs. When a security descriptor is missing, any user account may access any of the object's services. This is not the same as when an object has an empty DACL. In that case, no account may access the object. When there is no SACL for an object, that object may not be audited. An existing but empty SACL indicates that an object can be but is not currently being audited.

Rights versus Permissions

There are activities that do not apply to any specific object, but instead apply to a group of objects or to the operating system as a whole. Shutting down the operating system, for example, affects every object in the system. Operations of this nature require the user to have **user rights** to perform the operation.

Earlier in this chapter, I mentioned the Local Security Authority includes a Locally Unique Identifier when it creates an access token. The LUID describes which of the user rights that particular user account has. The Local Security Authority creates the LUID from security information in the Security Accounts Manager database. The SAM database matches users with rights. The LUID is a combination of the rights of that specific user account along with the rights of all the groups of which that account is a member.

Rights take precedence over permissions. That's why the Administrator account can take ownership of a file to which the owner of the file has set the No Access to Everyone permission; the Administrator has the Take Ownership of Files or Other Objects right. The Windows operating system checks the user rights first, and then (if there is no user right specifically allowing the operation) the operating system checks the ACEs stored in the DACL against the SIDs in the access token.

User accounts have the right to read or write to an object the user account owns even in the case of a **No Access permission**. The owner may also change the permissions of an object irrespective of the object's existing permissions.

NTFS File System Permissions

The **NTFS** file system is the bastion of Windows security. Being the platform upon which a secure Windows computer runs, NTFS is the gatekeeper of persistent security.

user rights
Actions that a user account can perform that apply to many or all objects in a system.

No Access permission
See *deny ACE*.

New Technology File System (NTFS)
The standard file system for Windows that provides secure object access, compression, checkpointing, and other sophisticated file management functions.

The LSA makes sure that running programs cannot violate each other's memory space and that all calls into the kernel are properly authorized. But access to files on disk must also be controlled, since running programs are loaded from disk files that could potentially be changed to anything. NTFS prevents unauthorized access to disk files, which is required for a truly secure system.

NTFS works by comparing a user's access token to the ACL associated with each file requested before allowing access to the file. This simple mechanism keeps unauthorized users from modifying the operating system or anything else they're not given specific access to.

Unfortunately, the default state of Windows is to provide full control to the everyone group at the root of all drives, so that all permissions inherited by files created therein are accessible by everyone. In order to receive any real benefit from NTFS file system security for applications and user stored files, you must remove the Full Control for Everyone permission and replace it with the appropriate user or group.

Using Windows Explorer, you can only replace permissions on existing files, which means that if you perform a permissions change across a large group of objects, they will all have the same resulting permissions. Using the CACLS command prompt tool, you can edit a large body of objects to insert or remove specific permissions without affecting the other existing permissions on the objects.

Managing NTFS File System Permissions

Managing NTFS file system permissions in Windows is simple. To change security permissions on a file or folder, browse to the file or folder object using the Windows Explorer, right-click the file or folder, select the Permissions tab, select the appropriate group or user account, and make the appropriate settings in the Access Control Entry list.

When a new file or directory is created, it receives a copy of the containing folder's (or drive's, if the object is created in the root) permissions (the DACL). In this way, objects are said to **inherit** permissions from their **parent**.

Inheritance is handled slightly differently in Windows 2000 than it is in Windows NT. In Windows NT, inherited permissions are simply the same as the parent objects and can be immediately modified. In Windows 2000, if the object is inheriting its permissions from a containing folder object, you'll have to uncheck the Allow Inheritable Permissions checkbox in order to create a copy of the inherited permissions, and then modify the existing permissions. You can create new ACE entries without overriding the inheritance setting.

inherit
To receive a copy of security information from the launching program, containing folder, or other such precursor.

parent
The preceding process (for programs) or containing folder (for objects, directories or files).

Encrypting File System (EFS)

Encrypting File System (EFS) is a file system driver that provides the ability to encrypt and decrypt files on the fly. The service is very simple to use: users need only check the encrypted attribute on a file or directory to cause the EFS service to generate an encryption certificate in the background and use it to encrypt the affected files. When those files are requested from the NTFS file system driver, the EFS service automatically decrypts the file for delivery.

The biggest problem with EFS is that it only works for individual users. That fact alone makes it useful only on client computers. Encryption certificates for files are created based on a user identity, so encrypted files can only be used by the account that created them.

NOTE

This is extremely shortsighted on Microsoft's part. If encryption certificates could be assigned to group objects rather than just accounts, encryption could be used to protect general files stored on a server.

EFS also has numerous accidental decryption problems that can occur when files are printed, when temporary files are created, and when files are moved. For these reasons, you should consider a third-party encryption package if you truly require encrypted storage on your system.

Windows Network Security

Windows network security is based on a few principle services:

- ◆ Active Directory
- ◆ Kerberos
- ◆ Group Policy
- ◆ Share Security
- ◆ IPSec

Each of these services works together to form a coherent whole: IPSec is defined by group policies which are stored in the Active Directory and can be configured to use Kerberos for automatic Private Key exchange. Share security is based on user identity as proven by Kerberos authentication based on password hashes stored in the Active Directory. Managing security policy through the Active Directory allows administrators to create group policies that can be automatically applied throughout the organization.

Active Directory

Active Directory is not a security service, but nearly all the security mechanisms built into Windows rely upon the Active Directory as a storage mechanism for security information like the domain hierarchy, trust relationships, crypto keys, certificates, policies, and security principle accounts.

Because nearly all of Windows's security mechanisms are integrated within Active Directory, you'll use it to manage and apply security. Most of the technologies covered in the sections to follow could be considered components of Active Directory because they're so tightly integrated with it.

Although Active Directory is not a security service, it can be secured: Active Directory containers and objects have ACLs just like NTFS files do. In Active Directory, permissions can be applied to directory objects in much the same way as they can be applied to files by NTFS.

Unlike NTFS file system permissions, you can set permissions for the fields inside specific objects so that different users or security groups can be responsible for portions of an object's data. For example, while you wouldn't want to give a user the ability to change anything about their own user account, allowing them to update their contact information is a good idea. This is possible using Active Directory permissions.

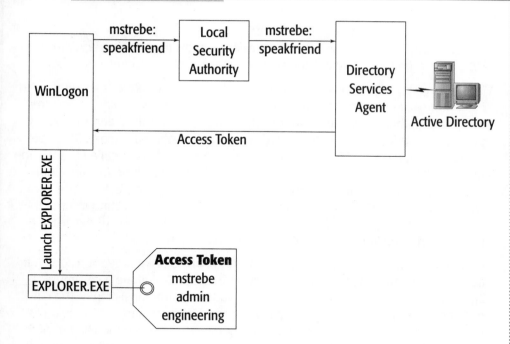

Kerberos
An authentication protocol that allows for a transitive trust between widely diverse domains. The primary authentication protocol for Windows 2000 and many UNIX distributions.

Key Distribution Center (KDC)
In Kerberos, a computer that manages user accounts. A domain controller.

Kerberos Authentication and Domain Security

Kerberos authentication was developed by the Massachusetts Institute of Technology (MIT) to provide an inter-computer trust system that was capable of verifying the identity of security principles like a user or a computer over an open, unsecured network. Kerberos does not rely on authentication by the computers involved or the privacy of the network communications. For this reason, Kerberos is ideal for authentication over the Internet and on large networks.

Kerberos operates as a trusted third-party authentication service by using shared secret keys. Essentially, a computer implicitly trusts the Kerberos **Key Distribution Center (KDC)** because it knows the same secret as the computer, a secret that must have been placed there as part of a trusted administrative process. In Windows, the shared secret is generated when the computer joins the domain. Since both parties to a Kerberos session trust the KDC, they can be considered to trust each other. In practice, this trust is implemented as a secure exchange of encryption keys that proves the identities of the parties involved to one another.

Kerberos authentication works like this:

A requesting client requests a valid set of credentials for a given server from the KDC by sending a plaintext request containing the client's name (identifier).

ticket
In Kerberos, encrypted time and identity information used to authenticate access between computers.

The KDC responds by looking up both the client and the server's secret keys in its database (the Active Directory), and creating a **ticket** containing a random session key, the current time on the KDC, an expiration time determined by policy, and optionally any other information stored in the database. The ticket is then encrypted using the client's secret key. A second ticket called the session ticket is then created, which is comprised of the session key and optional authentication data that is encrypted using the server's secret key. The combined tickets are then transmitted back to the client. It's interesting to note that the authenticating server does not need to authenticate the client explicitly because only the valid client will be able to decrypt the ticket.

Once the client is in possession of a valid ticket and session key for a server, it can initiate communications directly with the server. To initiate a communication with a server, the client constructs an authenticator consisting of the current time, the client's name, an application specific checksum if desired, and a randomly generated initial sequence number and/or a session subkey used to retrieve a unique session identifier specific to the service in question. Authenticators are only valid for a single attempt and cannot be reused or exploited through a replay attack because they are dependent upon the current time. The authenticator is then encrypted using the session key and transmitted along with the session ticket to the server from which service is requested.

When the server receives the ticket from the client, it decrypts the session ticket using the server's shared secret key (which secret key, if more than one exists, is indicated in the plaintext portion of the ticket). It then retrieves from the session key the ticket and uses it to decrypt the authenticator. The server's ability to decrypt the ticket proves that it was encrypted using the server's private key known only to the KDC, so the client's identity is trusted. The authenticator is used to ensure that the communication is recent and is not a replay attack. Tickets can be reused for a duration specified by the domain security policy, not to exceed ten hours. This reduces the burden on the KDC by requiring ticket requests as few as once per workday. Clients cache their session tickets in a secure store located in RAM and destroy them when they expire.

Kerberos uses the reusability property of tickets to shortcut the granting of tickets by granting a session ticket for itself as well as for the requested target server the first time a client contacts them. Upon the first request by a client, the KDC responds first with a session ticket for further ticket requests called a Ticket-Granting Ticket (TGT) and then with a session ticket for the requested server. The TGT obviates further Active Directory lookups by the client by pre-authenticating subsequent ticket requests in exactly the same manner that Kerberos authenticates all other requests. Like any session ticket, the TGT is valid until it expires, which depends upon domain security policy.

Kerberos is technically divided into two services: the TGT service (the only service that actually authenticates against the Active Directory) and the Ticket Granting service, which issues session tickets when presented with a valid TGT.

Trust Relationships between Domains

Kerberos works across **domain** boundaries. (Domains are called realms in Kerberos terminology—the two terms are equivalent.)

The name of the domain that a security principle belongs to is part of the security principle's name (e.g., titanium.sandiego.connetic.net). Membership in the same Active Directory tree automatically creates inter-domain keys for Kerberos between a parent domain and its child domains.

The exchange of inter-domain keys registers the domain controllers of one domain as security principles in the trusting domain. This simple concept makes it possible for any security principle in the domain to get a session ticket on the foreign KDC.

What actually happens is a bit more complex. When a security principle in one domain wants to access a security principle in an adjacent domain (one domain is the parent domain, one is the child), it sends a session ticket request to its local KDC. When the KDC determines that the target is not in the local domain, it replies to the client with a referral ticket, which is a session ticket encrypted using the inter-domain key. The client then uses the referral ticket to request a session ticket directly from the foreign KDC. The foreign KDC then decrypts the referral ticket because it has the inter-domain key, which proves that the trusted domain controller trusts the client (or it would not have granted the referral key) so the foreign KDC grants a session ticket valid for the foreign target server.

The process simply reiterates for domains that are farther away. To access a security principle in a domain that is two hops away in the Active Directory domain hierarchy, the client requests a session ticket for the target server against its KDC, which responds with a referral ticket to the next domain away. The client then requests the session ticket using the referral ticket just granted. That server will simply reply with a referral ticket that is valid on the next server in line. This process continues until the local domain for the target security principle is reached. At that point, a session key (technically, a TGT and a session key) is granted to the requesting client, which can then authenticate against the target security principle directly.

domain
A collection of computers that trust the same set of user accounts. Domain accounts are stored in the Active Directory.

187

The Ticket Granting Ticket authentication service is especially important in inter-domain ticket requests. Once a computer has walked down the referral path once, it receives a TGT from the final KDC in the foreign domain. This ensures that subsequent requests in that domain (which are highly likely) won't require the referral walk again. The TGT can simply be used against the foreign KDC to request whatever session tickets are necessary in the foreign domain.

group policy
A collection of computer and user configuration policies that are applied to computers based upon their association within an Active Directory container like a domain or organizational unit.

The final important concept in Kerberos authentication is delegation of authentication. Essentially, delegation of authentication is a mechanism whereby a security principle allows another security principle with which it has established a session to request authentication on its behalf from a third security principle. This mechanism is important in multi-tier applications, such as a database-driven website. Using delegation of authentication, the web browser client can authenticate with the web server, and then provide the web server with a special TGT that it can use to request session tickets on its behalf. The web server can then use the forwarded credentials of the web client to authenticate with the database server. This allows the database server to use appropriate security for the actual web client, rather than using the web server's credentials, which would have completely different access than the actual client.

Group Policies

Group policies are Windows's primary mechanism for controlling the configuration of client workstations for security as well as administrative purposes. Policies in general are simply a set of changes to the default settings of a computer. Policies are usually organized in such a way that individual policies contain changes that implement a specific goal—for example, disabling or enabling file system encryption, or controlling which programs a user is allowed to run.

Group policies are polices that are applied to groups like security groups or the members of an Active Directory container like a domain or organizational unit. Group policy is not strictly a security mechanism—its primary purpose is change and configuration management—but it allows administrators to create more secure systems by limiting users' range of actions.

Group policies can be used to control the following for computer policies:

- ◆ Registry settings related to security configuration and control
- ◆ Windows Installer package distribution
- ◆ Startup/Shutdown scripts
- ◆ Services startup
- ◆ Registry permissions
- ◆ NTFS permissions

- ◇ Public key policies
- ◇ IPSec policies
- ◇ System, network, and windows components settings

Group policies can be used to control the following for user policies:

- ◇ Windows Installer
- ◇ Internet Explorer settings
- ◇ Logon/logoff scripts
- ◇ Security settings
- ◇ Remote Installation Service
- ◇ Folder redirection
- ◇ Windows components
- ◇ Start Menu, Taskbar, Desktop, and Control Panel settings
- ◇ Network settings
- ◇ System settings

Mechanics of Group Policy

Group policy objects and any supporting files required for a group policy are stored on domain controllers in the SysVol share. Group policy objects are essentially custom registry files (and supporting files like .msi packages and scripts) defined by policy settings that are downloaded and applied to domain member client computers when the computer is booted (computer policy) and when a user logs in (user policy). Multiple group policies can be applied to the same computer, each policy overwriting the previous policy settings in a "last application wins" scenario—unless a specific policy is configured not to be overwritten.

Each group policy object has two parts: **computer policy** and **user policy**. You can configure both user and computer settings in a single group policy object, and you can disable the computer or user portion of a group policy object in the policy's Properties panel. I recommend splitting all policies to apply either to users or computers, because the policies are downloaded at different times and because the configuration requirements for the two types of security principles are highly likely to diverge over time, requiring the application of a different policy anyway.

Computer policies are applied at system initialization before a user logs in (and during periodic refreshes). Computer policies control the operating system, applications (including the Desktop Explorer), and startup and shutdown scripts. Think of computer policies as applying to the HKEY_Local_Machine portion of

computer policy
The portion of a group policy that is applied irrespective of which user account logs on.

user policy
The portion of group policy that applies to the logged on user.

189

the registry. Computer policies usually take precedence over user policies in the event of a conflict. Use computer policies whenever a configuration is required regardless of who logs onto the computer. You easily can apply a company-wide policy to computer policies.

User policies are applied after a user logs in but before they're able to work on the computer, as well as during the periodic refresh cycle. User policies control operating system behavior, desktop settings, application settings, folder redirection, and user logon/logoff scripts. Think of policies as applying to the HKEY_Current_User portion of the registry. Use user policies whenever a configuration is specific to a user or group of users, even if those users always use the same computers. By applying security-related settings to users rather than computers, you can ensure that those settings travel with the user in the event that they use someone else's computer—and that those policies don't apply to administrative or support personnel who may need to log onto the computer. (Of course, security group membership could be used to filter settings for support personnel as well.)

Group policies are called group policies because they're applied based on membership in Active Directory container security groups. Group policies are also hierarchical in nature; many policies can be applied to a single computer or user, and they are applied in hierarchical order. Furthermore, later policies can override the settings of earlier policies, so group change management can be refined from the broad policies applied to large groups to narrowly focused policies applied to smaller groups.

Group polices are configured at the following levels and in the following order:

Local Machine   Local group policy is applied first so that it can be overridden by a domain policy. Every computer has one local group policy that it is subject to. Beyond the Local group policy, group policies are downloaded from the Active Directory depending upon the user and computer's location in the Active Directory.

Site   These group policies are unique in that they are managed from the Active Directory Sites and Services snap-in. Site policies apply to sites, so they should be used for issues relating to the physical location of users and computers rather than for domain security participation. If your organization has only one site, this may not be obvious, but you should still apply policies this way because your organization may someday have multiple physical sites.

Domain   These group policies apply to all users and computers in the domain, and should be the primary place where you implement global policies in your organization. For example, if your company has a security policy document that requires specific configuration of logon passwords for all users, apply that policy to the domain.

Organizational Unit   These group policies apply to Organizational Unit member users and computers. Group policies are applied from top to bottom (parent then child) in the OU hierarchy.

You cannot apply group policies to generic folders or containers other than those listed above. If you need to create a container for a group policy, use an Organizational Unit.

Group policies are either all or nothing in their application—you cannot specify that only part of a policy will be applied. If you need to implement variations on a policy theme for different users, simply create one policy for each variation and apply the variants to the appropriate Active Directory container or security group.

A single Group policy can be applied to more than one container in the Active Directory because group policies are not stored in the Active Directory at the location where you apply them. Only a link to the group policy object is stored—the objects themselves are actually stored in the replicated SysVol share of the domain controllers in the domain.

shares
Constructs used by the Server service to determine how users should be able to access folders across the network.

Share Security

Shares are directories or volumes made available from a workstation or server for access by other computers in the network. Shares can be publicly available, or they can be given a list of users or groups with permission to access them. Shares use share-level security, which allows you to control permissions for shared directories, but not for anything contained within the directory. File-level security is superior to share-level security, but can only be used on NTFS volumes.

Although you can set up a reasonably secure small network with shares, share security techniques don't really scale well for larger networks and environments where security is required, because a new share must be created whenever security requirements change and because multiple shares with different security levels can be applied to the same directories.

Using and Securing Shares

File sharing is one of the most important uses of a network. Any directory on any workstation or server in the network can be set up as a shared directory. Although shares don't have the same level of security as NTFS directories on a dedicated server, Windows NT does provide a simple set of security features for shared directories.

Creating a Share

You can create a share with any volume or any directory within a volume. You can create shares in either NTFS or FAT partitions, although shares in NTFS partitions can be made more secure. To create a share, right-click a drive or a directory in an Explorer window and select the Sharing option. The Sharing Properties dialog box is displayed.

From this dialog box you can specify these options:

Not Shared/Shared As   Specify whether the volume or directory should be shared.

Share Name   Choose a name for the share. This name will appear as a directory name when users view a directory listing for the server. If the share will be accessed by users running Windows 3.*x*, or if your users use DOS applications, be sure to use a DOS-compatible name for the share (8 characters or less).

Comment   Enter a description of the share's purpose, or other information. (This is optional.) The contents of this field are displayed in the Explorer window to the right of the share name if the user selects the Details view.

User Limit   If Maximum Allowed is selected, the number of users accessing the share is limited only by the Windows NT license. If a number is specified, only that many concurrent users can access the share.

Permissions   Clicking this button displays a dialog box that allows you to change permissions for the share, as described later in this chapter.

Caching   Click this button to configure caching options for this share. Offline caching allows users to store the file locally on their hard disk so it's available even if they're not online or if the server is unavailable.

When a directory or drive is shared, it is listed in Explorer with a special icon that shows a hand underneath the drive or folder icon.

Accessing Shares

Although a server might have several shares configured—some entire volumes, some directories several levels deep—they all appear to users as a single listing under the server's name. Users can navigate to the server name using My Network Places icon, then open it to display a list of shares. Unfortunately, share names are not shown automatically in the Active Directory when you double-click on a computer—they must be manually added in the Active Directory hierarchy.

As an example, suppose we created several shares, including VOL_F for an entire NTFS volume, and IE4 for the \Program Files\Plus!\Microsoft Internet directory. A user who navigated to the server through My Network Places or Network Neighborhood would see a flat list of shares.

To make access to shares more convenient for users in the workgroup, you can create Desktop shortcuts to particular directories. You can also map a drive letter on the workstation to the share. This method has the benefit of fooling not only users into thinking it's a local drive, but also DOS and Windows applications that otherwise might not support network access. To map a drive to a share, right-click the My Network Places icon and then select Map Network Drive. Mapping drives is not normally necessary to access files from the Desktop Explorer or from Win32 applications.

To use this dialog box, choose a local drive letter, and then choose a server name and path to map the drive to. In Windows NT, the window at the bottom of the dialog box displays a list of servers and shares. In Windows 2000 and XP, you click the Browse button to search for a server and share. Select the Reconnect at Logon option to have the drive mapped each time the user logs on.

As an administrator, you have another option for displaying a list of shares on a server. The Computer Management snap-in's Shared Folders extension allows you to list shares on the local machine, add or remove shares, and monitor users who are currently accessing shares. The tool is available in the Administrative Tools folder and works just like every other MMC snap-in.

Default Shares

Windows automatically creates some shares, called administrative shares, which are accessible only to administrators and the operating system itself. These shares are used for remote administration and communication between systems.

Each drive is automatically given an administrative share, with the share name being the drive letter followed by a dollar sign. The ADMIN$ share is connected to the \WINNT directory on each server. There is also an IPC$ share, used for inter-process communication between Windows NT servers, and a PRINT$ share, which shares printer information between servers. Domain controllers have a SYSVOL$ share used to distribute group policies, scripts, and installation packages.

As you've probably noticed, these shares don't appear in the browse lists that you can view from the Explorer. The only way to list them is with the Computer Management snap-in, which was described in the previous section.

TIP

You can create your own "administrative" shares. Any share name ending with a dollar sign ($) will be hidden from browse lists. Users (administrators or not) can access the share if they know its exact name.

Administrative shares present a potential security risk. A hacker who has gained access to the Administrator account on a single workstation in the workgroup can access the system drives of other workstations, effectively allowing administrator-level access to the entire workgroup.

You can improve security by disabling the administrative shares. You can remove the shares from each drive's Properties window, or use the Shared Folder extension's Stop Sharing option. It's best to disable all of these and then add a share for any specific drives or directories that need to be available across the network.

Share versus File Security

Share level security is similar to file system security, but not nearly as sophisticated (or as secure) because Share Access Control Entries can be applied only to the share as a whole. Security cannot be customized within a share.

There is one significant advantage of share-level security: It works with any shared directory, whether it's on an NTFS or FAT volume. Share level security is the only way to secure FAT directories. However, the share permissions you set only affect remote users. Users logged onto the machine locally can access anything on a FAT volume, shared or not. Share level security also does not apply to users logged on locally or to Terminal Services clients.

Share Permissions

To set permissions for a share, click the Permissions button from the Sharing Properties dialog box. By default, the Everyone built-in group is given Full Control access to the share—in other words, share security is not implemented by default. The first thing you should do to secure a share is remove the Everyone group from the list. You can then add any number of users or groups, and give them specific permissions. The following are the permissions available for shares, and each can be allowed or denied:

Read   Allows users to list contents of the directory, open and read files, and execute programs.

Change   Allows users to create, delete, or modify files, as well as do everything the Read permissions allow.

Full Control   Allows all Read and Change permissions. In addition, users can change permissions and change file ownerships.

IPSec

Windows can be configured to use IPSec to secure communications between computers. Using default IPSec policy rules, you can configure clients to allow encryption and configure servers to request encryption or require encryption. A server that requires encryption will only communicate with hosts that have a valid SA that can be negotiated using IKE.

Windows 2000 supports both Authenticated Headers (AH) and Encapsulating Security Payload (ESP) in transport mode. Windows 2000 does not support ESP tunnel mode (IP encapsulation). This means that a Windows host cannot act as a bastion host and encrypt the communication stream between two private networks, it can only encrypt communications between itself and other hosts.

Windows 2000 uses IKE to negotiate encryption protocols and keys amongst hosts. As with any implementation of IKE, a private key is used for IKE authentication.

In the case of Windows 2000, the private key can be a valid Kerberos ticket, a Certificate, or a manually configured secret key.

Kerberos tickets   Make IPSec authentication seamless amongst hosts in the same domain, but only work when all the participants are running Windows 2000 or higher.

Certificates   Are appropriate for use in extranets, situations where trust does not transit between domains, communication with non-Windows hosts that can utilize certificates, or in environments where a Public Key Infrastructure is in place.

Manual secret keys   Are useful for encrypting communications between hosts that are not in domains and not in PKI environments where communications with non-Windows hosts are required, or when compatibility problems prevent the use of Kerberos or certificates.

Windows 2000 creates filters to determine which SA a particular host belongs to, in order to encrypt the communications with that host. These filters can be edited by the administrator to fix problems and for further customization or refinement. Automatically created filters tend to have problems if the host has more than one network adapter (as all Remote Access servers do) and in other situations.

Problems with IPSec

Microsoft believes that IPSec is the future of all communications amongst hosts in a network and sees it as something of a panacea for security problems. While it certainly could help with a number of problems, it's not compatible with more important security mechanisms like NAT and Proxy service, and it prevents firewalls from seeing the interior of TCP and UDP packets, thus eliminating their ability to filter based on packet type. This creates a conundrum for security administrators: If you allow IPSec to transit your firewall, you eliminate the firewall's ability to filter IPSec traffic.

Because IPSec transport mode doesn't play well with firewalls or private addressing allowed by NAT, which are far more important to holistic security, IPSec really only has a purpose in securing administrative connections to public hosts and in environments (like the military) where secure communications are required on the interior of already public networks. For most users, host-to-host IPSec will not significantly improve security and will dramatically increase the administrative burden.

IPSec puts heavy loads on servers (which must maintain numerous simultaneous encrypted streams), so extra processing power is required. In the case of terminal service and database servers, CPU power is at a premium, so requiring encryption will reduce the number of users that a server can support.

In sum, these problems mean that host-to-host IPSec is going to remain a network-to-network encryption as implemented by IPSec tunnel-mode VPN devices, not a host-to-host security service as implemented by Windows 2000's IPSec transport-mode. Once you have network-to-network communications established, there's little reason for most users to be concerned with additional encryption inside the private network.

Review Questions

1. Upon what foundation is Windows security built?

2. Where is the list of local computer accounts stored?

3. What represents user accounts in Windows security?

4. What process manages logging in?

5. What protocol is used to authenticate a user account in a Windows 2000 domain?

6. How is the user's identity passed on to running programs?

7. When you attempt to access a file, what does the LSA compare your access token to in order to determine whether or not you should have access?

8. What special right does an object's owner possess?

9. For what purpose is the System Access Control List used?

10. What is the difference between a right and a permission?

_____

11. What does the term inheritance mean in the context of file system permissions?

_____

12. Where are user accounts stored in a domain?

_____

13. In a Kerberos authentication, can a user in Domain A logon to a computer in Domain C if Domain C trusts Domain B and Domain B trusts Domain A?

_____

14. What is the primary mechanism for controlling the configuration of client computers in Windows?

_____

15. Can more than one group policy be applied to a single machine?

_____

16. Does share security work on FAT file system shares?

_____

Terms to Know

- ❑ New Technology LAN Manager (NTLM)
- ❑ objects
- ❑ owner
- ❑ parent
- ❑ permission
- ❑ process
- ❑ registry
- ❑ Security Accounts Manager (SAM)
- ❑ Security Descriptor
- ❑ Security Group
- ❑ Security Identifier (SID)
- ❑ security principle
- ❑ shares
- ❑ System Access Control List (SACL)
- ❑ Ticket
- ❑ user account
- ❑ user policy
- ❑ user rights
- ❑ Windows Explorer

Chapter

11

Securing Unix Servers

The security mechanisms available in standard UNIX (that being AT&T System V version 4), which essentially match those of BSD, are significantly simpler than those in Windows. Unix was originally developed as a "security simplified" alternative to Multics—as such, security is mostly an afterthought designed more to prevent accidental harm by legitimate users than to keep hackers at bay. Microsoft specifically designed the NT kernel to allow for much more expressive configuration of security than Unix in order to out-compete it.

But complexity doesn't equal security—in fact, in most situations, complexity is anathema to security. And, the default configuration of Windows after an installation bypasses most of Windows' sophisticated security mechanisms anyway, whereas Unix security is usually considerably stricter than Windows security out-of-the-box. In practice, Unix security can be configured similarly to Windows despite its inherent simplicity.

In this chapter, you will learn about:

 The history of Unix

 Understanding Unix file systems

 Configuration of Unix user accounts

 Creating Access Control Lists

 Setting execution permissions

A Brief History of Unix

To understand Unix security, it's important to understand why Unix was developed and how it evolved. In the mid 1960's, GE, MIT, and AT&T Bell Labs began development of an operating system that was supposed to become the standard operating system for the U.S. government. This system was called **Multics**, and its primary purpose was to support multiple users, multiple running programs, and multiple security levels simultaneously.

Multics
A complex operating system developed in the 1960s with many innovative concepts, such as multitasking. Multics was the precursor to the simpler and more portable Unix.

NOTE

In this book, "UNIX" in all capital letters refers specifically to AT&T System V version 4, and "Unix" in normal typeface refers to all Unix-compatible operating systems generically. Linux is Unix, BSD is Unix, and UNIX is Unix.

Unfortunately, because of its distributed development and the difficult problems it attempted to solve, the Multics development effort became bogged down and fell years behind schedule. In 1969, AT&T pulled out of the Multics development effort. Multics was eventually completed in the early seventies, but it languished on a few government-owned and commercial systems, without ever spawning an industry to support it or create applications for it. The last known running installation of Multics was shut down in 2000.

Ken Thompson, one of AT&T's programmers on the Multics team, decided to write a stripped-down version of Multics that threw out the security requirements that had bogged the project down and just allowed for the launching and control of multiple processes at the same time. With the help of Dennis Ritchie (co-developer of the C programming language), he had a running operating system within a year. Ritchie suggested calling the operating system UNIX as a dig at the overburdened Multics operating system. In a few short years, the system had been completely rewritten in Ritchie's C programming language, and included the C compiler, so that programmers had a complete system with which they could develop software.

Because AT&T was prevented from marketing or selling software by the Communications Act of 1957 in order to retain its monopoly status as the telephone provider for the entire country, AT&T allowed Thompson to provide UNIX to whomever wanted it for the price of the tape that stored it. It quickly became popular in academic environments and as an operating system for new computer systems whose designers couldn't afford to develop an operating system.

In the mid-1970's, some students at Berkeley bought a tape of the operating system, including the source code. Unlike most others who merely used the operating system or, at most, ported it to a new type of computer, the Berkeley students set out to modify and improve the system as they saw fit. When they began distributing their improved version of Unix, they called it the **Berkeley Software Distribution**, or **BSD**. BSD soon incorporated the Mach micro-kernel developed at Carnegie-Mellon University, which made the installation and incorporation of device drivers much easier and allowed for more distributed modular kernel development by more parties. By the early 1990's, BSD did not contain any code that was developed at AT&T, and Berkeley was able to place the entire distribution into the public domain. It survives today as the BSD 4.4, FreeBSD, NetBSD, and OpenBSD open-source distributions and as the operating system for innumerable network devices.

In 1983, the U.S. government split AT&T up, and the restriction that prevented them from selling UNIX commercially was lifted. AT&T immediately recognized the potential of their operating system and began selling it directly and licensing it to computer manufactures who needed compelling operating systems for their mainframes. AT&T officially licensed UNIX to IBM (named AIX), Hewlett-Packard (named HP-UX), Digital (named Digital UNIX and now Compaq Tru64), and many others.

AT&T realized the threat posed by BSD, which was technically superior to UNIX and not controlled by AT&T. AT&T refused to allow the UNIX trademark to be used to describe BSD and convinced their corporate customers that BSD was not well supported and so should not be used in a commercial enterprises. Largely, their tactics worked, and UNIX was pretty much officially split into the Academic version (BSD) and the commercial version (AT&T UNIX System V). (Microsoft is now using exactly this tactic against competitive open-source operating systems.)

The only major exception to this division of commercial and open-source versions was Sun Microsystems, which based their SunOS on BSD. After heavy marketing to Sun throughout the 1980's, AT&T finally convinced them to base a new operating system on System V, and Solaris was born. Solaris attempted to merge the two worlds and was mostly compatible with applications written for BSD and System V.

Microsoft simultaneously developed Xenix, which was based on the earlier AT&T System III UNIX, in the early 1980's, but sold it to the Santa Cruz Operation when they couldn't successfully market it. Xenix was the first Unix for Intel microcomputers.

Just after completing their domination of the commercial UNIX world, AT&T decided that its fortunes lay in telecommunications after all and sold UNIX to Novell. Novell completely mishandled the acquisition, and wound up selling it to the Santa Cruz Operation (SCO) less than two years later for about 10% of what they paid for it—but not before they opened the term UNIX to any operating system that could pass a suite of UNIX-compatibility tests, thus allowing BSD to

BSD (Berkeley Software Distribution)
A highly customized version of Unix, originally distributed by the University of California at Berkeley.

again be referred to as UNIX. SCO UNIX is now actually the original official AT&T System V version 4.

So, at this point, there really is no "official" Unix, merely a set of standards: BSD 4.4 and AT&T System V version 4. Nearly all versions of Unix are based on one of these two standard platforms.

Except the most important Unix: Linux. In 1993, a Finnish college student named Linus Torvalds developed his own operating system kernel as an experiment in creating lightweight and efficient operating systems for Intel computers. When he uploaded his running kernel to the Internet, thousands of independent developers downloaded it and began porting their software to it. The GNU foundation, a loose consortium of developers who had been attempting to develop their own version of Unix that would be free of license restrictions from AT&T or Berkeley, immediately ported the tools they had written for their as yet uncompleted operating system, and the Linux distribution was born.

Students, developers, hackers, scientists, and hobbyists from around the world began using Linux because it was completely free of all licensing restrictions except one: Anyone who wrote software for Linux had to release the software into the public domain, so that Linux would always remain free; nobody would be able to "embrace and extend it" back into a proprietary system by adding compelling features that would out-compete the free alternatives. Because it came with source code, Linux was quickly ported to every computing platform that anybody cared about.

Within five years, Linux became the largest distribution of Unix, and was compatible with software written for BSD and AT&T System V. Linux is now the second most widely deployed operating system after Windows, and is currently installed in more than twice as many commercial installations than UNIX or BSD. Within a few years, Linux is certain to displace most other versions of Unix, except for those that ship with computers like the BSD-based Mac OS X.

NOTE

BSD will always exist, because it is not limited to the restrictions of the GNU Public License (GPL). If you extend Linux, you must publish your extensions for everyone to use. For example, when TiVo developed their Television Personal Video Recorder on Linux, the Free Software Foundation pushed them to publish their source code, and they did so because they were license-bound by the GPL to do so. Because BSD is truly in the public domain, you can do whatever you want with it and sell it to anyone for as much as you want, and keep your code proprietary. For this reason, BSD is a more popular choice for embedded systems developers than Linux. This is one of the reasons that the MacOS is based on BSD's Mach kernel.

Just because Linux is the most popular Unix does not mean that it is technically superior to other Unix distributions; it's just free. BSD Unix remains faster and more stable than Linux (and even freer, since there are no licensing restrictions at all), and IBM's AIX is still the king of high-speed distributed computing. However, the Linux kernel programmers are moving quickly, and they have adopted a number of BSD's speed enhancements. It is highly likely that because of the interest in Linux, it will soon outclass all other versions of Unix in any meaningful comparison. Programmers often write for Linux rather than BSD, because they can guarantee that by writing for Linux their work won't wind up co-opted into someone's commercial product for which they won't be compensated.

Linus Torvalds does not sell or even designate an "official" version of Linux—he merely controls the kernel code. It is up to third parties to create installable operating systems with packages of tools, and there are many of them, all referred to as **distributions**. The Red Hat distribution is the most popular, but other distributions like Mandrake, VA Linux, TurboLinux, Yellow Dog, SuSe, Storm, and Stampede are also popular. These various distributions include a canonical set of tools, various applications, and management tools. They differ mostly in their ease of installation and setup, but some are tuned for various processors or situations. Anyone who wants to can create and market their own Linux distributions, and many institutions have created their own customized distributions of Linux for internal use.

distributions
A specific packaging of a Unix operating system and associated utility files and applications.

Unix Security Basics

Unix security is similar to Windows in that it is entirely permissions based, with user identity being determined by the login **process**. Like Windows, running processes either receive their user context from the logged in user who launches the process or from a predefined process **owner**.

To understand Unix security, you need to first understand how Unix organizes the various system objects that can be secured, how account security is managed, and how permissions are applied to file system objects.

Understanding Unix File Systems

In Unix, everything is a file system object. This includes print queues, running processes, and devices; even the kernel's memory space is represented as a file in the file system.

Unix implements permission-based security. So, because everything in Unix is a file, file system permissions can be effectively used to control access to devices, processes, and so forth. This simplifies security dramatically and requires fewer methods of checking for security.

The File System

All hard disks and their various **partitions** are **mounted** in a single unified directory in Unix. There are no drive letters or different disk objects as you would find in Windows or many other operating systems. Otherwise, the directory structure is very similar to most other operating systems in that it is a hierarchy of directories that can contain other directories or files.

The root of the file system is referred to as /, so using the change directory command below will take you to the root of the file system:

```
cd /
```

From there, other partitions and disks can be mounted and will appear as directories. For example, the /boot directory is usually a small partition at the beginning of the disk that contains the kernel. This convention stems from the fact that many computer boot loaders can only load the kernel from the beginning of a large hard disk, because they were written when all disks were relatively small and they can't access disk sectors beyond a limited range. The following graphic shows the typical first-level Linux directory structure.

process
A running program.

owner
The user account that has wide and separate access to a file. Typically, the owner is the user account that created the file.

partition
A low-level division of a hard disk. A partition contains a file system.

mount
To make a file system on a block device available. The term comes from the act of mounting a reel of tape on a tape reader.

```
[root@localhost root]# cd /
[root@localhost /]# ls -l
total 118
drwxr-xr-x    2 root     root         2048 Apr 15 16:20 bin
drwxr-xr-x    4 root     root         1024 Apr 15 15:31 boot
drwxr-xr-x   17 root     root        77824 Apr 16 08:08 dev
drwxr-xr-x   46 root     root         4096 Apr 16 08:07 etc
drwxr-xr-x    3 root     root         4096 Feb  6  1996 home
drwxr-xr-x    2 root     root         1024 Jun 21  2001 initrd
drwxr-xr-x    7 root     root         3072 Apr 15 16:25 lib
drwxr-xr-x    2 root     root        12288 Apr 15 14:58 lost+found
drwxr-xr-x    2 root     root         1024 Aug 29  2001 misc
drwxr-xr-x    4 root     root         1024 Apr 15 23:38 mnt
drwxr-xr-x    2 root     root         1024 Aug 23  1999 opt
dr-xr-xr-x   49 root     root            0 Apr 16 01:05 proc
drwxr-x---    2 root     root         1024 Apr 15 23:48 root
drwxr-xr-x    2 root     root         4096 Apr 15 16:18 sbin
drwxrwxrwt    4 root     root         1024 Apr 16 08:14 tmp
drwxr-xr-x   16 root     root         4096 Apr 15 16:33 usr
drwxr-xr-x   20 root     root         1024 Apr 15 16:17 var
[root@localhost /]#
```

CD-ROM drives are typically mounted in the /dev/cdrom directory, so that if you change directory to /dev/cdrom/install, you would be mapped to the same location as d:\install if that CD-ROM were mounted in a Windows machine.

Many Unix administrators create the /home directory in a separate partition to ensure that end users can't fill up the system partition where the operating system needs space to run. The /var directory, where log files are kept, is another popular directory to mount in its own partition. None of this is necessary, however—the entire file system can be created in a single partition, in which case these directories would represent just directories, not mounted disks or partitions.

The Unix mount command is used to attach a block device like a hard disk partition or a CD-ROM drive to the file system.

File System Structures

There are three primary file system structures that are used in Unix to manage files:

Inodes are the heart of Unix file systems. **Inodes** contain all the metadata (data about data) that describes the file, except its name—including the file's location on disk, its size, the user account that owns it, the group account that can access it, as well as the permissions for the user and group account. Inodes are stored in an array of inodes on the disk.

Directories are simply files that relate a list of file names to an inode index number. They contain no information other than the text of the name and the inode that contains details of the file. There can be any number of names that reference an inode, and when there are more than one, they are called **hard links**. When you delete a file in Unix, you're really just removing a hard link.

---

inode (index node)
A file descriptor in Unix systems that describes ownership, permissions, and other metadata about a file.

---

hard links
Multiple file names for a single inode. Hard links allow a single file to exist in multiple places in the directory hierarchy.

When the last hard link is removed, the kernel deletes the inode and reclaims the disk space.

File contents   are the data stored on disk, such as the text in a text file, or the information being read in or written out to a serial port, TCP/IP socket, named pipe, etc.

So when I say that in Unix everything is a file, what I really mean is that every process, network socket, **I/O port**, or mass storage device contains a name in the unified file system directory tree and an inode that describes its security permissions. They do not necessarily have actual file content stored on disk.

Inodes

Consider the following mythical directory listing from a Unix machine in the standard format of the 1s command:

```
[root@localhost sample]# ls -l
total 1
brw-rw----   2 root     disk     3,   0 Aug 30  2001 blockdevice
crw-------   2 root     root    10,   2 Aug 30  2001 characterdevice
drwxr-xr-x   2 root     root        1024 Apr 16 08:24 directory
-rw-r--r--   1 root     root           0 Apr 16 08:24 file
prw-------   2 root     root           0 Apr 15 23:51 pipe
srw-rw-rw-   2 root     root           0 Apr 16 08:07 socket
[root@localhost sample]# _
```

The various file types shown are:

◇ Standard **files** are data structures stored on disk.

◇ **Directories** are files that map file names to inode numbers.

◇ **Character devices** are I/O devices that transfer one character at a time, like a serial or parallel port.

◇ **Block devices** are I/O devices that transfer large blocks of data at a time, such as a hard disk drive or network adapter.

◇ **Sockets** are connections made between computers on a network using TCP/IP.

◇ **Pipes** are first in, first out (FIFO) communication streams between processes on the same computer or on computers in a local area network.

This listing displays much of the information contained in an inode, along with the file name that is contained in the directory. Inodes also contain pointers to the actual file data and a few other things, but for our purposes, this listing

---

I/O port
An interface to peripherals, like serial devices, printers, etc.

file
A sequence of data that is permanently stored on a mass-storage device, such as a hard disk, and referenced by a name.

directory
A file that contains the names of other files or directories.

character devices
A class of peripherals that transmit or receive information one byte at a time (i.e., processing occurs for each byte received). Typically, character devices are lower-speed devices like keyboards, mice, or serial ports.

shows almost everything in an inode that you need to know to understand Unix security.

You can determine the type of a file using the `ls` command by examining the first character of the mode field (the first character of the file.) I've named the files according to their type, so you can see that d represents a directory, for example.

Because all I/O devices and communication mechanisms are described by file names and inodes, all of the standard Unix file processing tools can be used to operate on them. For example, you can `cat` (list) the contents of a process file and see a textual representation of its memory on screen (although it will be impossible for you to interpret it).

Devices (and most of the other strange file types) are typically mounted in the /dev directory. This is a convention, not a requirement, and it's important to remember that a hacker may attempt to mount a device within their own /home directory.

User Accounts

User accounts for local security are stored in a plain text file in the /etc/passwd file. This file is a simple listing of accounts that are available along with some information about each account, as shown in the following picture.

```
[root@localhost etc]# cat passwd |more
root:x:0:0:root:/root:/bin/bash
bin:x:1:1:bin:/bin:/sbin/nologin
daemon:x:2:2:daemon:/sbin:/sbin/nologin
adm:x:3:4:adm:/var/adm:/sbin/nologin
lp:x:4:7:lp:/var/spool/lpd:/sbin/nologin
sync:x:5:0:sync:/sbin:/bin/sync
shutdown:x:6:0:shutdown:/sbin:/sbin/shutdown
halt:x:7:0:halt:/sbin:/sbin/halt
mail:x:8:12:mail:/var/spool/mail:/sbin/nologin
news:x:9:13:news:/var/spool/news:
uucp:x:10:14:uucp:/var/spool/uucp:/sbin/nologin
operator:x:11:0:operator:/root:/sbin/nologin
games:x:12:100:games:/usr/games:/sbin/nologin
gopher:x:13:30:gopher:/var/gopher:/sbin/nologin
ftp:x:14:50:FTP User:/var/ftp:/sbin/nologin
nobody:x:99:99:Nobody:/:/sbin/nologin
mailnull:x:47:47::/var/spool/mqueue:/dev/null
rpm:x:37:37::/var/lib/rpm:/bin/bash
xfs:x:43:43:X Font Server:/etc/X11/fs:/bin/false
ntp:x:38:38::/etc/ntp:/sbin/nologin
rpc:x:32:32:Portmapper RPC user:/:/bin/false
rpcuser:x:29:29:RPC Service User:/var/lib/nfs:/sbin/nologin
nfsnobody:x:65534:65534:Anonymous NFS User:/var/lib/nfs:/sbin/nologin
--More--
```

Anyone with access to this file can create or modify accounts in any way they see fit. By default, this file is writeable only by the root administrative account.

block devices
Peripherals that transfer mass quantities of information in large units (i.e., processing occurs for each large block of information received, rather than for every byte). Block devices are typically high-speed devices like hard disk drives or local area network adapters.

socket
A specific TCP or UDP port on a specific IP address, for example: 192.168.0.1:80. Sockets are used to transmit information between two participating computers in a network environment. Sockets are block devices.

pipe
An inter-process communication mechanism that emulates a serial character device.

The fields in each line in the passwd file are separated by a colon:

- ◇ Name—Account name.
- ◇ Password—MD5 hash of the account's password. In this case, the password field is merely a placeholder because shadow passwords are in use (see below).
- ◇ UID—User Identifier
- ◇ GID—Primary Group Identifier
- ◇ Display Name—User's full name
- ◇ Home Directory—Home directory (shell will start here)
- ◇ **Shell**—Path to the executable that should be loaded after a successful login

User accounts in Unix are represented in the system by simple integers referred to as **User Identifiers** or **UIDs**. UIDs merely indicate a unique serial number for user accounts, beginning with 0 for the root account.

shell

The program launched after a successful login that presents the user environment. Typically, shells allow a user to launch subsequent programs.

User Identifier (UID)

An integer that identifies a user account to the system.

root

The Unix superuser administrative account. Permissions are not checked for the root user.

WARNING

Unix UIDs are not unique on every machine: Root on one machine is the same UID as root on another. This can lead to unintentional elevation of privileges when accounts are moved between machines or connected via various authentication systems. Windows SIDs, on the other hand, are unique for every computer, so this security problem doesn't exist in Windows.

Besides editing the /etc/passwd file, you can create user accounts easily using these commands:

`adduser mstrebe`   adds a user account named mstrebe.

`passwd mstrebe`   changes the password for the account named mstrebe. Running passwd without specifying a parameter changes the password for the logged-in account.

`userdel mstrebe`   removes a user from the system.

Root

In Unix, there is only one specially privileged account: root, so named because it is the owner of the root of the file system.

The **root** account is used by the kernel to bypass permissions checking—permissions are not checked for the root account, so it is fundamentally different than all other user accounts. Root is the first account created by a new system during the installation, and it has a UID of 0.

> **NOTE**
>
> Root is not analogous to the Windows Administrator account, which is merely a normal account with elevated user rights. It is actually equal to the Windows LocalSystem account, which cannot be logged into (but can be exploited by writing a service that runs as Local System).

Because permissions are not checked for the root account, there is no way to lock the root account out of any file. Root users are all-powerful in Unix, so access to the root account must be strictly controlled.

> **NOTE**
>
> There's nothing special about the name "root"—it's just a name, and it can be changed. A root account is any account with a UID of 0. Changing the name of the root account will be confusing to administrators of other systems and some software, but will also confuse hackers, so for security purposes, you should strongly consider changing the name of the root account by editing the `/etc/passwd` file.

The traditional Unix security warning is that you should never actually log in as root; rather, you should use the su (set user) command after you've logged in normally to obtain root privilege, as such:

```
su root
```

You'll be prompted for a password and receive a new shell. When you exit from this shell, you'll be back in your normal account's shell.

> **NOTE**
>
> I'm not nearly as religious about this as most people. There's no technical difference between logging in as root and "suing" to root, except that you're far less likely to forget about your elevated privileges if you su to root rather than log in as root. For normal users, this could mean something, but I've been a network administrator for so long that I have a hard time remembering why things aren't working when I don't have elevated privileges. I also tend to administer a lot of special purpose machines that don't necessarily have user accounts for normal users, so logging in as root is normal.

My warning is that you should only log in as root when you're actually performing administration. Log in with your normal user account most of the time. If you do that, you'll find that you su more often anyway because it's more convenient.

Groups

Groups in Unix are analogous to user accounts—they are simply named representations of a Group Identifier (GID) as stored in the file /etc/group (most system configuration files are stored in the /etc directory in Unix).

```
[root@localhost etc]# cat group |more
root:x:0:root
bin:x:1:root,bin,daemon
daemon:x:2:root,bin,daemon
sys:x:3:root,bin,adm
adm:x:4:root,adm,daemon
tty:x:5:
disk:x:6:root
lp:x:7:daemon,lp
mem:x:8:
kmem:x:9:
wheel:x:10:root
mail:x:12:mail
news:x:13:news
uucp:x:14:uucp
man:x:15:
games:x:20:
gopher:x:30:
dip:x:40:
ftp:x:50:
lock:x:54:
nobody:x:99:
users:x:100:
slocate:x:21:
[root@localhost etc]#
```

Groups provide a way to elevate the privileges to a file higher than those allowed to everyone, but lower than those provided to the owner of the file. Unix maintains three sets of permissions for each file system object: permissions for the owner, permissions for the file's group, and permissions for everyone. By setting permissions for the file's group and then making select user accounts members of that group, you can provide more permission to a file for specific users. You can specify all the members of a group by simply listing them with commas behind the group name in the group file.

For example, say you have a set of instructions for using a piece of equipment that you maintain (so you need Write access to it) and you want to provide those instructions to the people who use that equipment (so they need Read access to it), but you don't want anyone else to be able to read it. To set these permissions, you would give the owner (you) Read and Write permissions, set the group permissions to Read only, and set the Everyone permissions to None. You would then create a group for the users who need to access the file and set the file's GID to match that group. Finally, add each of the users to that group in order to provide them with access to the file.

You can create and manage groups using the following Unix commands:

groupadd groupname   allows you to create a group.

newgrp groupname   allows a user to switch their group context between the groups that they belong to.

To delete groups and add or remove members, edit the /etc/group file.

Wheel Group

As with user accounts, there is one group, group 0, that has elevated permissions. This group is often called "wheel," but its name is not nearly as standardized as "root" is for UID 0. (In Linux, GID 0 is typically referred to as root.) Members of the wheel group are like root in that the system does not perform security checks on their activities, so they are in essence root users. Various utilities in Unix may only operate for members of the wheel group.

Shadow Passwords

One major problem with Unix security is that the /etc/passwd file must be accessible by various user accounts in order for a number of service logon mechanisms to work correctly, but if it is accessible, users could change their UIDs or groups to elevate their own privileges. The solution to this problem is **shadow passwords**.

The system implements the shadow passwords mechanism by making a copy of the passwd file called "shadow" that contains the same information, but is not accessible by users other than root. This file actually stores the passwords used by the system for logons. Because the passwd file does not contain actual passwords, the true password file does not need to be exposed to other processes. The following screenshot shows a listing of the /etc/shadow file. Notice the long string of strange characters after root: those characters are the MD5 hash of the root password. None of the other accounts on this machine have passwords, so they cannot be used to log in.

shadow passwords
A security tactic in Unix that separates password information from user account information while remaining compatible with software written for the earlier combined method.

```
[root@localhost etc]# cat shadow |more
root:$1$bAOcÈOfñ$ZOceFiYNBZZHAFYTuR/t00:11792:0:99999:7:::
bin:*:11792:0:99999:7:::
daemon:*:11792:0:99999:7:::
adm:*:11792:0:99999:7:::
lp:*:11792:0:99999:7:::
sync:*:11792:0:99999:7:::
shutdown:*:11792:0:99999:7:::
halt:*:11792:0:99999:7:::
mail:*:11792:0:99999:7:::
news:*:11792:0:99999:7:::
uucp:*:11792:0:99999:7:::
operator:*:11792:0:99999:7:::
games:*:11792:0:99999:7:::
gopher:*:11792:0:99999:7:::
ftp:*:11792:0:99999:7:::
nobody:*:11792:0:99999:7:::
mailnull:!!:11792:0:99999:7:::
rpm:!!:11792:0:99999:7:::
xfs:!!:11792:0:99999:7:::
ntp:!!:11792:0:99999:7:::
rpc:!!:11792:0:99999:7:::
rpcuser:!!:11792:0:99999:7:::
nfsnobody:!!:11792:0:99999:7:::
--More--
```

File System Security

Once you understand Unix user accounts and file systems, understanding file system security is simple.

There are four levels of Read, Write, and Execute permissions maintained for every object in the file system:

- ❖ The root user (and wheel group) has all permissions; permissions are not checked for the root user.
- ❖ The owner of the file object has the permissions specified by the first three access entries in the inode.
- ❖ Members of the file's system object's group have the permissions specified by the second block of three access entries in the inode.
- ❖ Everyone else has the permissions specified by the final block of three access entries in the inode.

In practice, this system can be nearly as expressive as the complex Access Control List structure used by Windows, except that, rather than creating a large number of access control entries for a few groups of users on a large number of files, you create a large number of groups (one for each file system object, if necessary) to obtain precise control over how users can access files. Because there are no access control lists, file access in Unix is considerably more efficient than other secure file systems.

NOTE

Windows has numerous security problems due to the complexity of its security subsystem. Because there are many ways that various objects might be secured, there are numerous processes that are responsible for security. This means that Microsoft has much more code to comb through than Unix, and there's a greater possibility of error. It also means that users have to understand a lot more about the system and its security features, and they are more likely to make mistakes when securing a computer. It's like having a castle with hundreds of small doors to guard instead of one big one.

While most versions of Unix do not implement any analogue to the "deny ACE" in Windows, you can mimic this behavior by allowing wider access to the Everyone group than you allow to the object's group. For example, if you allow Read/Write access to the Everyone group, but only allow Read access to the object's group, then members of the object's group will only have Read access.

To change permissions on a file in Unix, use the chmod command. Permissions are grouped into three octal fields, each represented by a number from 0 to 7 that represent the following:

1= Allow Execute Access

2= Allow Write Access

4 = Allow Read Access

You add up these values to determine the exact permission, so a 6 equals Read and Write permission. You then conjoin all three values in Owner, Group, Everyone order to come up with the parameter for chmod:

```
chmod filename 0764
```

A 0764 means that Owners have Execute, Read, and Write permissions, members of the file's group have Read and Write permission, and everyone else has Read permission only. The preceding "0" indicates that the file's SetUID bit is not set, which is explained in the section on execution permissions.

To change a file's owner, use the chown command:

```
chown filename user
```

Typically, chown can only be executed by the root user.

NOTE

The term "world" is frequently used to describe "everyone" in Unix—so "world writeable" means that all users have write access to a file.

Access Control Lists

While neither AT&T System V version 4 UNIX, BSD, nor Linux support Access Control lists, some versions of Unix (HP-UX and AIX specifically) do support the more complex Access Control List method of permissions checking.

For the most part, ACLs in the various versions of Unix that support them work the same way as they do in Windows: for any given file, a list of permissions for arbitrary users or groups can be used to specify permissions more explicitly than can be specified using traditional Unix permissions. In Unix, these permissions are essentially stored in a text file stored in an associated file stream that can be edited with a standard text editor, or modified using a set of commands to add, delete, or enumerate permissions.

Unfortunately, ACLs are not widely supported in the Unix community, and every implementation of them is different amongst the various vendors. This lack of conformity ensures that they will never be widely implemented, and because no clear authority remains to define the constitution of standard Unix, it's unlikely that any real uniformity will ever occur. Solaris and Linux have committed to support ACLs in future releases, but that may be overcome by events; most people have realized that permissions alone are not capable of truly protecting information from dedicated hackers and will move instead to a true Public Key Infrastructure.

NOTE

Ultimately, Linux will subsume and replace all other versions of Unix, so whatever form of ACLs it implements will become the standard.

Execution Permissions

The only other thing you need to know about file system security is that the setuid and setgid flags can be set on an executable permission in order to modify the user account under which the file is executed.

Normally, an executable file inherits its user security context from the user who executes the file. For example, if user "postgres" launches a database executable, that database inherits the UID of user "postgres" in order to access files itself.

But this is a problem for executables that launch automatically at boot time. Daemons and services that launch automatically, will all be launched under the root context because there is no logged-in user during the boot process. This means that every daemon would have full access to the system, and any flaw or poorly coded daemon that a hacker could exploit would provide full access to the system.

The Unix solution to this is the setuid and setgid bits contained in the executable file's inode.

If the setuid flag is set on an executable file, then the executing program (process) inherits its UID from its own file's UID rather than from the user who started the executable.

This means, for example, that a daemon could have an owner other than root who would only be able to access files that are necessary for the daemon to operate. The setgid flag works the same way, and causes the file to inherit its GID from its file GID rather than the logged-on user's primary group.

WARNING

Programs that operate with SetUID or SetGID permissions can open very serious holes in your security. Be extremely cautious about using them.

To create a SetUID executable (also referred to as SUID executables), execute the following command:

```
setuid bash root
```

Note that this command will create a shell that always has root permissions—exactly what a hacker would attempt if they could, and what you should never do. If you do this for test purposes, remember to change it back to normal by executing this command:

```
setuid bash -
```

You can do the same thing to a file's group using the setgid command, which gives the executable whatever permissions are held by that group.

SetUID Security Problems

There are numerous security problems associated with SetUID programs; obviously, since they can operate as the root, any exploit that can take control of them and cause them to launch a new process (like a shell) effectively has control of the system.

But there are more subtle ways in which SetUID can cause problems. For example, say a user copies a shell executable to a floppy disk on a system that they have root access to, and uses SetUID to set the shell to load as root. If they can mount this floppy on a system upon which they are a normal unprivileged user, then by running that shell they will have root access. UID 0 on their machine is the same as UID 0 on every other Unix machine, so because the shell program on the floppy has root execution privilege, it can be used to exploit other machines. In many cases, mount is restricted to normal users for this reason. Some newer versions of Unix can be configured to ignore SetUID bits on removable or networked file systems. You should check this exploit specifically on your system to ensure that it doesn't work.

SetUID Shell scripts

In most versions of Unix, Shell scripts can be marked as SetUID programs and run as the root user. You should avoid doing this to the extent possible, because if the text of a script can be modified by anyone, that user can exploit the script to launch a new shell under the root context. Aside from the obvious method of modifying a script, a user could potentially hook into or replace any executable called by the script (or even modify a program in the executable's search path to mimic a normal system executable) to exploit root context.

For example, say a shell script that executes as root changes into a user's directory and then executes a `find` command. If the user has replaced the `find` command with another shell script in their own directory, that `find` command could be executed instead of the system `find` command and exploited to launch a new shell, modify the user's permissions, or perform any other action on the system. These sorts of exploits have been used in the past to hack into Unix machines with regularity.

daemon
A Unix executable that is launched automatically at boot time and normally runs at all times. Similar to a service in Windows.

Finding SetUID and SetGID Programs

You should regularly monitor your systems for the presence of SetUID and SetGID programs in order to prevent hackers or users from loading them in and using them as Trojan horses. The methods a potential hacker could use to load a SetUID program onto a system are too numerous to enumerate, but you can avoid them all by using the `find` command to search for SetUID files.

The following system command (when executed as root) will search for executables with their SetUID or SetGID bits set. By running this regularly and comparing the output with prior output, you can determine when new SetUID programs have been loaded onto your system.

```
find / -type f -perm 4000
```

Daemons and Daemon Security

When Unix boots, the boot loader loads the kernel without checking permissions of any sort and starts the kernel. The kernel begins checking file system permissions as soon as the file system is mounted. Once the kernel has loaded, all subsequent processes are loaded in user mode, where their memory is protected from foreign processes by the kernel.

Daemons (services) in Unix are not special applications with a specific service interface like they are in Windows; they are merely executable programs that are launched by a script that is read in at boot time. Daemons launch with the user identity of the user account that owns the executable file system permission.

Many older (and often exploited) daemons require root access to do their work. Sendmail, the standard mail server for Unix, is notorious for its root user context requirements and the many exploits that it has been susceptible to.

Daemons that require root access to operate are almost always examples of lazy programming by programmers or network administrators who don't want to bother really thinking about how a daemon should be using the system. In every case that I can think of, a more secure alternative exists that operates correctly in the context of a user account that is specifically created for it, and these should be chosen over daemons that require root access. For example, Postfix, a simple alternative to Sendmail, is more secure, easier to configure, and more feature-rich than Sendmail.

To the extent possible, avoid any software that requires running in the root context. You should also avoid installing software to run as root that does not require it, but allows you to do so anyway. For example, MySQL can be configured with a root user context, but it also runs perfectly fine in its own user context. The more security-minded programmers of PostgreSQL won't allow it to run in root context and automatically set up a postgres user as part of the normal setup process.

Review Questions

1. Why is Unix security so simple?

2. Why did AT&T originally give UNIX away to anyone who wanted a copy?

3. Why are there so many variations of Unix?

4. In Unix, every system object is represented and controlled by what primary structure?

5. What is the primary security mechanism in Unix?

6. Which component stores permissions?

7. Where is user account information stored on a Unix system?

8. How are permissions handled for the root user in Unix?

9. What is the GID of the wheel or superuser group?

10. What are the basic permissions that can be set for owners, group members, and everyone else in an inode?

_____

11. Which two commands are typically used to modify ownership and permissions on an inode?

_____

12. What does it mean when an executable has its SetUID flag enabled?

_____

13. What makes a daemon different than a normal executable in Unix?

_____

Chapter
12

Unix Network
Security

This chapter covers the major contemporary Unix network security mechanisms. There are a number of obsolete Unix protocols and security mechanisms that are not discussed here because they are no longer used—either because better alternatives exist now or because their security was weak and is now considered compromised.

This chapter provides an overview of the basic network security mechanisms available to Unix including their relative merits, security posture, and administrative difficulty. It's not possible to cover the configuration or administration of these protocols in a single chapter, but pointers to other resources for configuring them are provided.

In the chapter, you will learn about:

 The basics of Unix network security

 Unix Authentication mechanisms

 Firewalling Unix machines

Unix Network Security Basics

Standard Unix (AT&T System V) does not include facilities to implement either single-signon (one password and user account in the network) or pervasive network security. Security accounts are only valid on individual machines, machines do not "trust" other machine's accounts per se, and every network service implements its own security mechanisms. Unix security is similar to Windows "Workgroup" mode security in this respect, where trust amongst machines does not exist.

Also consider that no true universal network file system exists in Unix. While Windows has had "Windows networking" since its inception to allow for file and print sharing, Unix did not have anything that could be called a standard file sharing mechanism until the early nineties, when NFS became the de facto file sharing standard. Prior to that, FTP was the closest thing to a file sharing standard, but it only allowed for copying files, not mounting and using them remotely.

Without a standard network file sharing mechanism, there was little point in having a single network logon—traversing machines wasn't that much of an issue. But as networks of single-user computers became popular in the late 1980's, Unix began to show its age.

Of course, numerous solutions to these problems have cropped up in the 30 years since Unix was developed. Originally, network access simply meant connecting to a Unix machine using a terminal application and logging in using a local user account. This method is still used by telnet, remote shell, secure shell, and numerous other **remote logon** protocols.

When Sun developed the **Network File System** and **Network Information System**, they simply adapted Unix security to a network environment. In these situations, all machines share a central account database, but they log on locally using these accounts. Because UIDs are synonymous throughout the network (supposedly), this mechanism was relatively seamless, but terribly insecure—any user logged onto a local machine could simply change their UID in their own passwd file to match a target account on the NFS server, and then log in. The NFS server would simply trust their UID and serve them supposedly secure files.

remote logon

The process of logging on to a remote machine in order to execute software on it.

Network File System (NFS)

A file-sharing protocol developed by Sun Microsystems for use in Unix environments. NFS allows clients to mount portions of a server's file system into their own file systems.

Network Information Service (NIS)

A simple distributed logon mechanism developed by Sun Microsystems for Unix, originally to support single sign-on for NFS.

224

The first real attempt to create true network security, where one logon account was valid throughout a security domain and where computers could participate in robust trust relationships, was the Athena project at MIT, which evolved into Kerberos. Kerberos solved the problem so well that Microsoft replaced their own relatively sophisticated Windows NT Domain model security with Kerberos when they released Windows 2000. While not perfectly secure, Kerberos solves so many different security problems that it will clearly be the standard single logon methodology for quite some time.

Unfortunately, none of the existing network services supported Kerberos, and they had to be modified and recompiled to support it. For proprietary network services, adding support for Kerberos was difficult and in many cases still has not happened.

Remote Logon Security

Local Area Networks (LANs) are new to Unix. Unix was developed in the mid 70's, but LANs didn't come onto the scene until the mid-'80s. Linking computers together seamlessly was an esoteric problem when Unix came out—the major problem originally was linking a large number of **terminals** to a single computer.

This explains why Unix security is so self-centric—Unix was pretty much set in stone before networking computers together was really that much of a problem. Originally, the problem was trying to get enough serial ports connected to a single computer so each user could have his own terminal.

Remote logon allows multiple users to connect to a single computer and run their software on it. Originally, remote logon was accomplished by connecting multiple terminals each to a serial port on the Unix computer. When modems and PCs became popular, administrators began connecting modems on both ends so that remote users could dial in. This mimicked terminal connections over serial lines, but replaced the serial lines with phone lines and modems.

When local area networks first came on the scene in the 1980's, Unix adapted by adding the Telnet service, so that microcomputers connected to the LAN could run a Telnet client and connect remotely over a network as if the network were a serial connection to the host computer. Telnet naïvely transmitted data the same way a serial connection did—in the clear. This meant that anyone with a sniffer on the local network could steal passwords.

The `rlogin` service is similar to telnet, but it does not prompt for a username—rather, user and security information are read in from the Unix machine's `/etc/rhosts` file. It also sends passwords in the clear. Another service, `rsh`, is a similar service that executes commands on the remote host without providing a login shell, and it suffers from the same security problems.

Secure shell (SSH) solves all of these remote logon problems by integrating public-key security to authenticate both users and machines and thus eliminates the possibility of man-in-the middle and other redirection or emulation attacks. SSH is also capable of encrypting the entire communication stream to eliminate all security vulnerabilities except the possibility of bugs in the server service.

Local Area Network (LAN)

A network in which all participants can communicate directly without the need for routing at the network layer. The term is somewhat obsolete, as many LAN-sized networks implement routing for various reasons since the advent of the Internet.

terminal

A remote display and keyboard/mouse console that can be used to access a computer.

secure shell (SSH)

A remote logon protocol that uses strong cryptography to authenticate hosts and users.

To solve the remote logon problem, use only SSH for remote logon connections. For dial-up users, setup your Unix server as a Remote Access server that accepts PPP connections, and run SSH over the PPP connection. This will ensure that all communications and password exchanges are encrypted.

NOTE

You can find out more about SSH at www.ssh.com. All modern versions of Unix come with SSH clients and servers built in. You can down load a free SSH client for windows called "putty" from www.chiark.greenend .org.uk/~sgtatham/putty/.

Remote Access

Remote access refers to the problem of accessing resources on a remote Unix machine without actually logging on and running programs on those machines.

Examples of remote access include:

- ◇ Storing files
- ◇ Transmitting e-mail
- ◇ Retrieving a web page

None of these problems involve remotely controlling a **shell** on the Unix machine; rather, they access a service running on the Unix machine and receive data from it.

Any programmer can write a **daemon** that allows remote computers to connect to it and receive data. Because the daemon is accessing files locally using the daemon's own **user context** (either from the account that executed the daemon or the owner of the executable file), all file access is controlled by that user account on the local machine.

This means that it's up to each and every network service to provide its own method of authenticating the clients that connect to it. This lack of central authentication authority is the primary cause of security problems in the Unix environment. No matter how strong security is for one service, another poorly secured service can provide a portal for hackers to take control of a machine.

Many services perform no authentication whatsoever. Simple Mail Transfer Protocol (SMTP) does not include any form of authentication—it will accept connections from any user and deliver any properly formatted e-mail message transmitted to it. This lack of authentication is why the **spam** problem exists. Various jury-rigged methods to authenticate e-mail have been wrapped around SMTP to attempt to eliminate spam, but there is no standard extension to the SMTP protocol for security even today.

There are no rules about what a daemon must do to perform authentication—some do nothing, and allow all attempts to access the service to succeed. Others read the passwd file and try to authenticate against the traditional user accounts list. Others maintain their own files with lists of users and passwords. Still others use proprietary authentication mechanisms like **one-time-passwords** or **smart cards**. Others authenticate against **Kerberos** or an **LDAP** server. In many cases, services are distributed as source code and require the end-user to compile in whatever security library they want to use for authentication.

---

remote access
The process of accessing services on a remote server without executing software directly on the remote machine.

---

shell
An executable program that runs immediately after logon and is used as a springboard to launch subsequent programs.

---

daemon
An executable in Unix that runs automatically as a service (i.e., with a unique user context) when the computer is booted.

---

user context
The user identity under which a process executes that determines which files and resources the process will have access to.

---

spam
Unsolicited e-mail. Unscrupulous spam transmitters typically exploit unsecured mail servers so they won't have to pay for bandwidth.

---

one-time passwords
An authentication method that uses synchronized pseudorandom number generation on both the client and the server to prove that both sides know the same original seed number.

The lack of a standardized authentication protocol for Unix was one of the reasons that it was so frequently hacked. There are numerous problems with implementing proprietary logon mechanisms. The programmers may not be particularly rigorous about security and may make naïve mistakes that hackers could exploit. Even well meaning programmers may not think through the problem entirely, or they may underestimate the risk and choose a lower level of security than most users will require. Finally, the sheer number of mechanisms means that the same users will need multiple methods to access various services, increasing the odds that users themselves will sabotage security for the sake of convenience.

Pluggable Authentication Modules (PAM)

Clearly, a unified method for managing authentication methods is necessary to ensure that service writers don't need to keep reinventing the wheel—and so that end users don't have to compile in support for their favorite authentication mechanism.

The **Pluggable Authentication Modules (PAM)** library has recently emerged as the solution for standardizing authentication in Unix. Linux, BSD, and Solaris currently support it. By compiling each daemon to support the PAM library, developers can avoid writing their own (potentially insecure) authentication mechanism and can allow end users a choice in establishing their own authentication mechanism.

PAM is a modular library that allows administrators to configure which authentication mechanisms they want to allow without recompiling daemons: Unix passwords, Kerberos, smart cards, one-time-passwords, even Windows authentication are all options. Administrators can configure the PAM library once and rely on any "PAMed" application to use that configuration for authentication.

TIP

Configuring PAM is how you would enable the use of alternative forms of authentication in Unix, such as biometric scanners, one-time-passwords, and smart cards.

smart cards
Physical devices with a small amount of non-volatile memory that stores a random number only available to the device. Authentication software can push a value on to the card, which will be encrypted using the random number and returned. Smart cards thereby create an unforgeable physical key mechanism.

Kerberos
A distributed logon protocol that uses secret keys to authenticate users and machines in a networked environment.

Lightweight Directory Access Protocol (LDAP)
A Protocol for accessing service configuration data from a central hierarchical database. LDAP is frequently used to store user account information in Unix and is supported as an access method by Microsoft Active Directory.

Pluggable Authentication Modules (PAM)
An authentication abstraction layer that provides a central mechanism for connecting various authentication schemes to various network services in Unix. Services trust PAM for authentication, and PAM can be configured to use various authentication schemes.

Configuring PAM is simply a matter of editing the application's PAM configuration file in the /etc/pam.d directory. Each file's PAM configuration file is named the same as the service, e.g. login or imapd. The service's configuration file allows administrators to control which types of authentication are valid (or invalid), various account restrictions, how to control passwords, and what post-authentication session setup is required for each specific service.

PAM is usually distributed with a standard set of authentication modules configured to authenticate services against Unix passwords and/or Kerberos. If you intend to change these settings, configure a new service to use PAM, or otherwise customize PAM security settings, read up on the latest PAM configuration documentation from your Unix vendor by searching their website on "pluggable authentication modules."

Distributed Logon

Distributed logon (also called **single signon**) is a simple concept: When attaching to a remote networked service, the user's current **credentials** trusted by the local machine are transmitted automatically to the remote service, which, if it trusts the credentials, will automatically allow access without the user being interrupted for credentials.

Distributed Logon is essentially a convenience—with it, users need not remember a plethora of logon names and passwords (or running over and re-inserting their smart card on the remote machine and other infeasible measures).

As with everything in Unix, there are innumerable ways to achieve distributed logon.

Common methods include the following:

◆ Distributed `passwd` files

◆ NIS and NIS+

◆ Kerberos

Each of these methods is discussed in the following sections.

Distributed *passwd*

The first method used for achieving distributed logon was simply to copy the same `passwd` file around the organization. While this didn't actually provide seamless logon, it did allow for the same account name and password to be used on every machine. Achieving this distribution is technically easy but labor intensive.

Administrators have hacked various methods to simplify `passwd` distribution, including `cron` scripts using `ftp`, using `rdist` to automatically move the file, and so forth. These administrative hacks frequently opened up security holes of their own.

NIS and NIS+

Network Information Service, originally called **yellow pages** (or **yp**) was developed by Sun Microsystems to simplify logon distribution and allow for the seamless mounting of NFS volumes. The concept is simple: A single master NIS server maintains a database of account names and passwords (and other

---

distributed logon
Any client/server protocol for verifying user identity. The purpose of distributed logon services is to allow users to log on once and use their credentials on any machine within the security domain. This provides the illusion of logging into the network as a whole rather than a single computer.

single signon
See *distributed logon*.

credentials
Information used to prove identity. Typically, this is a combination of a user account name and a password.

yellow pages (yp)
The original name for *NIS*.

information). NIS slave servers periodically refresh their own local password map based on the contents of a master NIS server. Client machines use modified login processes (as well as other services) to attach to the NIS server to retrieve logon credentials. The group of machines configured to trust the master NIS server is called a NIS domain.

NIS also does for groups what it does for user accounts: groups (called netgroups in NIS) on the master are the basis for valid GIDs on all machines in the NIS domain.

NIS for Windows Administrators

The NIS architecture is the same as the original Windows NT domain model, where a Primary Domain Controller maintains an official database of user accounts. The accounts are replicated to backup domain controllers that provide logon services, and clients are attached to the domain to trust the domain controllers for secure logon credentials.

The following terms are congruent in the two environments:

Domain = Domain

Primary Domain Controller = NIS Master

Backup Domain Controller = NIS Slave

Domain Member Server = NIS Client

Domain Member Workstation = NIS Client

A newer version of NIS called NIS+ was developed by Sun to shore up some of the early problems with NIS security. NIS+ is significantly more secure than NIS because it encrypts and authenticates communications between clients and servers, but it suffers from stability problems, a lack of wide support across different versions of Unix, and overly complex server-side administration. NIS+ stores logon information in database files rather than in plain text files. A number of sites that have attempted to use NIS+ have abandoned the effort in favor of simply shoring up the security of NIS.

NIS itself has numerous security flaws that are well documented—data is not encrypted between the clients and server, password maps can be retrieved and decrypted using popular password crackers, and so forth. As with nearly all pre-Internet protocols, NIS is LAN-grade security that simply isn't strong enough to keep the hacking hordes at bay.

WARNING

NIS is not compatible with shadow passwords. There have been some attempts to make NIS compatible with shadow passwords, but those modifications do not work correctly as of this writing.

To set up a NIS master server, you need to install the NIS server. In some distributions, the NIS server is called `ypserv`, in others it is called `nis-server`. In either case, the NIS master server's configuration is set by the `var/yp/securenets` file.

Most distributions of Unix install the NIS server by default; In Red Hat Linux (the most popular distribution of Unix), all that is necessary to run the NIS server is to correctly set the NIS configuration and rename the `ypserv` link in `/etc/rc.d/rc3.d` to begin with an "S" rather than a "K" (this change should be made in `/etc/rc.d/rc5.d` if you boot to directly to X-Windows rather than the text console).

Configuring clients is simple: Make sure the machine's host name and domain are set in `/etc/sysconfig/network` (i.e., it's not `localhost.localdomain`) and configure `ypbind` to run as part of the startup process by appending `usr/sbin/ypbind` as the last line in `/etc/rc.d/rc.local`. For complete information on setting up NIS servers, slaves, and clients, check out the NIS HOWTO for your distribution. The Red Hat NIS HOWTO can be found at: `www.redhat.com/mirrors/LDP/HOWTO/NIS-HOWTO/index.html`.

NOTE

For more information about establishing and managing a NIS infrastructure, read *Managing NIS and NFS (2nd ed.)* by Hal Stern et al. (2001, O'Reilly).

Kerberos

Kerberos is an authentication protocol that uses secret key cryptography to provide seamless logon amongst computers in a **security domain** (called a **realm** in Kerberos). Kerberos was developed by MIT, and is basically open source under a BSD style license. MIT will provide it to anyone who wants it.

TIP

Official documentation for Kerberos can be found at: `web.mit.edu/kerberos/www/`

security domain
A collection of machines that all trust the same database of user credentials.

realm
A Kerberos security domain defined by a group of hosts that all trust the same Key Distribution Center.

Kerberos is becoming the standard distributed logon mechanism in both Windows and Unix environments that require higher security, and it is clearly the future of distributed logon in both environments. The two platforms are somewhat compatible; with effort, Windows and Unix can be configured to logon interchangeably using Kerberos.

Key Distribution Center (KDC)

In Kerberos, an authentication server.

Distributed Computing Environment (DCE)

An early initiative by the Open Software Foundation to provide distributed login mechanism for Unix and Windows. DCE is supported in many commercial Unix distributions and by Windows.

Kerberos in Unix is analogous to Kerberos in Windows: you have **Key Distribution Centers** (called domain controllers in Windows parlance) and you have clients. Kerberos v.5 specifies a Master KDC and numerous slave KDCs to which changes are propagated on a regular basis. You can optionally use **DCE (Distributed Computing Environment)** as your KDC database, so that you can keep a single database of users at your site. (Windows uses Active Directory, a modified Exchange engine, to maintain the database of users and makes it available via LDAP.)

NOTE

A discussion of the Kerberos security mechanisms can be found in Chapter 10, because Kerberos is a "here now" security solution for Windows. This section concentrates on the current Unix security issues associated with Kerberos.

The road to Kerberos on Unix is a long one. Because Windows is controlled by a single vendor, Microsoft was able to "Kerberize" their server services and their clients in a single release. Unix doesn't have a central point of control, and as of this writing, there's no pre-built "Pure Kerberos" distribution available. Installing Kerberos currently in Unix is like making a patchwork quilt of services and being rigorous about which services must be chosen. Kerberos also lacks a "Kerberos wrapper" that can be used to shore up security on any client service (although Cornell University is working on a project called "Sidecar" that will do exactly this).

NOTE

Configuring Kerberos is complex and well beyond the scope of this book, but a pretty good step-by-step procedure can be found at http://www.ornl .gov/~jar/HowToKerb.html.

Using Kerberos

Kerberos works by either replacing the standard login mechanism on a host with a kerberized logon or by running the kinit program after logging in (if Kerberos is not being used to provide local security). When you log on (or `kinit`), your credentials are sent to the KDC, which uses them (and the current time) to encrypt a **Ticket Granting Ticket (TGT)** that is transmitted back to your machine. Your host then decrypts the ticket using your stored credentials. TGTs have an expiration (8 hours, by default; 10 hours in Windows) period and are encrypted using the current time each time they're used. Think of a TGT as your "all day pass" at an amusement park: Once you've paid for it, it's valid all day.

Whenever you attempt to subsequently access a Kerberos service, your TGT is again encrypted and transmitted to the KDC, which responds with an encrypted service specific **ticket** that can be provided to a **kerberized** service to gain access to it. Tickets usually have a very short expiration time and must be used within five minutes of their grant. This is analogous to using your "All Day Pass" to get free "Ride Tickets" for a specific attraction at the fair from the central ticket booth (the KDC's Ticket Granting Service). You can then take the ride tickets to the specific attraction to be admitted.

> **NOTE**
>
> Kerberos is extremely sensitive to time synchronization amongst hosts in the domain. You must make sure that all of your hosts are correctly synchronized to the same Network Time Protocol (NTP) server for Kerberos to work correctly.

Kerberos Security

Theoretically, Kerberos security is very strong. By authenticating with a KDC, you get a ticket that can be used to prove your identity to any service in your organization. Keys are automatically managed by your system, so login to various services is seamless. It sounds wonderful, and in Windows, it really works. But Kerberos just isn't completely integrated into any Unix distribution, and without complete integration, it loses much of its appeal and security.

The major problem with Kerberos is its "all or nothing" nature—you can't just add Kerberos to the mix and secure a few protocols, because users will use the same account names and passwords with the as-yet-unsecured services, thus compromising them. You have to convert your entire network services infrastructure to use services that are compatible with Kerberos for authentication, or the whole thing isn't really secure. Every service you provide that you want to provide seamless logon for has to be replaced with a "kerberized" version that knows how to trust the Kerberos authentication mechanism.

Ticket Granting Ticket (TGT)
An encrypted value stored by a client after a successful logon that is used to quickly prove identity in a Kerberos environment.

ticket
In Kerberos, an encrypted value appended with the time to prove identity to a network service.

kerberized
A service or services that has been modified for compatibility with Kerberos.

PAMed
An application that has been modified to allow for *Pluggable Authentication Modules*.

WARNING

Don't use the same user accounts and passwords on your Kerberos systems as you use on non-kerberized services. Non-kerberized services can't protect the passwords, so they will be revealed to sniffers if users are in the habit of using the same passwords on all systems. Best: Kerberize all of your services, or none of them.

This is why deploying Kerberos is so complex. It is possible to use **PAMed** applications that are configured to check Kerberos for applications that haven't been kerberized, but this is problematic because the user's credentials may have to run from the client to the service host in whatever form the service uses before PAM can use Kerberos to validate the password.

WARNING

Don't use PAM to "kerberize" every service on your machine, because many services transmit passwords in the clear. Depending upon its configuration, PAM may not check the password until it's received on the server, meaning that it has traveled through the network in whatever form the PAMed protocol uses. PAM then receives the password and checks it against a Kerberos KDC. For protocols that transmit passwords in the clear, like Telnet and FTP, using PAM to check Kerberos passwords would reveal the passwords to a sniffer.

Despite the promise of Kerberos to eliminate the vast majority of simple attacks against Unix, it is not going to achieve widespread use until a Unix vendor releases a pure Kerberos distribution that any system administrator can deploy. This is a few years away from actually happening, so unless your organization has significant network administration resources available to properly deploy Kerberos, it's likely to drain more resources away from more immediate security solutions than it is to provide better security in the short term.

File Sharing Security

File sharing security describes those measures taken to protect files that are transmitted on the network.

There are two major types of file sharing protocols:

File transfer protocols allow users to transfer entire files between computers using a specific client program. They are relatively simple programs that are designed to distribute software and documents to consumers in one direction. Examples of file transfer protocols include FTP, TFTP, and HTTP.

File sharing protocols (also called network file systems) allow programs to request just the small segments of a file that are actually in use, and they allow files to be locked momentarily by users to prevent conflicting write operations where one user's changes overwrite another user's changes. Essentially, these protocols simulate a hard disk drive by using a network—they allow the full set of semantics that the operating system can use with local files. **File sharing protocols** also allow multiple users to access a file in read/write mode, so that updates to the file made by one user are available immediately to all users that have the file open. File sharing protocols can be mounted on the current file system and browsed seamlessly. Examples of file sharing protocols include SMB (Windows) and NFS (Unix).

NOTE

Microsoft also frequently refers to Server Message Block (SMB) protocol as the Common Internet File System (CIFS). Microsoft changed the name when they submitted it to the IETF as an Internet standard, but has been inconsistent in applying the new name. Most outside the Microsoft camp still refer to the protocol as SMB.

These protocols and their implications on security are covered in the next few sections.

File Transfer Protocol (FTP)

The **File Transfer Protocol (FTP)** is the venerable granddaddy of file sharing solutions. FTP is a simple client/server protocol that allows servers to publish a directory in their file systems to the network. FTP users can then use an FPT client program to authenticate, list files, download files, and upload files. Because FTP is simple and widely supported, it's a very popular mechanism for transferring files across the Internet.

---

file sharing protocol
A protocol that allows a rich set of semantics for serving files to clients. File sharing protocols are distinguished by their ability to provide small portions of files and provide locking mechanisms so that multiple users can write to the file simultaneously.

File Transfer Protocol (FTP)
A simple protocol that allows the complete transfer of files between servers and clients. File transfer protocols cannot support simultaneous multiple users. File Transfer Protocol is also the name of the oldest and most widely implemented file transfer protocol.

FTP is what is says it is: A file transfer protocol. It is not a true file-sharing protocol, because it is not really capable of simulating a local file system.

FTP lacks all of these semantic mechanisms, and only allows for the uploading and downloading of complete files.

Companies often use anonymous FTP to publish software to the public. Anonymous FTP is the same thing as normal FTP, but a special account called "anonymous" is provided that will accept any text as a valid password. Typically, public FTP servers will ask you to enter your e-mail address as the password so they can record it in a log, but there's no way to validate the address. Some companies attempt to secure their FTP sites by requiring customers to call first for a valid account/password combination, and then always provide the same account/password. This doesn't work, because hackers keep track of these in databases. Once a single hacker customer has obtained the working account and password, they all know it.

Using FTP

Configuring an FTP server is simple. If your Unix distribution has an FTP server service installed by default, you need only configure the `/etc/ftphosts` file to determine what domains you wish to allow to log into your server. Permissions for uploading and downloading files are determined by the FTP directory's file system permissions, as explained in Chapter 11. You can configure a welcome message that will be displayed to FTP users by creating a file containing the welcome text and storing it in the FTP root directory as `.message`, for example, `/home/ftp/.message`.

FTP clients are even simpler: Type `ftp hostname.domainname` at any command prompt (Windows or Unix) and you'll get a logon prompt from the FTP server. Use the `ls` command to list files, `get file` to download a file, and `put file` to upload a file to the FTP server.

FTP Security

FTP has three major security problems:

All public services are a security liability.   Like any service, FTP is a potential liability because any service that answers connections on the Internet could potentially contain bugs that allow hackers to exploit it. In the specific case of FTP, hackers discovered a major security flaw in the most popular version of WU-FTP (Washington University FTP) in April of 2001 that allowed hackers to gain remote control of any server running the wu-ftp daemon. It took six months for a patch to be made generally available.

Passwords are transmitted in the clear. This means that hackers can potentially intercept valid account names and passwords while in transit on the Internet.

Anonymous writable FTP servers can be exploited. Hackers will exploit FTP servers that allow file uploads from the public. Besides the simple problem of stealing your disk space to store (probably) illegal content like pirated software and copyrighted material, allowing write access to an anonymous FTP server allows hackers to test a number of different file system exploits against your machine. For example, buffer overruns can be embedded inside files so that when the file is uploaded, the hacker can gain root access to your server.

FTP has too many security problems to detail completely, and the specific exploits vary from distribution to distribution. No matter what version you have, allowing anonymous write access spells immediate trouble. As a test for this book, I opened anonymous write access to an FTP server inside a virtual machine. Fourteen minutes later, an automated port scanner found the new machine (on an unlisted IP address), ran a test write against it, and automatically began uploading content to it—including a number of files with different buffer overrun exploits embedded in the filenames. It was extremely difficult to remove some of those files, because their strange names prevented the normal file system tools from working.

Don't use FTP on public or private servers if you can avoid it—HTTP provides an easily controlled and more robust file transfer methodology for anonymous files and can be easily secured using SSL. Use anonymous FTP for read-only shares if you can't avoid using FTP. Don't use anonymous FTP access to a writeable share if you can't avoid using anonymous FTP. If you think you have to use writable FTP access for some reason, you'll change your mind after a few minutes.

Network File System (NFS)

Sun Microsystems developed NFS as a "true" networked file system to replace FTP. With FTP, files actually have to be transferred from the server to the local file system, where they can be modified by various processes and then moved back to the server. This makes it impossible for multiple users to use the file simultaneously, and worse, provides no information about whether a file is in use or has been modified since the last time it was downloaded. Clearly, a protocol like FTP does not provide enough file sharing semantics to allow for true **file sharing**.

NFS was designed to allow transparent file sharing on a Local Area Network, and for that purpose, it does a very good job. However, NFS implements no real security on its own.

file shares
A directory tree that is published by SMB for remote attachment by SMB clients. Analogous to an NFS export.

Using NFS

NFS requires `portmap` to be running; it runs by default in all modern Unix distributions, and NFS is installed by default in almost every Unix distribution. An NFS server creates NFS **exports** by listing them in the file /etc/exports, according to a simple path and rules format:

```
/var/exportedfiles  *.mydomain.dom(ro)
/                   admin.mydomain.dom(rw)
```

After editing the NFS exports file, you need to restart the `rpc.mountd` and `rpc.nfsd` daemons—the easiest way is to simply reboot. In this example, the first line allows all computers in the mydomain.dom domain to have read only (ro) access to the files in /var/exportedfiles. The second line allows the computer admin.mydomain.dom to have read/write access to the entire file system on the computer.

For an NFS client to mount the NFS export, use the standard mount command as follows:

```
mount nfshost.dom:/var/exportedfiles /mnt/importedfiles
```

In this example, `nfshost.dom` is the name of the host, /var/exportedfiles is the NFS export on that host, and /mnt/importedfiles is the mount point in your local file system where you want to mount the NFS export.

NFS Security

Sometimes, security is a matter of usage. NFS is less secure than FTP, but because of that, nobody attempts to use it on the public Internet, which means it's subject to far less exploitation. Don't consider using NFS on an Internet-connected network that doesn't have strong Internet firewalling.

The major flaw in NFS is that it trusts the connecting client to accurately present its UID. This means that anyone who has set up their own host and "stolen" the UID from another legitimate user on the network can access their files. Of course, this is a serious architectural problem with NFS that makes it completely inappropriate for use on the public Internet.

TCP Wrappers is a tool commonly used to shore up this security problem in NFS. By wrapping NFS with TCP Wrappers, you can use the `hosts.allow` and `hosts.deny` files to prevent unknown machines from connecting to your NFS server. However, TCP Wrappers only authenticates the machine, not the user, so while this limits the domain of the problem to computers under your control, it doesn't truly secure the service.

export
A directory tree that is published by NFS for remote mounting by NFS clients. Analogous to an SMB share.

TCP Wrappers
A process that inserts itself before a network service in order to authenticate the hosts that are attempting to connect.

Various other patches have been incorporated into NFS to attempt to shore up security:

 ◆ NFS was modified to automatically map access attempts from root to the nobody user on the local machine. Basically, this means that root users who access NFS will have no rights, rather than all rights.

 ◆ NFS also performs subtree checking to make sure that a user hasn't changed into a directory below the NFS file system share (or that a link hasn't accessed a file outside the share).

 ◆ By default, NFS will only export to machines that send requests on ports below 1024. This is because services on these ports must be configured by the root user. This security hack is basically ineffective, because hackers are always the root users of their own machines, and when they gain access to machines inside your LAN, they usually do it through a remote root access that allows them to set services up as they please.

These various changes do little to really secure NFS. Any hacker who has gained remote root access on an NFS client inside your network will have no problem accessing files on the NFS server. All of these security fixes can be disabled on an export-by-export basis to speed up NFS as well.

Never allow public access to NFS exports. Never use NFS on publicly available machines, because if they get exploited, hackers can subsequently exploit the NFS server easily. If you use NFS in your local network, always use TCP Wrappers to limit the number of machines that can reach your network. Be very frugal with read/write access to NFS shares.

HyperText Transfer Protocol (HTTP)

HyperText Transfer Protocol (HTTP) is the protocol of the World Wide Web. Obviously, HTTP is designed for public access so security is of paramount importance—so much so that HTTP security is the subject of its own chapter in this book. In this chapter, it's presented as a pure file sharing mechanism without discussing its primary context on the Web.

Under the hood, HTTP is much like FTP with a few extensions. Like FTP, HTTP is a file transfer protocol, not a file sharing protocol, so it's not appropriate for multi-user write access. This is not an issue, however, since the Web uses a pure publication mechanism where clients don't normally expect to be able to modify web pages.

> **NOTE**
>
> The HTTP WebDAV (Web Distributed Authoring and Versioning) extensions add semantics to allow for multi-user file locking so that the Web can be used as a true file-sharing protocol. WebDAV was developed to allow easier website editing on live servers by multiple authors, but it is now being incorporated into office programs to allow traditional file sharing over the Internet.

The primary extension that makes HTTP different in the minds of users is the concept of the embedded link that browsers can use to automatically request new documents. Links contain the full, globally unique path to the document, and when a user clicks on them, the browser requests the document from the server. The link request is actually determined and negotiated by the browser—a browser could be configured to run using anonymous FTP and work essentially the same way that HTTP works.

Links aren't what makes HTTP special. HTTP's PUSH and GET semantics that allow form submission and the passing of parameters between pages, as well as the extensions that allow server-side session information to be retained between page loads are what makes HTTP different than FTP. With an FTP-based hypertext system, there would be no method to submit a form, except to write a file back to the FTP server—and that would come with all the problems that anonymous writable FTP sites have.

Configuring a Unix web server is easy: Download the Apache web server from www.apache.org, install it according to the instructions provided with it, and edit the /etc/httpd.conf file to create the root of the www service. From that directory, the files within it are available publicly (usually, although TCP Wrappers and most web servers allow you to limit which machines can attach to the server using their own mechanisms). Although other web servers exist, Apache has stood the test of time and stood up to literally billions of hacking attempts, with few real exploits having succeeded against it. Apache is also among the fastest web servers, and it has reasonably good default security mechanisms to keep novice webmasters from making simple security mistakes.

HTTP Security

There is no protocol more public than HTTP. You are inviting the world onto your server when you use HTTP. Because every web server program written has been exploited at one time or another, you should assume that hackers will be able to exploit your web server if they want to. HTTP security is so critical that it is covered in the next chapter.

Samba

Samba is an open-source implementation of Microsoft's Server Message Block protocol, also called the Common Internet File System. SMB is the file sharing protocol used by Windows, originally in Local Area Networks. Despite its LAN origins, SMB works surprisingly well over the public Internet. When properly used, it can be made secure enough to use on the public Internet. Aside from Samba, commercial SMB/CIFS servers and clients are available for most versions of Unix. SMB runs on all versions of Windows, MS-DOS, OS/2, and Macintosh computers natively as well. After FTP, SMB is the closest protocol there is to a universal file sharing protocol.

SMB is a true file-sharing protocol, with a rich enough semantics to allow multi-user write locking. To attach to an SMB server from Unix you can use smbclient, which is much like a standard command-line FTP client. If you're using an open-source Unix that has SMB support compiled into the kernel, you can use the much easier smbmount and smbumount commands, which work exactly like mount and umount work for NFS exports.

> **share**
> A portion of a file system that the SMB service (server.exe in Windows, samba in Unix) exports for access by SMB clients. Access to the share can be configured on a per-user or per-group basis.

NOTE

For Windows machines, SMB is built right in. By simply specifying a path to the server in the form \\sambaserver.mydomain.dom\sharename, a user can provide logon information and begin using the file system. Windows will attempt a "silent logon" behind the scenes using the user's logon credentials, so if the Samba server has a matching user name and password, the logon will be seamless. Otherwise, Windows will prompt for a username and password combination to allow access.

Samba Security

To avoid en-masse the problems involved with sending UNIX UIDs across the network (as well as to ensure Windows compatibility), SMB transmits user names and passwords between the client and the server for authentication. You can configure SMB to use clear text or encrypted passwords; most Unix installations use clear text passwords because it's easier and because early versions of Samba did not support encrypted passwords; also, each new version of Windows seems to break Samba's password encryption mechanism, and it takes a few months for Samba to catch up.

Samba is configured by making changes to the /etc/smb.conf file. In this file, you establish **shares**, or directories that SMB will expose to SMB clients. You can specify an unusual number of security options for a Unix file sharing protocol, including what access various users will have, what the default permissions for created files will be, and whether writing is allowed.

Interestingly enough, Samba doesn't use local Unix accounts for SMB security; rather, the Samba daemon authenticates users against a separate list of users. This means that Samba users need not have Unix accounts on the Samba server, but it also means that individual file system permissions can't be used to secure files on an individual basis. In practice, this means that Samba user accounts can't be exploited by testing them against other protocols or trying to log in directly with them using Telnet or SSH, which significantly improves security.

If you set up a public Samba server, use the same caution that you would with an FTP server. Set up a separate host inside your DMZ to transfer files rather than making an internal machine available on the Internet. Don't allow connections originating from that machine; rather, connect to it from within your network to move files off it. Be certain to encrypt passwords. Use a dedicated firewall to filter connections to the server, and use IPChains or IPTables to filter all protocols except ports 135, 137, 138, and 139 directly on your Samba server.

NOTE

Windows 2000 allows direct SMB over TCP (without NetBIOS) on port 445. Remember this when you're configuring your firewall policy.

Overall, because of its foreign-OS origin and high code quality, Samba is the most secure commonly used file sharing protocol for Unix. Prefer it to NFS for LAN servers, and consider it over FTP for public servers.

Firewalling Unix Machines

The same software used to turn a Unix machine into a firewall to protect an entire domain can also be used just to protect an individual Unix machine; this is similar to personal firewall software discussed for PC home computers in Chapter 6. While standard Unix doesn't include much in the way of TCP/IP security mechanisms, freely available packages have become so popular that they are either included in most Unix distributions or they can be added to any Unix distribution.

While **IPChains**, **IPTables**, FWTK, and TCP Wrappers can all be used to block access to local services and provide some flexibility for access, their simple pass/fail mechanisms often are not rich enough to provide complete authentication and security for services. Use a dedicated firewall device to protect your network. Use these Unix security mechanisms to protect public servers individually.

IPTables and IPChains

A relatively recent addition to the open-source versions of Unix operating system is the ability to perform packet filtering and Network Address Translation in the operating system's kernel. Most commercial Unix distributions do not include any form of integral packet filtering, and it cannot be added without modifying the kernel's source code.

IPChains and IPTables provide a packet filtering mechanism that, while traditionally associated with routers, can also be used to protect a host. IPChains implements a stateless packet filter; IPTables is a newer mechanism that implements stateful inspection. For a router, the distinction is important, but to protect an individual machine they are functionally equal.

Packet-filtering rules are applied to every packet as it arrives, as the packet transits the Linux routing stack, and when the packet exits. In the case of local host protection, we're only worried about packet arrival.

IPChains and IPTables only inspect packets at the TCP and IP layers; protocol inspection must be provided by a higher-level service. TIS FWTK (described later in this chapter) is an excellent proxy server package that interoperates well with other security mechanisms on a Unix server.

IPChains
A stateless packet filtering mechanism for Unix kernels.

IPTables
A stateful packet filtering mechanism for Unix kernels.

245

IPChains/IPTables Security

IPChains and IPTables filter packets before they are delivered to the IP stack for processing, allowing you to protect your computer from malformed packets and other IP-level attacks. They provide the full range of options for packet filtering on source and destination IP addresses, source and destination ports, packet type, and most other TCP/IP header data elements.

Since they do not inspect the data portions of packets, you will need a proxy service to ensure that the traffic traversing a particular port conforms to the protocol for that port. For example, IPChains will allow traffic to flow over port 80; it won't inspect the payload to ensure that the traffic truly conforms to the HTTP protocol. See the section on FWTK for more information on protocol inspection.

IPChains evaluates every packet received by the network adapters in the firewall computer according to a set of rules you established when you installed IPChains. The rules are applied in order one-at-a-time until IPChains finds a rule that matches the packet and specifies a terminal action, such as ACCEPT or DROP. Since the rules are applied in order, it is very important to craft the rules in the right order.

A useful feature of IPChains (and the feature that gives it its name) is the bundling of sets of rules into chains. IPChains starts out with three—INPUT, FORWARD, and OUTPUT. You can establish additional chains and use a rule in INPUT, FORWARD, or OUTPUT to direct packet analysis to the appropriate chain for that type of traffic. This structured rule management makes it easier to plan the security of the host and thereby makes it easier to secure the host.

IPChains is administered using the ipchains command, which takes as its arguments the rules to be established or modified in the IPChains packet filter.

NOTE

Step-by-step instructions for installing IPChains on the Internet can be found at the following location or just search on "IPCHAINS" from any search engine: www.tldp.org/HOWTO/IPCHAINS-HOWTO.html.

TCP Wrappers

TCP Wrappers is a security package that "wedges" itself into a daemon's connection process and intercepts connections before the actual service gets them.

TCP Wrappers works by replacing the daemon's executable file with a simple TCP daemon called `tcpd`. The actual service daemon is moved to another location, then `tcpd` hands off the connection to the actual service daemon only after it has authenticated the attaching client.

NOTE

TCP Wrappers was written by Wietse Venema while he was employed at the Eindhoven University of Technology after a particularly destructive hacking attack. Wietse also wrote the RPC Portmapper service replacement that is crucial to securing NIS while at Eindhoven, and the Postfix e-mail daemon when he worked for IBM. Postfix is my favorite drop-in replacement for the notoriously insecure Sendmail. Wietse has probably contributed more to real-world Unix network security than any other single individual, since his software can be applied to existing systems without much effort.

TCP Wrappers works by searching its access control file for the service requested and checking the requesting client against the `/etc/hosts.allow` and `/etc/hosts.deny` files. Because TCP Wrappers stops at the first match, an allowed host will be allowed even if it appears in the deny file. TCP Wrappers also logs everything it can about the connection in the syslog.

TCP Wrapper also allows the execution of arbitrary scripts upon connections to various services, which can be exploited to create *honey pots*, or seduction servers, whose purpose is to be exploited in order to keep hackers away from production machines. It can also be used to create booby traps, servers who counterattack in response to an attack.

WARNING

Booby traps are technically illegal in the United States (the FBI does not consider self-defense hacking to be anything other than hacking), and are likely to attract the attention of legions of hackers.

Because the functionality provided by TCP Wrappers is so important (and so sorely lacking in Unix prior to its release) it now comes with many distributions of Unix. If your machine respects the `/etc/hosts.allow` and `/etc/hosts.deny` files, then you've got it. Otherwise, get it.

Firewall Toolkit (FWTK)

The FWTK is the strongest and oldest of the freely available proxy firewalls. You can download versions for Linux, NetBSD, Solaris, as well as just about any other flavor of Unix. Although FWTK is traditionally used to create firewalls, it can easily be used to secure firewall services running on a server itself.

FWTK was created for the Defense Advanced Research Projects Agency (DARPA) by Trusted Information Systems (TIS) when DARPA realized that no packet filter would be secure enough to filter protocol content. After fulfilling the terms of their contract with DARPA (which included making the code public domain), FWTK further extended the firewalling concept into a commercial suite known as the Gauntlet Firewall.

FWTK is not a packet filter. Instead it comes with protocol-scrubbing proxies for Telnet, rlogin, SMTP, FTP, and HTTP. In addition, it comes with a generic TCP pass-through redirector (a SOCKS proxy). FWTK also extends its security controls into the Unix LAN environment, providing centralized network login and resource control using the `netacl` and `authserv` utilities.

FWTK does not filter packets before they are delivered to the IP stack for processing. You must use some other package to protect your computer from malformed packets and other IP-level attacks (IPChains or IPTables are good choices for packet filtering).

FWTK is a proxy server; it examines the data portions of IP packets to ensure that the traffic traversing a particular port conforms to the protocol for that port (that only HTTP requests and replies are going over port 80, for example). This ensures, for example, that a hacker doesn't use port 80 to access a Trojan horse with its own protocol, because your packet filter allows only packets to port 80 for HTTP services.

FWTK evaluates data received by the network adapters in the firewall computer according to a set of rules established in its net-perm rule table. The rules are defined according to the port to which the data was sent, while permissions are defined according to the source and destination of the data.

You enable FWTK by replacing the services to be proxied in the `inetd.conf` file with the corresponding FWTK filter for that protocol (see Example FWTK Configuration Entries below). You then configure the FWTK protocol proxy to locate the real service. This is the same method used by TCP Wrappers to check `hosts.allow` and `hosts.deny` before allowing access to an executable. FWTK performs considerably more checking than TCP Wrappers for the protocols that it specifically proxies.

The FWTK proxies read their configuration from the net-perm table, which describes for each protocol those hosts (source and destination) that are allowed to use the proxy.

NOTE

You can find step-by-step instructions for installing FWTK on the Internet—go to `http://www.fwtk.org`.

Review Questions

1. Why doesn't UNIX have a standard-file sharing mechanism?

2. What is the most secure protocol for remotely logging on to a Unix computer?

3. What is the primary authentication mechanism used by SMTP?

4. What does PAM do?

5. What type of encryption does NIS use to protect user credentials?

6. What cryptographic mechanism does Kerberos use to protect user credentials?

7. What is the difference between a File Transfer Protocol (FTP) and a file sharing protocol?

8. Does SMB provide any mechanism for securing user credentials over the network?

9. How does TCP Wrappers protect a service?

10. What do IPChains and IPTables provide?

_____

11. What functionality does FWTK provide?

_____

251

Chapter

13

Web Server
Security

This chapter discusses the best practices used to keep web servers secure when they are publicly available. Web and e-mail servers are the two most difficult security problems you will encounter, because (in most cases) they must be open to the public in order to fulfill their purpose.

With the exception of exploits based on specific bugs, most web server security problems are generic in nature. Most of this chapter deals with practical security measures for any web server. Because 90 percent of the Internet is run on Apache and IIS, those two web servers are covered specifically.

You've probably heard about security problems with cookies, ActiveX controls, Java applets, and multimedia plug-ins like Real Player. These technologies are problematic, but they only affect the client side—they are not a problem for servers that inspect them or provide them. Serving ActiveX or Java applets is not a security problem for servers, and can frequently be used to provide enhanced server-side security by creating a proprietary interface to your web application that would be far more difficult to hack than a typical HTTP-based interface, if you can entice users to actually download your controls. This chapter doesn't discuss the security ramifications of web browsing—that problem is well covered in the rest of this book.

In this chapter, you will learn about:

     Security Flaws in Web Server Applications

Web Security Problems

Bugs in the web server application are the most threatening security problem you will run into when securing web servers. Flaws in the operating system and web server applications are routinely exploited by hackers, and no matter how well you've secured your server, there's very little you can do to prevent these sorts of attacks. In closed-source operating systems, only vendors can repair their code, and the level of support varies widely. Microsoft has been very proactive about patching their web server, Internet Information Server (IIS); in fact, a constant torrent of patches flows from them on almost a weekly basis. Novell, on the other hand, has allowed known flaws in their web server to go for many months without being patched.

In open-source operating systems, theoretically anyone can fix the flaw, but only the writers of the code are familiar enough with it to actually fix the problem in a short period of time. For this reason, you have to stick with open source solutions that are being actively maintained and developed by its community. Many older or less popular open-source solutions languish in near-abandonment, and security flaws in them may take a long time to be repaired.

NOTE

Washington University's wu-ftp daemon, the most popular FTP daemon, contained a flaw that went six months between exposure and repair, because the University did not have an active development effort for the software. This flaw was widely exploited. In contrast, the longest IIS has gone between the exposure of a serious flaw and the release of a patch is three weeks.

Administrative and author access to the server is the next major web security problem. If your web server is outside your network and you've included some file transfer service to allow the website to be updated, hackers can attempt to exploit that service to gain access to the server.

Finally, poorly secured web servers will be exploited. Fortunately, securing a web server is relatively easy to do. This chapter will cover the basics and provide direction to more information.

Implementing Web Server Security

Implementing web server security is relatively simple and methodical.

The first security decision you need to make is which web server to choose. This can be a bit of a conundrum. The World Wide Web consortium actually recommends Macintoshes running the older (non-Unix based) System 9 as the most secure web servers available. While they may in fact be less exploited, these servers do not scale well at all, and System 9 is not nearly as stable an operating system as Unix or Windows. Apple's own web application server, WebObjects, isn't supported on System 9, because Apple knows that the operating system is not robust enough to withstand public use. These web servers achieve security only through obscurity, not through some inherently superior design. If they were widely used, hackers would cut through them like Swiss cheese.

On the other side of the coin, popular web servers are the target of so much hacking effort that they get exploited routinely even though the vendors are aggressive about patching them. Since 1999, a new serious remote exploit in IIS has been found about once per month. Although Microsoft has always quickly released patches, there's inevitably a few days of vulnerability between the appearance of the attack and the availability of a patch.

Apache has fared much better, with an order of magnitude fewer serious problems, but Linux, the host operating system usually used under Apache, has been exploited more than Windows 2000, the host OS under IIS, in that same time period.

Your choice of a web server and operating system platform is a catch-22. Choose a small market server and operating system and you'll probably be secure for now, but if an exploit comes along, it may never be patched. Choose a large market operating system and you're almost guaranteed to be exploitable at some point, but not for very long.

There's no correct answer here. My company uses OpenBSD running Apache for external servers, and we put all of our web servers behind a dedicated firewall that blocks access to everything but port 80.

Apache is a bit more secure from a theoretical standpoint than IIS, because it uses a separate user account database, so web accounts are not valid machine accounts. It also suffered at least an order of magnitude fewer serious exploits than IIS, bespeaking a higher quality of coding and an understanding of Internet security by its developers. The new 2.0 version runs equally well on Unix and Windows, and some reports show it outperforming IIS on Windows. It brings its separate user accounts to that platform as well, making it a solid choice on either platform.

I would consider the following configurations to be reasonable in most to least secure order:

1. OpenBSD running Apache 2
2. Windows 2000 running Apache 2
3. Linux (kernel 2.4.4 or later) running Apache 2
4. Windows 2000 running IIS 5

> **TIP**
>
> The World Wide Web Consortium's WWW security FAQ can be found at www.w3.org/Security/Faq/.

Common Security Solutions

Although Windows and Unix are completely different platforms and even though IIS and Apache have very little code in common (though both are based on the early NSCA server), there are a number of security principles that all web server platforms share.

The following sections are the best practices followed by secure websites irrespective of platform.

Install the Minimum

Web server security begins during the installation. When you install the operating system, install the minimum number of services possible, and only choose those you actually need to serve your website and applications and to administer the website. This almost always means choosing a "custom" installation. Default installations usually install the most popular options for a LAN server, not appropriate options for a public web server.

When you install your web server, choose only those options that you need to use. Avoid extras like indexing services that you won't use, service daemons like FTP, and web-based site administration tools that are poorly secured and can be exploited by hackers.

Don't leave file system permissions in their default state. Before you begin loading files, secure the web root directory correctly so that files you move into the director will be created with correct security.

As a rule, avoid moving files (drag and drop in Windows or mv command in Unix) between directories, because their permissions are not changed to match those of a new parent directory. Use copy operations (Copy and Paste in Windows or cp in Unix) to ensure that a new copy is created in the destination directory that will inherit the permissions of it's parent directory.

bugs
Errors in programming code.

Beware of Features

Every line of code potentially contains a bug, especially in "dense" languages like C++ (the language that IIS and Apache were both written in). The more code, the more potential **bugs** exist.

Larger, more expansive web servers (like Apache and IIS) have literally thousands of undiscovered bugs. Simpler, single-purpose web servers on smaller market operating systems like OS/2 and Mac OS 9 are far harder to exploit because they have less code and fewer features.

The bugs in a portion of an application that are exercised by most users are well debugged. Vendors have found most of the problems in the well-tested areas of a web server. But the esoteric sections of code, where seldom-used features are implemented, are far less tested. It is in these areas where bugs that affect you are most likely to live.

NOTE

A perfect example of this effect cropped up during the production of this book. All versions of Internet Explorer are subject to a remote-root exploit due to major flaw in it's support for Gopher—a rarely used protocol pre-dating HTTP that supports Hypertext but does not support images or multimedia content. Microsoft's solution was to remove support for Gopher.

There is a paradox here: To avoid problems, deploy only well-tested code. But hackers also test popular software and are more likely to find problems in them than in small-market web servers.

Use Only Dedicated Web Servers

For public web servers, dedicate a machine to the purpose of web service. Any other services running on the machine will only increase the likelihood of the server being exploited.

Don't even consider simply throwing a web server application on an existing server and opening it up to the Internet. If you do this, you will certainly be exploited.

Avoid traditional business applications that have been recently **web enabled**. For the most part, these web-enabled applications are packages of poorly tested scripts that connect directly to your accounting or database application. They are thrown out the door as quickly as possible to compete in the market, usually without rigorous testing of user-provided web input. They typically install the web server with its default security settings and do little to modify them—often leaving notoriously insecure "sample websites" in place. Do not consider making them available on the public Internet.

Use SSL for Sensitive Information

Secure Sockets Layer, also called HTTPS, is the standard for encrypting communications between a web browser and a web server. SSL does not perform authentication—it merely encrypts the data between a server and client for authenticated or anonymous users to protect the data from sniffing attacks. SSL also does not secure data stored on the server.

SSL is a great way to improve security in a multivendor environment. Because there is no universal password encryption standard for the web besides unencrypted basic authentication, it is widely used on public websites. SSL can be used to encrypt the contents flowing between the browser and the server, thus encrypting both the account name and password in a basic authentication session. SSL is supported by all common web browsers and servers, so this is the perfect solution for secure authentication.

SSL can be a tremendous drag on server performance for popular websites, because the web server's CPU is relied upon to encrypt and decrypt many simultaneous sessions. Use hardware-based SSL accelerators to solve this problem or limit SSL encryption to just the information that requires security—like the logon page.

Put Servers Behind a Security Proxy

Reverse proxies can be used to inspect URLs before delivering them to a public web server. Many security proxies can also be used to load balance a single website across a number of actual web servers.

By simply inspecting URLs, you can eliminate most of the buffer overruns and security problems that a web server might be subject to. For example, you're used to seeing a URL in the following form:

```
http://www.google.com
```

web enabled
An application that has an HTTP interface, allowing its primary functionality to be used over the Internet.

But hackers know that most web servers will do their best to try to deliver a document, and will also interpret URLs like:

```
http://www.google.com%4063.241.3.69
```

Type this URL into Internet Explorer and see what happens. Scary, isn't it? To the uninitiated, you would think that Google will come up and deliver some sort of specific content or directory. The %40 is the ASCII hex code for @, which changes everything. In a URL, the content before an @ sign is interpreted as a username, so in this URL, the actual website being delivered is indicated by the 63.241.3.69 IP address.

But this trick is frequently used by hackers to confuse people into clicking on links that will actually take them to a hacker's website, where security flaws in their web browser can be exploited.

Try this URL:

```
http://63%2E241%2E3%2E69
```

This is another simple example of URL obfuscation. This is actually an IP address with the periods replaced by the sequence %2E. The percent sign tells the web browser to interpret the next two characters as the hexadecimal value for the ASCII representation of a character. 2E is the ASCII value for period, which is why this works.

TIP

You can decode encoded URLs using the tables at www.asciitable.com.

Using URL encoding allows hackers to push buffer overruns because they can send any sequence of codes to the URL input buffer on the web server.

The upshot of all of this is that by using a security proxy in front of your web server, you can search every inbound URL for characters like %, which are almost always signs of attempted hacking, and drop them.

You can configure a security proxy to allow you to inspect a URL and drop the connection if it contains characters that are likely to be used by hackers. You can also configure a security proxy to perform more complex connection checking than the server or host operating system provides.

Use a VPN for Intranet Servers

Do not connect intranet servers to the Internet and think that the web server's logon authentication mechanisms will keep you secure. Buffer overruns, the most common type of exploit against a web server, can be perpetrated without logging in. Logon authentication is private network security and is not appropriate for securing servers connected to the public Internet.

To connect remote users, put your website behind a firewall with a dedicated VPN server. Connect to remote users using a VPN and allow individual users to connect by using a PC-based VPN client. Chapter 6 details ways that home users can connect to company assets securely over the Internet.

Use IP Address and Domain Restrictions for Extranet Servers

If you implement an extranet, use public web-server grade security and implement SSL to encrypt communications.

Use the operating system's IP filtering to allow only your client's expected addresses. Use TCP Wrappers or your web server's domain restrictions to drop connections from unknown sources. While a dedicated hacker who tries to exploit your site won't be stopped by this sort of protection, it will absolutely eliminate casual hacking attempts.

Use IP Address and Domain Restrictions for Public Servers

Domain restrictions on a public server? Why would you limit your audience on a public server? Because you run a business that doesn't service France, or Russia, or Israel, or China, or India, or 130 other foreign countries. The biggest current threat of hacking activity comes from foreign nations, yet 99 percent of websites don't service more than one language or country. Why allow hackers from anywhere when you don't allow customers from anywhere else? You can significantly shore up the security of your website by performing domain restrictions against foreign country code **Top Level Domain Names (TLDs)**.

This can provide a significant legal advantage—many hackers don't hack inside the boundaries of their own nation, because they can be held legally accountable there, but they have no fear of prosecution in foreign countries. Limiting access to your website to countries that will prosecute hackers is a good way to dramatically reduce the amount of hacking activity you will see against your site.

You will want to redirect to a website that explains to legitimate customers what's going on if they can't access your website, and give them a phone number or e-mail address to contact so you can explicitly allow them if they run into a problem accessing your site. This should be rare, but some people do come from IP addresses that don't have valid reverse DNS lookups, and so won't resolve to a domain name. If you're going to restrict domain names, you have to restrict addresses that don't have reverse DNS names as well, or hackers can get around the domain restrictions by using an unregistered address.

Top Level Domain Names (TLDs)
The first specific level of the domain name hierarchy, TLDs are used to apportion the domain name system into sections that can be administered by different Internet Naming authorities. Each country has it's own country-code TLD (ccTLD) like `.us`, `.ca`, `.uk`, `.sp`, `.fr`, `.de`, and so on. There are also six common general purpose (non-country specific) TLDs (gTLDs): `.com`, `.net`, `.org`, `.edu`, `.gov`, and `.mil`. Some new gTLDs such as `.biz`, `.info`, `.pro`, and `.aero` have been released, but there has been no significant interest in them. The Internet Corporation for Assigned Names and Numbers (ICANN) administers the TLD hierarchy.

260

Even if you don't bulk-block foreign TLDs, you should comb through your access logs looking for numerous attempts from strange domains or IP addresses. Block these specifically when you find them to prevent hackers who have already knocked on the door from coming back.

Force User Logon for Sensitive Data

As an additional measure to otherwise strong security, you can protect sensitive information using file system permissions. This will cause the web server to prompt the user for logon information and will apply the operating system's security measures to the problem of securing content.

In both IIS and Apache, you can configure a single user account to be used by anonymous browsers, and you can also force users to logon using a local user account. This requires them to have a local user account (IIS) or a web service account (Apache) on the web server.

When you do this, you can subsequently use file system permissions to secure documents on IIS. Apache does not pass authentication through to the operating system however, so document security remains in the context of the Apache user.

Aside from file system permissions, you can also configure security differently in the various virtual directories within your website. This can be configured using Apache's virtual HTTP user accounts, which (like Samba accounts) are not true Unix user accounts. IIS does not have a facility to manage user accounts that are not real Windows user accounts, which can be a security disadvantage, because any account valid on the website is also valid on the server.

Be aware that this logon information is usually sent in the clear, so it can be sniffed. Use only unique account names and passwords on public sites.

Although both Apache and IIS can be configured to allow encrypted passwords, the mechanisms for implementing them are by no means universal. Apache (80 percent of the web server market) supports only MD5 authentication, which is only compatible with Internet Explorer 5.0 (and later) and Opera. Netscape Navigator, Mozilla, Konquerer, and most other popular web browsers are not compatible with encrypted passwords in any form. IIS uses only Windows authentication for encryption and its encrypted authentication is only compatible with Internet Explorer.

This basically means that non-Windows clients are basically out of luck when it comes to encrypted passwords, and that if you intend to implement encrypted passwords, you're limited to clients who use Internet Explorer 5.0 and later (which comes with Windows 2000, Me, and XP), and Opera. This is usually not acceptable for public websites, so encrypted passwords is not an option for public websites.

The only universal solution to this problem is to first use SSL to encrypt all data between the browser and server and then use basic authentication. When you do this, the account name and password (as well as the authentication semantics) are encrypted.

Centralize Risky Content

Put your scripts and executables in a single directory, where file system permissions can be maintained correctly. If you distribute scripts and applications all over the place, you have to be especially vigilant to ensure that the permissions are not accidentally changed during a copy or move operation or because permissions are broadly changed in the directory for some other reason. Centralizing this content in a single location makes it easy to determine what the permissions should be.

Place Your Web Servers in a DMZ

Don't place web servers directly on the public Internet if you can avoid it. Place them on your firewall's DMZ interface or use two firewalls (one between the web server and the Internet, and one between your private network and the web server) to secure your web servers.

Running a general-purpose operating system like Windows or Unix on the Internet is a bad idea. Operating systems and their TCP/IP stacks are optimized for performance, not security, and there are a number of low-level vulnerabilities that both platforms have been susceptible to in the past. Even with good OS filtering in place, you're better off protecting your web servers with a dedicated firewall.

Don't Allow Connections to the Private Network

Don't allow web servers in the DMZ to establish connections to the interior of your network. Just because you've set up an IP address filter on your website to allow only your web server to connect means nothing, because when hackers exploit your web server, they will use the legitimate vector through the firewall to reach the interior of your network.

Place a firewall between your internal network and your web servers as if they were public computers.

Don't Store Sensitive Data on Web Servers

Don't store any data on your web server that isn't stored elsewhere. And don't store sensitive information on your web server.

Always treat public web servers as though hackers will eventually get in and exploit them. Make backups when you update your site content so that you can quickly restore a server to operation if it gets defaced. Never store confidential or sensitive information on a web server, because hackers can steal it when they break in.

The purpose of many web servers is to collect data from the public, like account and credit card information. If you can't store the data locally and you can't connect from the DMZ to the internal network to store the data safely, what can you do? There's a catch-22 for sites that must retrieve important data from clients: If it shouldn't be stored on the web server and the server should be shielded from the rest of your network, then how should you retrieve it?

The answer to this question is to set up a secure directory (or table, if you're talking about a database) and set it up on a separate virtual directory with custom security settings. Program your web application to store data retrieved from clients in this more secure area. Then access this private section of your web server from your interior servers to retrieve the data provided by users on a regularly scheduled and frequent basis, and remove it from the web server. Because interior servers are connecting out to the DMZ, there's no need for a hole through your firewall; the server in the DMZ can't reach machines on the interior, but machines in the interior can reach the server in the DMZ. This avoids creating connections from the web server that could be exploited by hackers who may have gained control of the machine.

Minimize Services

Don't use the default installation of your operating system on a web server. Both Windows and Unix install a large number of extraneous services that hackers can exploit to hack the machine. Disable all services that aren't required for your website.

In particular, Windows machines should disable the Server service to prevent the machine from allowing SMB/CIFS logons. This is the second most important vector for hackers, after pushing buffer overruns, because Windows will always allow the Administrator account to log in without the normal account lockouts. Hackers can run automated tools to try thousands of passwords if your web server is running the Server service. Aside from stopping the service, you should unbind TCP/IP from both the file sharing and the Microsoft networking client in the Network Control Panel, and block ports 135, 137, 138, 139, and 445 from entering or leaving the web server.

WARNING

Most administrators know that port 139, the NetBIOS session port, should be blocked on a public server to prevent attempts at blocking passwords. Most don't know that the new SMB over TCP port introduced in Windows 2000, which provides the same functionality, is on port 445 (the NetLogon port). Hackers can map drives directly using this port as well. Furthermore, a bug in Windows 2000's login timeout security feature allows over 1200 password attempts per second to be thrown at this port. The entire English language could be cracked in under a minute, and every first and last name registered by the IRS in another two.

Windows users should also disable FTP, NNTP, and SMTP if they're not going to be used. These protocols are installed by default with the IIS Web Server, but you can uncheck them in the installation details panel when you install IIS or disable the services after they are installed.

On Unix machines, disable Telnet, rlogin, and all the other remote logon protocols besides SSH. Run SSH on a non-standard port (other than 22) so that automated attack tools can't find it, and use TCP Wrappers to prevent all hosts but your own from attaching to the server.

It's common to map FTP to the WWW root on your web servers if you provide hosting services for those outside your organization. This allows clients to update their own web pages via FTP logons. Be aware of the security problems with FTP (unencrypted passwords, numerous security flaws in FTP server executables, etc.) before you do this. Consider using WebDAV instead of FTP to reduce the number of services your server requires.

Delete unnecessary executables on dedicated web servers. Windows does not need cmd.exe to operate. Don't use Perl on your Unix machine? Remove it. This is a "last stand" against hackers who have already compromised your machine, but it's remarkably effective—breaking into an empty store doesn't do any good, and the vast majority of hacking exploits are "chain reactions," where a hacker finds a small hole and uses other executables on the web server to make the hole wide enough to squeeze completely through.

NOTE

Unfortunately, Microsoft built the Server service into the service control manager (along with a few other services like the Event log) so it cannot be removed from a web server.

Run Vendor-Provided "Lockdown" Tools

Many vendors provide automated **lockdown programs** that check for common security problems. These applications are sometimes able to remove more unnecessary services than you could remove on your own because of their tight integration with the operating system and because the vendor knows more about their operating system then most end users.

Check out `www.bastille-linux.org` for Linux servers, `www.openbsd.org` for BSD Unix, and Microsoft's IIS lockdown tool at `www.microsoft.com/windows2000/downloads/recommended/iislockdown`.

Stay Patched Up-to-Date

Right now, if you install Windows 2000 Server and Internet Information Server 5 from the CD-ROM that came with your server and place it on the public Internet to serve web pages, your server will be exploited by a variant of the Nimda worm within 30 minutes. Guaranteed. When we tested an unpatched version of IIS on the Internet for this book, the Nimda worm found it within 15 minutes of its first boot, pushed its buffer overrun, and began uploading its code to further exploit other servers.

You absolutely cannot deploy a web server without the complete set of security patches from the vendor and expect it to stay secure. You can't even connect it to the Internet just for the time it takes to download the requisite patches and remain secure—you'll be exploited during the patch download process.

To safely deploy a web server these days, you need to install and configure the server inside a firewall that blocks port 80 (HTTP). Once you've got the server completely configured and patched up-to-date (and only then) you can move it out onto the public Internet. You could try disabling the web service to do the patching, but the operating system itself is vulnerable to numerous exploits. Besides, you can only disable the services once the installation has been completed and you've logged in. There's a reasonable chance that your server will be exploited before you can log in for the first time. Don't try it.

Once your server is deployed, subscribe to every security mailing list you can find in order to get an early warning about new threats. Vendors only mention a threat once they've got a patch ready, which can be days or weeks after an exploit has appeared. Independent advisories have no such conflict of interest, and often break the news about exploits before vendors do.

If an exploit appears that you may be vulnerable to and the vendor hasn't released a patch yet, you're in no-man's land. You can either shut your web

lockdown programs
Software designed to automatically configure the security options of an operating system or other application to be optimal for a specific purpose.

server down and wait for a patch, get a good backup and prepare for frequent restorations, implement a proxy server, or purchase a third-party proxy filtering application (like FWTK for Unix machines) that may be invulnerable.

TIP

eEye security produces a TCP Wrapper-like service called SecureIIS that looks for buffer overruns and other URL malformations and blocks them before they get to IIS. It's a good thing. Check it out at www.eeye.com.

Analyze CGI and Script Security

Besides delivering files, HTTP also allows programs to be remotely executed on the web server through the Computer Gateway Interface (CGI) mechanism. If you specify the path to an executable in a web browser (and the web proxy–user account has execute permissions), the server will launch the executable and deliver its text output to the web browser, rather than delivering the file itself. It's a simple and powerful mechanism that allows HTTP to act as the user inter-face to incredibly complex programs. It's also the means by which innumerable hacking exploits can be perpetrated. Poorly written CGI applications are likely to contain unchecked buffers that can be overrun and flaws like taking a filename as a parameter without checking whether that file is in an appropriate directory. These same problems have existed in web servers, so there's no reason to think that custom software would be any more secure.

Modern web browsers also allow the execution of text files instead of its delivery; these text files are called scripts, and the browser determines whether to deliver the text or execute it by examining the file's extension. If the extension is regis-tered as a scripting language extension on the server, then the server will run the script through a scripting language module or executable program and deliver the output of that process to the web browser. This is referred to as server-side scripting.

Scripting allows simpler, less sophisticated programs to be run on the server. They are easier to write, simpler to debug, and able to take advantage of the (hopefully) secure environment provided by the scripting module. Unfortunately, simpler programs lower the bar for programming talent, and it's common for scriptwriters to accidentally circumvent security without understanding the rami-fications of their actions. Fortunately, exploiting individual programming mis-takes on a single website takes time and dedication; poorly written scripts will not be subject to the automated hacking attempts that widely deployed prob-lems like buggy web servers will be.

The solution to server-side scripting and CGI is simple: Don't use custom CGI programs or scripts without serious security testing. Here are a few simple things to look for in scripts or programs you write or evaluate.

Never take file names or database path information directly as a parameter even if you're certain that your own pages are generating the file names. Rather, create your own aliases for files that need to be accessed and pass those semantic aliases to refer to filenames and database paths by looking them up on the server side. This prevents access to unintended files.

Parse every input from a user for characters outside the legitimate range before inspecting its value. If you find any illegitimate characters, discard the entire input value.

Avoid creating files to the extent possible. If it's not avoidable, be certain to set the file's permissions such that only the web server has access to the file, or that the file is only readable to web users if the file needs to be subsequently delivered to the http user.

Never call another executable from a script or CGI program on the server if you can possibly avoid it. This is usually done through the exec or eval calls in scripts. Most unintentional security problems occur because programmers execute software that they didn't write (and can't secure) from within their own relatively secure programs. Write your own code instead.

Never use command shells as the execution environment for a script. In Unix, use a scripting language specifically designed for web scripting or text processing, like Perl, PHP, or Python. These languages, while not perfect, have built-in security measures to prevent many of the simple problems that running scripts from a shell environment can allow.

WARNING

Downloading freely available scripts for common purposes like form mailing or cookie-based logon mechanisms is exceptionally dangerous. Most of the popular scripts have known exploits, and adding them to your site will make your site vulnerable to those exploits. Even if you're doing the same thing as a freely available script, writing a custom script at least requires hackers to exploit your unknown script.

Avoid Web-Based Server Managers

Web-based server managers are popular on both Windows and Unix machines—IIS comes with one installed out of the box, and Webmin is a popular open-source administrative website for Unix machines.

Don't use either one. Both have significant security problems, not the least of which is the fact that by default, they're open to public hacking attempts.

On Windows servers, use the far less exploitable Terminal Services in administrative mode. It's free and gives you complete access to the host operating system. Password exchanges are secure, and you can configure the server to encrypt the entire session if you want. Remove the Administrative Site, the default site, and the sample sites before you make the server public.

On Unix machines, learn to configure the system from the command shell and use SSH as your remote administrative tool.

Apache Security

The Apache HTTP server project is the second most successful open-source development effort, after Linux. Apache is based on the public domain NCSA HTTP daemon developed by the National Center for Supercomputing Applications at the University of Illinois. After the original author left the University in 1994, development of NCSA stalled and various webmasters began writing their own extensions, and a small group of them began coordinating their changes and distributing them to one another. Within a short period of time, this core group began releasing complete compiled versions of their servers and coordinating the implementation of new features: Apache was born.

NOTE

Apache's name is derived from "A Patchy Server." It was originally the NCSA web server with a bunch of patches applied to fix various problems.

About a year after the first public release of Apache, it became the most popular web server on the Internet and remains so today. Versions of Apache are available for all operating systems. Apache 2.0 was released in 2002 as a complete redevelopment, designed to be efficient on all supported platforms rather than being developed primarily for Unix and running through POSIX emulation on other platforms.

TIP

Apache is actually faster and more secure than IIS when running on a Windows 2000 server. Windows webmasters should seriously consider replacing IIS with Apache 2.0 to avoid the constant barrage of hacking attempts that are IIS specific.

Apache configuration is performed by editing the `/etc/httpd/conf/httpd.conf` file and modifying the directives contained therein. The graphic below shows some of the virtual directory configuration options for an Apache web server.

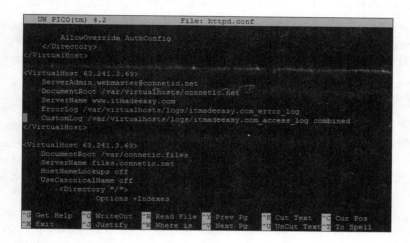

```
UW PICO(tm) 4.2                    File: httpd.conf

        AllowOverride AuthConfig
    </Directory>
</VirtualHost>

<VirtualHost 63.241.3.69>
    ServerAdmin webmaster@connetic.net
    DocumentRoot /var/virtualhosts/connetic.net
    ServerName www.itmadeeasy.com
    ErrorLog /var/virtualhosts/logs/itmadeeasy.com_error_log
    CustomLog /var/virtualhosts/logs/itmadeeasy.com_access_log combined
</VirtualHost>

<VirtualHost 63.241.3.69>
    DocumentRoot /var/connetic.files
    ServerName files.connetic.net
    HostNameLookups off
    UseCanonicalName off
        <Directory "/">
                Options +Indexes

^G Get Help   ^O WriteOut   ^R Read File   ^Y Prev Pg   ^K Cut Text    ^C Cur Pos
^X Exit       ^J Justify    ^W Where is    ^V Next Pg   ^U UnCut Text  ^T To Spell
```

The Apache HTTP daemon process runs as root, but spawns a new user context for every web session served. This means that users who browse web pages are served by a process using the user account defined by the `user` directive.

There are three major levels of directives in Apache:

◆ Global directives determine the configuration of the server as a whole.

◆ Server Root directives determine the configuration of the default website.

◆ Virtual Host directives determine the configuration of individual **virtual hosts**.

TIP

The official source for Apache configuration settings is `httpd.apache.org/docs-2.0/`.

Use User-Based Security

Apache user-based security, like most secure network services in Unix, uses it's own user/password file, so web accounts are not the same as operating system user accounts. This is a very important security feature, because it does not provide an open door to the operating system for someone who has intercepted web credentials.

---

virtual host
A web server administration feature that allows a single web server to serve numerous websites as if they were hosted by their own server. The web server inspects the URL header, IP address, or port number from the client connection to determine which virtual host should deliver a specific page request.

Apache can be configured to use different user password files for each virtual server, which means that if you host multiple websites on a single server, you should configure apache to use a different list of users for each website. Information on how to do this is included with the official documentation.

Because Apache user security is not passed through to the operating system, you can't rely on file system permissions to secure documents against specific web users. File permissions can only be set for the standard apache user.

taint
In Perl, a flag indicating that the information contained in the flagged variable was directly entered by a web user and should not be trusted. Taint is copied with the variable contents and can only be removed by interpreting the variable's contents, rather than simply passing them through to a function or another application.

TIP

Unlike IIS, Apache does not spin off the session using the authenticated user's credentials, so security checking is up to the server process. Apache has to parse user files and check credentials for every page access, so you can speed up processing for a large number of users by using DBM formatted user files rather than text files.

Apache supports MD5 message digest authentication to securely exchange passwords. Most popular web browsers, including Internet Explorer versions 5 and higher, support MD5 authentication. Use MD5 authentication to encrypt credentials when you use user authentication unless you absolutely have to support users with obsolete web browsers, or use SSL with basic authentication.

Ensure Proper Directory Security

Make sure that your ServerRoot directory (where the Apache executable is stored, as defined by the ServerRoot directive) is properly secured against modifications by the anonymous web user account. This directory and all of its subdirectories should be owned by root (chown 0), the group should be set to the root (wheel) group (chgrp 0), and permission should be set to disallow writes by group and everyone (chmod 0755). If anonymous web users can modify this directory, you open up the possibility of a remote-root exploit.

Scripting Security

Use Perl as your scripting language, and enable taint checks. **Taint** is a flag on a variable that indicates that the data that it contains came directly from a web user. As this variable is copied around from one variable to another, the taint is copied with it. If taint checks are enabled, Perl will not allow data from a tainted variable to be used to open or execute files. Taint basically forces you to use proper data checking procedures on user input. No other web scripting provides this security feature.

WARNING

If you download a script that says you must turn of taint checks to use it, it's a sure sign that the script is not secure. If you can't get your own scripts working with taint checks enabled, keep working until you can. Disabling taint checks is an admission of security failure.

Internet Information Services Security

Internet Information Services is Microsoft's web server for the Windows platform. Like Apache, IIS is based on the public domain NCSA web server developed by Rob McCool at the University of Illinois. IIS 1.0 was little more than NCSA with a Windows interface and was available for download from Microsoft. NT Server 4 shipped with IIS 2, but was quickly supplanted by the considerably superior IIS 3. During the lifecycle of NT 4, IIS 4 became the standard, introducing numerous new features, like name-based virtual hosting and numerous security fixes. IIS 4 also introduced an entirely new tree-based management console. IIS 5 is a security fix version of IIS 4 that shipped with Windows 2000. IIS 5 includes WebDAV support and numerous other esoteric features; otherwise, IIS 5 is basically the same as IIS4 and difficult to tell apart.

NOTE

Microsoft changed the name from Internet Information Server 4 to Internet Information Services 5 for the version included with Windows 2000. So now you have to search on both terms to find information on the Web.

Microsoft includes IIS for free with the operating system when you buy Windows NT/2000 server. However, there's a serious "gotcha" embedded in Microsoft's licensing terms when it comes to web service:

- ♦ Anonymous users are free.
- ♦ Users who authenticate with the server require a $40 client access license per user or an Internet Connector License ($2000) for unlimited logons.

Microsoft has concocted this convoluted licensing scheme to extract money from those who use IIS to create intranets and extranets, while remaining competitive for public websites. They know that most companies deploy Windows-based websites, not because they've performed a competitive analysis of server technologies, but because their programmers only know Visual Basic—and once a site is developed on Visual Basic, the users are locked into Windows and IIS.

Microsoft's position is basically that they charge per authenticated user for server services. Since anonymous users don't authenticate, there is no additional cost to support them. It's blatantly obvious that anonymous users are only free because Apache and Linux exist.

Microsoft packages the Internet Connector license as an operating system license, not an IIS license. This means that the same licensing applies whether you use Apache or IIS to serve "authenticated" pages—quite clever, since this way you're required to pay for an Internet Connector License for authenticated users even if you run Apache to serve your pages. However, since Apache uses its own user authentication accounts, users are not logged into actual Windows accounts, thus technically nullifying Microsoft's licensing argument—no Windows-based authentication is being used.

TIP

If you're worried about licensing issues (such as trying to figure out how much you're supposed to pay Microsoft for various modes of access), use Linux or BSD with Apache for your public website.

A "workstations" version of IIS called Peer Web Services exists; it's the same software, but it is subject to the limitation that Windows NT 4 Workstation, Windows 2000 Professional, and Windows XP will only serve 10 simultaneous IP-based logons. However, there is no per-client charge for authenticated users when running on these operating systems.

IIS is simple to install and configure. The management console shown here is from a default installation. It can take a moment to figure out what's going on, but like all Microsoft MMC console apps, the configuration is easy to figure out once you're used to the paradigm.

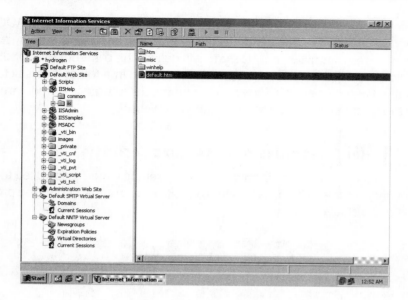

The "Default Website" and "Administration Website" nodes are both virtual hosts, which are distinguished either by IP address, TCP port number, or host header domain name. The default website runs on port 80 and is served in the absence of any more specific information about which website the user wants. IIS allows you to create as many virtual hosts as you want.

There are many properties in IIS that can be configured globally for all sites, both for performance and security. These properties are basically the same as the properties that can be configured for individual hosts; the global configuration merely creates the default template that all sites inherit. Setting the master configuration before you begin adding websites is a good way to start off with better security. The master properties for the IIS server shown here is the gateway for global configuration.

Under the default website, the IISHelp, IISAdmin, IISSamples, and MSADC nodes are **virtual directories** that are linked into the default website as subdirectories, so that `http://hostname.dom/IISHelp` will deliver the content pointed to by the IISHelp virtual directory even though it's not stored in a folder that is actually contained in the www root directory where the default site is stored. Virtual directories can also be redirects to a different website.

virtual directory
A portion of a website with its own specific configuration and security settings. A virtual directory appears as a directory inside the website, but may be located anywhere on the Internet.

Use Virtual Directories to Customize Security

Virtual directories have their own IIS security settings and can be used to modify security settings within a website. The following graphic shows the properties panel of a virtual directory.

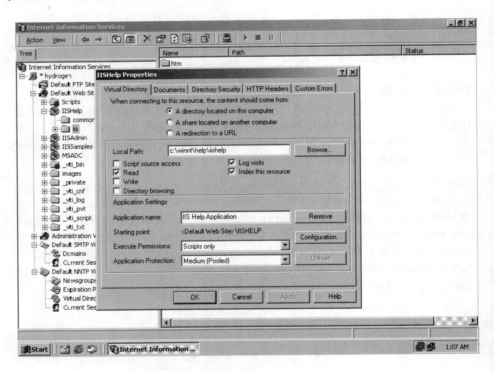

With virtual directories, you can change the following on a directory-by-directory basis:

- ❖ Access to scripts
- ❖ Directory browsing
- ❖ Read and write access
- ❖ Logging of access

- Indexing of files
- Execution permissions (none, scripts, executables)
- Partitioning of CGI, ISAPI, and script applications
- Enable sessions
- Associate document types with scripting engines

You can manage snippets (small applications or scripts with an associated user interface that are intended to be included in other web pages) by using virtual directories. Place a specific snippet in its own directory, and use virtual directories to include it in the rest of your websites. This way, you can control its security settings globally and store only a single copy of it.

Avoid IIS User Authentication

The IIS host process (The World Wide Web Server service) runs under the account credentials configured in the services control panel—by default, the LocalSystem account. But every user session connected starts under the context of the IUSR_COMPUTERNAME user account, which is created when IIS is installed. This can be changed to any other user account if desired. If users authenticate with the server, then a new session is started using the credentials supplied. The three authentication methods shown here are available in IIS.

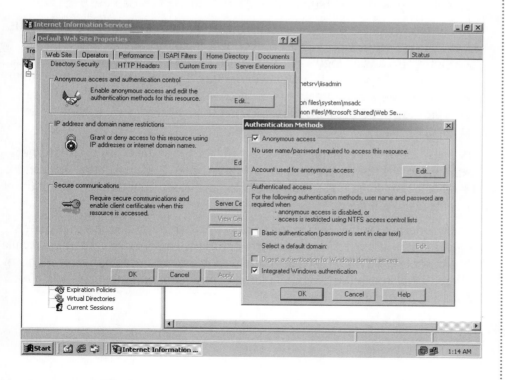

You can configure IIS to use three types of user authentication for any website.

Anonymous Access is the default mechanism. When a session is connected, the connection process is spun off using the IUSR_COMPUTERNAME user account context by default or whatever other user the administrator configures. If you use the NTFS file system, all public web directories and their contents need to be configured to allow read access for the anonymous web user. They should not be configured to allow write access.

Basic Authentication is the traditional method of user logon supported by all web browsers and servers. User accounts and passwords are transmitted in unencrypted form, and since they are valid Windows accounts, they can be used to exploit the server directly using other services, if those services are running and open to the web. If you choose to use basic authentication, use SSL to encrypt the web session and protect user credentials from sniffing attacks.

Windows Authentication (also called NTLM Authentication or pass-through authentication) is a proprietary mechanism only supported by IIS and Internet Explorer. NTLM transmits the password in encrypted form using the standard Windows hash algorithm.

If the web server attempts to load a page that the default web user does not have permission to access, the web browser will prompt for different credentials. Assuming the logon is successful, the web server will open a new process using the supplied user credentials and again attempt to load the page.

IIS falls flat when it comes to user authentication from a security standpoint. IIS does not support service-only user accounts, which means that any valid web account is also a valid logon account, which of course means that it can be used to connect to the server via any other configured network service. Although IIS also doesn't use a separate list of user account for virtual hosts, you can use NTFS file system permissions to restrict access to different virtual hosts based on groups.

IIS does not support encrypted passwords for browsers other than Internet Explorer, so it is not widely used for public websites. Because passwords cannot be reliably encrypted unless you intend to limit access to Internet Explorer users only, its utility is limited.

Finally, Internet Explorer will automatically provide the credentials of the user logged onto the client machine before it prompts for separate credentials. While this isn't specifically a server-side security problem, it can provide a mechanism whereby the credentials of your legitimate intranet or extranet users could be suborned by hackers on the Internet.

Use NTFS Permissions to Correctly
Secure Documents and Scripts

When you install IIS, the Scripts directory (where most scripts are stored) is set to "full control" for the Everyone group. Set these permissions to Read and Execute for only those accounts that will be used by web users.

Use a Security Proxy

IIS is subject to a phenomenal number of buffer overruns, and because its root process runs by default as the LocalSystem account, exploits provide even wider access to the machine than the administrator account allows. If you serve a public website using IIS, use a security proxy to shore up security.

Microsoft's Internet Security and Acceleration Server is a good and relatively inexpensive choice that provides an astounding array of security services. It can be run directly on the web server or as a firewall in front of an array of web servers, where it can assist in load balancing across the pool of servers. Check out ISA Server at www.Microsoft.com.

eEye's SecureIIS security filter is another good (and inexpensive) way to eliminate most of the egregious security problems in IIS. eEye's filter runs on each web server and checks inbound URLs and user input for suspicious characters and invalid length. Check it out at www.eeye.com.

Review Questions

Terms to Know
- bugs
- lockdown programs
- reverse proxy
- taint
- Top Level Domain Names (TLDs)
- virtual directory
- virtual host
- web enabled

1. Over 90 percent of the public Internet is served from which two web server applications?

   _____

2. What is the most threatening security problem facing public web servers?

   _____

3. Which is more secure: Closed source or open source operating systems?

   _____

4. Which is more secure, IIS or Apache?

   _____

5. Why should websites only be deployed on dedicated web servers?

   _____

6. Where are bugs most likely to be found in a program?

   _____

7. What service does SSL perform?

   _____

8. What's the best way to secure intranet servers?

   _____

9 What is the universal encrypted authentication mechanism?

   _____

10. How do you configure Apache?

_____

11. What is taint?

_____

Chapter
14

E-mail Security

All modern businesses require Internet **e-mail** of one form or another. E-mail is the first truly new method of communication to come along since the invention of the telephone, and its effect on business efficiency has been just as dramatic as its vocal predecessor.

As with all public services, running an **SMTP** service entails the risk that the service itself could be exploited to run arbitrary code on the mail server. In fact, this has occurred with every major e-mail server system, including **Sendmail**, **Exchange**, and Lotus Notes. The only solution to this problem is to keep e-mail servers in your DMZ or outside your firewall so that if they're exploited, they don't allow further access to the interior of your network. E-mail servers must stay up-to-date on server software and security patches to prevent exploits related to bugs.

This chapter will teach you how to mitigate e-mail security risks. You will learn about:

 E-mail encryption

 E-mail Virus protection

 Spam Prevention

 Securing mail clients

electronic mail (e-mail)

A queued message delivery system that allows users to transmit relatively short text messages to other users over the Internet. The messages wait in a mail queue until they are downloaded and read by the ultimate recipient.

Simple Mail Transfer Protocol (SMTP)

The Internet protocol that controls the transmission of e-mail between servers. SMTP is also used to transmit e-mail from clients to servers but usually not to receive it, because SMTP requires recipient machines to be online at all times.

Sendmail

The most popular e-mail service, Sendmail is open-source and was originally part of the BSD. Many commercial e-mail services are based on Sendmail.

E-mail Encryption and Authentication

The only way to make e-mail truly secure is to encrypt it. Encryption protects against sniffing, accidental misdirection, loss of attached document security, and even forgery.

WARNING

E-mail encryption foils all attempts to strip attachments or scan for viruses, because the e-mail server cannot decrypt the mail to check it. Be certain that you only receive encrypted mail from trusted sources.

All e-mail encryption methods use public key encryption to secure messages. To establish secure e-mail, your e-mail encryption package will create a private key for you and a public key that you can send to those who need to receive secure e-mail from you.

NOTE

This chapter discusses public e-mail security methods. Numerous methods exist to secure private e-mail services within a single organization, but these proprietary systems cannot be effectively used on the public Internet because they only work with e-mail servers of the exact same type. Private mail system security is rarely important since purely private e-mail systems cannot be attacked from the Internet, so server-to-server encryption systems have little real value.

Forgery can be prevented through public key encryption. The ability to decrypt a message with a specific public key proves that it was encrypted with the corresponding private key, which in turn proves that the message is from whomever sent you the public key. However, unless both parties know that all e-mail should always be encrypted and that unencrypted e-mail should not be trusted, forgery can still occur by the transmission of an unencrypted message.

In the early days of encrypted e-mail, you had to manually encrypt messages by piping the message through an external encryption program. More modern e-mail encryption packages automate the encryption process by keeping track of those to whom you've sent a public key, and subsequently encrypt mail to those recipients.

Every encryption system is different, and both recipients must be using the same system in order to exchange encrypted e-mail. Fortunately, two systems have emerged as the market leaders: **Secure Multipurpose Internet Mail Extensions (S/MIME)** and **Pretty Good Privacy (PGP)**. PGP is proprietary but free. S/MIME is an open standard supported by multiple vendors, but free implementations are rare. Both systems are somewhat free to use, but S/MIME requires you to have an X.509 Digital Certificate installed that gives the Root Certificate Authorities something to charge you for if you can't figure out how to generate your own certificates or if you want to have transitive trusts between organizations.

Encrypted e-mail hasn't caught on because it's an extra layer of hassle. End users have a hard time obtaining **rooted** digital certificates; businesses are hesitant to pay for or administer rooted certificate services. Finally, if an end user has problems with his or her e-mail system and looses their ring of public keys, they won't be able to open mail from their associates until they bother them for a new key.

S/MIME

S/MIME is the future of encrypted e-mail. Developed by RSA Security (originators of the first commercial public key encryption implementation), it's an open standard that has wide industry support, except from the open-source community, which doesn't like the fact that S/MIME is based on rooted X.509 certificates that come only from commercial entities. There's no reason why the open-source community couldn't make their own Root CA, but without the resources to verify subscriber's true identities, it would become a hornet's nest of fraudulent certifications. Organizations can create their own non-rooted certificates as well, using the Windows Certificate Server service or Open SSL, but it's a fairly complex process.

S/MIME encryption is built into the e-mail client or is an add-on package for the e-mail client once the encryption certificate is installed. To use S/MIME encryption, obtain a digital certificate from some certificate authority and install it into your e-mail client.

TIP

Check out www.bacus.pt/Net_SSLeay/smime.html for explicit instructions on creating S/MIME-compatible digital certificates for open-source users.

Exchange
Microsoft's e-mail and messaging server. Exchange was originally designed for private interoffice messaging, with Internet functionality provided as an add-on. It uses the proprietary Microsoft MAPI protocol for exchanging mail between Exchange servers and clients, SMTP for transmitting e-mail on the public Internet, and can be configured to allow POP3, IMAP, and WebMail access as well.

Secure Multipurpose Internet Mail Extensions (S/MIME)
MIME with extensions that provide encryption.

Pretty Good Privacy (PGP)
A freely available encryption package that supports file and e-mail encryption for nearly all computing platforms.

rooted
A transitive trust system that relies upon a hierarchy that culminates in a single entity that all participants implicitly trust.

S/MIME doesn't specify an encryption algorithm or standard. The original S/MIME implementations used RC2 40-bit encryption (the same as early SSL encryption), which is extremely weak and can be cracked in a trivial amount of time using brute force methods. This algorithm was originally used because it was the strongest grade of security that the U.S. would allow to be exported.

TIP

Thawte provides free, uncertified personal certificates at `www.thawte.com/getinfo/products/personal/join.html`.

Another popular algorithm is 56-bit DES, which is also now considered weak. The minimum secure standard for S/MIME today is Triple-DES, which provides 168-bit security. Unfortunately, the stronger the algorithm is, the less likely any specific implementation is to support it.

TIP

VeriSign sells personal "Digital IDs" (X.509 certificates) that come with $1000 worth of fraud insurance for $15/year at `www.verisign.com/products/class1/index.html`.

To use encrypted e-mail on the client side, you simply download your certificate from a trusted provider and import it into your mail client. Once done, you have the option to encrypt e-mail that you send to anyone. You must first send them an e-mail containing your public key, which will be installed in their **key ring** when they open the attachment.

PGP

PGP (and the newer OpenPGP) e-mail encryption works essentially the same way, but instead of using S/MIME, it uses PGP to encrypt mail. PGP is also not supported natively by most e-mail applications, but can be added as a module or extension to most of them.

PGP is a little less transparent than S/MIME, but it's easier to administer for small sites or individuals because you can easily generate your own key pairs rather than obtaining them from a certificate authority.

key ring
A database of public keys that have been received by a user.

Although PGP lacks any concept of rooted transitive trust, it does use a **grass-rooted** methodology called a **web of trust**, where individuals who use the system sign the posted public keys of those individuals that they know personally to certify that they know the person has honestly posted the key—in other words, they vouch for their identity. The more users that have vouched for an individual, the more likely it is that you will know one of them.

The idea is that when everyone has vouched for everyone they know, the result will be a "six degrees of Kevin Bacon" effect where you know someone who knows someone who knows someone who signed the key of the person you're authenticating, and so transitive trust exists without a central certifying authority. It's a nice idea, but it takes massive participation for it to actually be of any real value. It is perfectly fine for business partners, however, because they can simply certify each other and be assured that they're talking to real individuals. Thawte is building a web of trust system for its S/MIME-based, free personal certificates as well.

grass-rooted

A trust system that has no hierarchy, instead it relies upon massive participation to provide a transitive trust mechanism that requires no supporting commercial organization.

web of trust

The PGP grass-rooted transitive-trust mechanism for encrypted e-mail.

285

Mail Forgery

Mail forgery is about as uncommon as standard document forgery, but it's much easier to perpetrate. It is rare only because it takes truly criminal intent to forge e-mail.

There is no SMTP authentication mechanism. This lack of inherent security allows mail forgery to occur. But despite this, there are a few things you can do to make mail forgery difficult.

It's pointless to forge e-mail unless you can get a human to do something based on the contents of the message. Given that this is the case, you can mitigate the effectiveness of an e-mail forgery attempt by making a few acceptable-use policies concerning the e-mailing of highly sensitive information. For example, you should never mail passwords, but many users may not know this. If everyone knows that passwords are never e-mailed, then a forged e-mail from an administrator asking a user for a password will immediately be exposed as a forgery. You should also make policies concerning the request for e-mail attachments (at the very least attachments containing sensitive information). If everyone within your organization knows that only links to documents should be e-mailed, then requests for attachments will also be foiled. With just these two policies, the majority of mail forgery exploits can be prevented.

You can configure your e-mail server to reject SMTP connections from any e-mail server that doesn't have a valid registered domain name. People you do business with have a mail server with a registered domain name, so you aren't going to lose mail from them. You can take this a step further by rejecting mail from domains that you don't do business with. For example, if you work at a small business, it's likely that you don't do business internationally, so there's no point in receiving mail from most foreign countries. By dropping connection attempts from countries that you have no business interest in, you can eliminate the source of numerous mail forgery attempts, a tremendous amount of spam, and the origin point of numerous automated e-mail–based Internet worms and viruses.

If an e-mail message is important, use encrypted e-mail even if you don't need privacy. E-mail encryption not only secures the contents of e-mail, it proves that the message came from the same person who sent you the public key.

None of these measures eliminate the possibility of mail forgery, but they do reduce the risk substantially.

E-mail Viruses

E-mail is the new favorite vector of virus writers. Personal information managers that store contact information are also used as e-mail clients, putting the information that an e-mail virus needs to propagate in the same execution environment as the virus itself. More than 99 percent of all virus strikes now enter via e-mail—in fact, non e-mail virus strikes are now exceptionally rare, because e-mail has all but eliminated the use of removable media such as floppy or zip disks to transfer documents among computers.

The fact that most viruses propagate via e-mail is actually a serious advantage for network administrators.

For computers inside a corporation, an e-mail gateway virus scanner can eliminate the need to deploy virus scanners on every workstation. You need only run a virus scanner on your e-mail server to detect viruses as they come through the gateway, and you can be almost certain that your individual workstations will be protected. That is, as long as your virus definitions are up-to-date and your virus scanner vendor releases updates fast enough to make sure that even new viruses are caught. If a virus does slip through your e-mail gateway, workstation scanners won't catch it either. But to remove the virus once you do update your virus definitions, you will need scanners on your workstations.

WARNING

Beware of e-mail virus hoaxes. Hoaxes are just as common as actual viruses, and can be just as destructive. Recently, a friend called me saying he'd gotten a virus warning that urged him to "check for the virus" by looking up certain files, and if they existed, to delete them. Of course, the files were critical system files, and we had to re-install the operating system to restore them.

Outlook Viruses

Outlook and **Outlook Express** have special security problems related to their incorporation of Windows Scripting directly into e-mail. These two e-mail clients will execute scripts automatically that are contained in an e-mail message.

Most outlook viruses operate by rifling through your Outlook contacts and then e-mailing themselves either to all of your contacts or randomly selected contacts. The authentication problem is that they look like they've come from you, so

Outlook
Microsoft's extremely popular, but poorly secured, e-mail client and personal information manager.

Outlook Express
A stripped-down version of Outlook that handles only the minimum set of features necessary to propagate e-mail viruses.

your colleagues will be off guard when they open the e-mail and may even be induced to open an attachment.

The scripts are included in e-mail as a special type of attachment and can be easily stripped at the e-mail server, so the solution to this problem is the same as the solution to stripping attachments.

Commercial Gateway Virus Scanners

There are numerous virus-scanning packages to choose from. They all use the same type of technology to search for the signature characteristics of viruses. They operate like a spell checker searching through a document for misspelled words. Code quality varies a bit, but most of them do the job. Other technologies that attempted to predict "virus-like" behavior had too many false positives and didn't always catch new types of viruses, so they did not gain widespread acceptance. This effect is much like the attempts now being made to detect "hacker-like activity" in intrusion detection systems, which are being bested by simple signature-based intrusion detectors.

Where the scanners vary is mostly in the speed at which the vendors find and post new virus definitions, the ease with which you can update your definitions, the cost of their software, and the automation of deployment.

I could go on at length about the merits of various commercial virus scanners, but there's a simple bottom line: Symantec AntiVirus is better in every category than any of its competitors, and is priced at about the mid-range of virus solutions. It's simple to install, it automatically deploys clients, and it automatically receives updates. Symantec is very fast in deploying new virus definitions, and it costs less than $25 per workstation. Every time I've walked into a client site where they use another enterprise virus scanner, I wind up replacing it because either the code quality is low and causes problems for users or the update mechanism is prone to failure, or the vendor isn't fast enough to catch new viruses and deploy updates so new viruses slip through.

When you buy Symantec AntiVirus Enterprise Edition, you get the scanning software for servers and e-mail servers along with the package. If you buy retail versions of their desktop scanner, you don't.

Unfortunately, none of the major vendors really provide decent support for Unix- or Linux-based machines, but viruses don't usually attack those platforms, so virus-scanning software is usually not necessary for them. Unix avoids viruses by remaining incompatible with Microsoft Office, the engine behind 99% of all current virus activity.

AMaViS

Unix isn't all that susceptible to viruses, so virus scanners are uncommon in the Unix world. But there is a place for them: When Unix e-mail servers host e-mail for Windows clients. In this situation, you need to scan for Windows viruses, but you need to do it on a Unix machine.

Many commercial vendors (such as Kaspersky) provide solutions for this problem by selling special Unix e-mail gateway scanning software. Unfortunately, they charge for their software per mailbox, which means that if you host thousands of e-mail boxes on a mail server, you'll pay tens of thousands of dollars for the same software that someone else paid mere hundreds for.

AMaViS, an open source solution for scanning e-mail, is my favorite solution to this problem. It does an end-run around silly licensing practices by allowing you to use a single workstation license virus scanner for Unix to check all the e-mail that flows through it. Furthermore, it decompresses attachments to make sure that viruses aren't hiding inside ZIP files, and it's reasonably efficient. You do have to use it in conjunction with a commercial Unix virus scanner, so make sure that the vendor's **EULA** doesn't expressly forbid this type of use. You can check it out at www.amavis.org.

end user license agreement (EULA)
A contract between the developer of software and the users of software. The contract limits the user's right to use and distribute the software as specified by the developer.

Attachment Security

Every mail client suffers from one problem: Hackers can send a Trojan horse or virus to users as an executable **attachment** and, by inducing the user to open the attachment, the content may execute automatically. This is a fundamentally different problem than Outlook viruses, because these viruses or Trojan horses don't rely upon the execution environment of the e-mail client, they rely upon being extracted from the e-mail message and executed by the user in the execution environment of the host operating system.

Attachments, a relatively new feature of e-mail, allows files to be encoded in a format that can be transmitted as text. **Multipurpose Internet Mail Extensions (MIME)** is the protocol that describes how e-mail attachments should be handled. The web also uses MIME to transfer multimedia content in web pages.

Some e-mail clients are better than others at helping to mitigate this problem by requiring you to actually download the file before it can be executed, but this won't stop a user who has been fooled by the body text. The latest mail clients will automatically quarantine attachments that are considered too dangerous to e-mail, as well.

There are four ways to deal with attachments (in order from most to least secure):

- ◇ Strip all attachments.
- ◇ Allow only the specific attachment types you commonly use.
- ◇ Strip only known dangerous attachments.
- ◇ Don't strip attachments.

These methodologies are discussed in the following sections, except for the last one because it's not a security measure.

Strip All Attachments

Configuring your e-mail server to strip all attachments is usually relatively simple, but somewhat draconian. It limits e-mail to a communication mechanism only, but it prevents e-mail hacking (except e-mail forgery) and virus activity.

Exchange and most open-source e-mail servers can be easily configured to strip attachments. Consult your e-mail server's documentation for information on how to configure it for e-mail security.

attachment

A file encoded in text form for transmission in an e-mail message, such as a word.doc or picture.jpg file.

Multipurpose Internet Mail Extensions (MIME)

An IETF protocol for encoding and transmitting files along with metadata that determines how the files should be decoded and what applications should be used to interpret them.

290

TIP

Many attachment strippers only work during the transfer to individual mail-boxes and can't be used to strip attachments on a relay mail server. MIMEDefang can strip attachments as a mail relay, as well as perform a number of other utility functions on e-mail passing through the server. Check it out at www.roaringpenguin.com/mimedefang.

Even if your e-mail server doesn't support the functionality required to strip attachments, you can add the functionality to any network by putting a Unix-based **relay server** between the Internet and your mail server. Configure your **MX records** to send e-mail to the relay server and configure the relay server to forward to your interior proprietary mail server. You can then use one of many methods available to the open source community to strip attachments on the open-source e-mail server before they are forwarded to your proprietary server, guaranteeing that it never even sees the attachments. This same method can be used to add e-mail virus scanning to any e-mail server.

Attachment stripping needn't be completely draconian. You can configure the e-mail server to decode and move attachments to an FTP directory on the mail server where administrators could forward the files to end-users if they actually needed them for a legitimate purpose. Don't go too far to make the process convenient, however. The attachment could be automatically replaced by a link to the attachment, making the whole process so seamless that you might as well have done nothing.

Allow Only Specific Attachments

The next best security measure for attachments is to allow only the document types you actually use to be transmitted as attachments. This would include office documents, Acrobat files, Visio diagrams, CAD drawings, etc. By stripping superfluous attachments at your border e-mail server, you can eliminate most of the problem while still allowing the business use of e-mail attachments.

This is significant security degradation from complete stripping, because most of the office documents that people use can contain macro viruses, but it's far better than nothing and is practical for every organization.

relay server
An intermediate e-mail server configured to route e-mail between e-mail servers.

Mail Exchanger (MX) Records
DNS entries that identify the host names of e-mail servers for a specific domain.

Administrators won't always know what document **extensions** people legitimately use, but you shouldn't let that discourage you. If a person can't get an attachment through, they'll let you know and you can reconfigure the server to allow that type, as necessary. Using this methodology, you'll always have the minimum set of attachment types that you actually know you need.

Strip Only Dangerous Attachments

At a bare minimum, you should at least strip the attachment types that represent an extreme risk and have almost no legitimate reason to be e-mailed. These attachment types are usually directly interpreted by the base operating system and have the potential to allow widespread intrusion if they are opened.

You can eliminate this problem by configuring your mail server to strip attachments that have executable extensions. You should always strip, without exception, the following attachment extensions on your mail server:

Executable (.exe) The standard extension for programs in systems descended from MS-DOS. Originally, .exe files were programs larger than 64Kb that required paging memory extensions and 16-bit processors to execute.

Command (.com) The standard extension for MS-DOS command programs. These programs were less than 64Kb in size and could be directly executed on all Intel 8-bit processors.

Command (.cmd) Windows NT command scripts (batch files that use NT specific command line programs).

Batch file (.bat) A text file executed by COMMAND.COM (MS-DOS through Windows ME) or CMD.EXE (NT, 2000, XP, .NET) that contains shell commands to be executed.

Program Information File (.pif) An accessory file for Windows 3.1 systems that specified icons and program associations for DOS executables. While these files were replaced in Windows 95 and later, modern versions of Windows still respect the files and will launch the executables they specify.

Screen Saver (.scr) A binary file that acts as a screen saver. This extension is frequently used by hackers because the system will launch it as an executable automatically and most systems that strip attachments aren't configured to stop it, because many administrators don't know about it.

JavaScript (.js or .jse)   A Windows Scripting host file written in JavaScript. These files are automatically executed by the Windows Scripting Host built into Explorer.exe and can call any system objects available in Visual Basic and perform any function on your computer. The language and capabilities are essentially the same as an Office macro or an IIS server-side web script.

Visual Basic Script (.vb, .vbe, .vbs)   A Windows Scripting Host file written in Visual Basic. This is the same thing as a .js script, but using Visual Basic syntax rather than JavaScript syntax.

HTML Application (.hta)   A web page that runs in the Microsoft HTML Host, a simple browser without the security restrictions of Internet Explorer. This is an executable file type that can perform any function Internet Explorer can perform without the security sandbox that makes web pages somewhat safe. HTAs are just as dangerous as JS or VBS scripting host files. Very few administrators or users know what HTA files are, so they are a new threat that most people do not expect. HTA support is automatically included in Internet Explorer 5 and later.

Microsoft Installer Package (.msi, .mst, .msp)   An automated program installer package (.msi) or transform (.mst) or patch (.msp). Clicking on an MSI file will automatically install a program that can perform any action on your computer, including installing services that will execute automatically and automatically launch the file that it installs. MSI files are extremely dangerous attachments. Installer packages were developed for Windows 2000 and Windows XP.

Registry Files (.reg)   Text files that update values in the Registry and can be used to disable systems, reconfigure services, or perform other limited mischievous acts. Registry files don't actually execute code, but they can reconfigure a computer to launch programs the next time they are started, connect to remote servers on the Internet, or an array of other attacks.

Program Links (.lnk)   Shortcuts to executable files, which can contain parameters to control how the program executes. Hackers could use LNK files to send shortcuts to CMD.EXE that include command line parameters to perform nearly any action.

Executable extensions aren't the only problem. They represent extensions that will run on any Windows system, but Windows automatically runs the program associated with any registered extension. So by choosing a common program that has an execution environment associated with it, hackers can get right through attachment stripping programs.

Microsoft considers the following attachment types so dangerous that Outlook 2002 automatically quarantines them, as well as the extremely dangerous extensions listed above. You should also strip these attachments on your mail server irrespective of who sends them:

Extension	File Type
.ade	Microsoft Access project extension
.adp	Microsoft Access project
.bas	Microsoft Visual Basic class module
.chm	Compiled HTML help file
.cpl	Control Panel extension
.crt	Security certificate
.hlp	Help file
.inf	Setup information
.ins	Internet Naming Service
.isp	Internet communication settings
.mda	Microsoft Access add-in program
.mdb	Microsoft Access program
.mde	Microsoft Access MDE database
.mdz	Microsoft Access wizard program
.msc	Microsoft Common Console Document
.mst	Visual Test source files
.pcd	Microsoft Visual Test compiled script (also used by PhotoCD)
.sct	Windows Script Component
.shs	Shell scrap object
.url	Internet shortcut
.wsc	Windows Script Component
.wsf	Windows Script file
.wsh	Windows Script Host Settings file

Beyond this list, there are certainly many types of applications that can be used to gain control of a system. For example, many administrators of cross-platform networks install **Perl** as an administration scripting language, so the .pl and .pls extensions it uses will be just as dangerous as any other scripting language. Because these applications are more rare, hackers are less likely to target them unless they know you're using these applications.

As you can see, the list of known dangerous attachments just for Office and Windows is large, and this isn't a complete set. To be safest, you should configure your e-mail server to strip all attachments except the types you actually use.

Foreign E-mail Servers

You can solve nearly all e-mail security problems without regard to the type of mail client used in your organization by turning your e-mail server into an e-mail firewall. An e-mail firewall strips e-mail attachments, cleans scripts out of e-mail files, and drops connections from hosts that don't have legitimate DNS names, come from parts of the world that you don't do business with, or come from open relays.

But as with all firewalls, beware the unchecked border crossing: All your server-side security is for naught if you allow users to set up their e-mail clients to also check their own personal e-mail accounts at work. By allowing **POP3** to transit through of your firewall, you will be allowing users to circumvent every e-mail security measure you enforce on your corporate e-mail servers. You'll find that users will actually tell business associates to send files to their personal accounts because you strip attachments on the server. To enforce e-mail security, you have to block POP3 and **IMAP** access going out from your network to the Internet at your firewall, and you may have to block access to web-based e-mail providers like Hotmail and proprietary e-mail protocols like **AOL**.

Post Office Protocol, version 3 (POP3)

An e-mail client protocol used to download e-mail from mail servers into mail client programs.

Internet Mail Access Protocol (IMAP)

A client e-mail access protocol typically used in situations where it's appropriate to allow users to leave e-mail on the mail server rather than downloading it to their client computer.

America Online (AOL)

A popular graphical BBS system that has transformed into the largest consumer Internet service provider. Due to its non-Internet origins, AOL uses a proprietary e-mail mechanism that (among other things) does not support true MIME attachments or use standard ports for transmitting e-mail.

Spam

In the context of the Internet, **spam** is unwanted, unsolicited e-mail. The name comes from an early newsgroup poster who referred to unsolicited e-mailers as those who would throw a brick of Spam at a fan to distribute it as widely as possible—spam was probably being used as a euphemism, but the term stuck.

spam
Unsolicited, unwanted e-mail.

spammers
Those who send spam. Usually, the term is applied to those who steal bandwidth to send spam, as opposed to legitimate e-mail marketers who send spam.

open relay servers
E-mail servers that perform no authentication whatsoever on transmitted e-mail.

NOTE

The posting user may have already been familiar with the term from its original connotation in early Internet chatrooms, which referred to pasting the word "spam" repeatedly into the chat sessions to interrupt the conversation. "Spam" was chosen for this usage in tribute to the Monty Python sketch, "Spam," where the waiter keeps listing menu items that contain various amounts of Spam. Hormel has been gracious about the co-opting of their trademark by the Internet community.

Rather than making any attempt to determine who might want their product, spam marketers simply send an advertisement to every e-mail address they can find. While it is annoying, receiving spam isn't that big of a deal for most people. Consistently using a "spam account" on a public free e-mail provider like Hotmail whenever you have to enter your e-mail address on a website can easily defeat spam. Reserve your "real" e-mail address for sending to people whom you actually know personally.

There are two types of **spammers**. The first is large, legitimate marketing companies who don't care about annoying people and who use their own resources and bandwidth to transmit e-mail. Like any other infrastructure costs, bandwidth and e-mail servers cost money, so these marketers have at least some cost to send e-mail, small as it is. The real plague issues forth from the second type of spammers, the legion smaller illegitimate marketers who steal the greater resources of others like parasites to transmit e-mail. Many unscrupulous e-marketers don't have the equipment or bandwidth required to transmit the massive volumes of e-mail that they want to transmit, so they steal the bandwidth of others. By scanning for mail servers and then testing to see if they can send e-mail back to themselves through the server, spammers identify and target **open relay servers**. Open relays are mail servers that will relay e-mail for anyone, not just those on the local domain, because they haven't been properly secured or because they use obsolete versions of the SMTP service software.

When they find open relays, they send a single message with hundreds or thousands of recipients at a time. They pay only for the bandwidth to transmit a single message with thousands of names, whereas the sender (the exploited relay) pays for the bandwidth to transmit every message. By exploiting open relays, spammers can transmit a few orders of magnitude more spam then their own pipes could handle—at no cost to themselves.

Spam is a common plague on the Internet that occurs because SMTP does not have an authentication mechanism built into the protocol and because most early implementations of mail servers did not validate the source of e-mail transmissions.

Sending spam is not illegal. Exploiting open relays to send spam is. However, like individual hackers, these marketers are difficult to find and even more difficult to prosecute. Because they almost always cross state lines, you have to get the federal government to prosecute them. But because it's difficult to quantify the value of bandwidth or determine how much was stolen, it's difficult to prove that the $5000 threshold has been crossed in order to get FBI attention. So by spreading their crime across many thousands of victims rather than concentrating on a few, relay spammers can avoid prosecution. Most victims never find out, unless they pay for metered bandwidth or have congestion problems so severe that they call in a network analyst to determine what's happening.

Authenticating SMTP

Stopping relay spammers is simple: Close your open relay. A closed relay only sends e-mail that originates from machines that have either authenticated with it by providing credentials or which are assumed to be allowed based on some property like their IP address.

There are numerous effective ways to close relays:

- ◆ Only relay mail for computers in the same domain or an allowed domain list.
- ◆ Only relay mail based on some authentication mechanism.
- ◆ Use a separate service like the web to receive mail content and generate the actual e-mail directly on the mail server.

There's no standard way to authenticate with an SMTP server. Most e-mail servers support a range of authentication methods, and various clients support their own range of methods. Not all clients are compatible with all server methods.

Fortunately, Outlook (the most popular client) is compatible with Sendmail, **qmail**, Exchange, and **Postfix**—the four most popular e-mail servers—using its default AUTH mechanism. The various standard authentication mechanisms are described below.

qmail
A popular e-mail service for Unix systems.

Postfix
A popular and highly secure e-mail service for Unix systems.

297

Host- and Network-Based Authentication

An e-mail server with network-based authentication only relays mail from recipients inside the local IP domain and only receives mail for recipients in the hosted domain list. So, for example, a mail server with an IP address of 10.4.7.3/16 named mail.connetic.net will only send e-mail for hosts with an IP address in the 10.4.0.0/16 network and will only receive e-mail for addresses that end in connetic.net.

Setting up SMTP to reject mail from unknown hosts is relatively easy. In most e-mail systems, you can simply reject relaying for hosts outside your local domain and be done with the problem. Your e-mail server will not relay mail if you set this up.

But you will quickly find that roaming users with laptops or users who work from home won't be able to send mail through your server if you do this. This may not be a big problem: Home users can simply set their SMTP server to be their own ISPs mail server, and roaming users can set their SMTP host to be that of their dial-up ISP. You don't have to use your company's SMTP server to send e-mail.

TIP

Specifications for closing open relays vary for every individual mail server, and some older mail servers cannot be closed and, therefore, must be replaced to avoid exploitation by relay spammers. An exhaustive list of instructions for closing open relays can be found at http://mail-abuse.org/tsi/ar-fix.html.

The remaining users who will have problems are those who travel frequently amongst ISPs. These users may not know the name of their temporary ISP's SMTP server, how to configure their mail client settings, or even which ISP is servicing them. This happens most frequently to traveling executives and sales people, who are least equipped to deal with it and most likely to rely on e-mail. To solve this problem, you need to use authenticated SMTP or perhaps a web mail interface.

Web E-mail Interfaces

Web e-mail interfaces are websites that are integrated with mail servers to provide a site from which users can send and receive e-mail. Web e-mail interfaces are typified by Hotmail, the first really popular public web e-mail site, but they don't have to be public.

You can run one on your own e-mail server to easily provide a web interface for your users. Using a web e-mail interface can provide a reasonably secure mechanism for traveling users to check their mail from their own laptops, the computers of business partners, Internet cafes, handheld web-enabled devices, and anything else that can access the web. They eliminate the need for e-mail client software and custom configurations. They aren't as easy to use as a true client, but they are reasonably secure and can be used from any computer without requiring the user to know anything more than a website URL and their account credentials.

WARNING

Be sure to use SSL rather than unencrypted HTTP for all web e-mail interfaces, as passwords are unencrypted. Also, stay up-to-date on security mailing lists and patches for your web e-mail interface, as these services (like most popular website scripts) have been exploited.

Exchange comes with Outlook Web Access, which is a website that has the look and feel of outlook. Web Mail and the more popular Squirrel Mail are open source alternatives that can be freely downloaded and run on any Unix mail server. These applications solve the SMTP problem by generating mail locally on the e-mail server.

WARNING

Outlook Web Access has been subject to numerous different exploits. Be sure to check Microsoft's security site for Outlook Web Access security problems, solutions, and recommendations before you consider setting it up in your environment.

POP Before SMTP Authentication

The most compatible method used is POP before SMTP authentication (also called SMTP after POP authentication, of course). POP before SMTP is a simple and effective trick that opens up e-mail relaying to any computer IP address that has previously authenticated with the POP service. Basically, it's a simple transitive trust mechanism that assumes that a computer from which a valid POP authentication originated must have a legitimate user operating it. While this isn't always true, it's more than satisfactory for SMTP relay purposes.

Sadly, this simple method doesn't work well with Outlook (the most popular e-mail client), Outlook Express, or Netscape Messenger, because these clients always check SMTP first. This means that users will get an initial error message when Outlook tries to send e-mail, because the server won't relay for them, but they will receive their e-mail. They can subsequently press the Send/Receive button again to send e-mail.

TIP

You can automate POP before SMTP authentication for these clients by creating two e-mail accounts. The second account uses the same settings as the first, but because the check of the first account provided POP authentication, the SMTP service is open for the second account to transmit. Be sure to set the second account as the default SMTP account. You can't avoid the error indication, but you can teach users to ignore it.

Many other e-mail clients can be configured to check SMTP first or natively check POP before transmitting with SMTP and work seamlessly with POP before SMTP authentication.

Systemic Spam Prevention

Systemic spam prevention measures attempt to stop spammers using broad methods that aren't specific to any single server, they attempt to prevent spammers from sending mail in the first place or delete spam that has been sent. Some of these measures attempt to stop spammers from sending mail, others attempt to block mail from open relays assuming that the open relay must have been exploited, and others analyze e-mail to find individual spam that they then block on a message-by-message basis.

Mail Abuse Prevention System

MAPS is a service that scans the web looking for mail servers that are open relays by attempting to transmit an e-mail message back to itself through the mail server. If MAPS receives the e-mail they attempted to send, it adds the mail server's hostname and IP address to its list of open relays.

Mail administrators can subscribe to the MAPS service to receive a copy of their database of open relays (the Realtime Blackhole List), and thereby block e-mail coming from open relays in an attempt to block e-mail that originates from spammers.

In theory, this makes sense. In practice, it's a huge waste of effort. While the idea is noble, the implementation is fundamentally flawed. Simply put, it just doesn't actually work that well.

Firstly, it can take months for the MAPS server to find a mail server that is an open relay. New, unsecured mail servers appear on the Internet by the thousands every day. In those months, you've been getting spam from all these new open relays because MAPS hasn't found them yet. Spammers exploit different mail servers every day. They jump from mail server to mail server like mosquitoes, and they know to avoid mail servers that have been blacklisted by MAPS. The large spam organizations subscribe to MAPS, so they know which servers to remove from their open relay lists!

Secondly, MAPS won't find legitimate spammers that don't exploit open relays; they use their own secured e-mail servers. While MAPS has blacklisted notorious spammers, they can't list everyone, and sending spam is still not a crime unless you exploit open relays. So, because MAPS doesn't stop legitimate spammers, it doesn't stop spam. MAPS has been successfully sued by legitimate spammers who have used the courts to force MAPS to remove them from their spammer's blacklist.

Thirdly, if you subscribe to MAPS, you'll also find that about once per quarter an executive in your company will come to you claiming that some crucial business partner can't send e-mail to him because your e-mail server is blocking mail from them. Why? Because that crucial business partner's e-mail server is (or was) an open relay. Whether or not they are being exploited by relaying spam, they can't send you e-mail, because they are on the MAPS list.

It also takes months of hassle and effort for MAPS to de-list a formerly open relay from their service and distribute that delisting to their clients. This means that having that crucial business partner secure their e-mail server won't mean that you can immediately receive mail from them.

Finally, hosting an open relay isn't a crime, and there are legitimate reasons to do it, especially if you have a lot of traveling users whose e-mail configurations cannot be controlled easily because they use a myriad of different e-mail programs. Clever administrators can prevent spammers from abusing an open rely by detecting "spam-like" bulk mailing activities and then denying the originating host access to the mail server, but they can't stay off the MAPS list, because the MAPS open relay probe is a single message that wouldn't be detected.

Ultimately, open relay blocking lists are not effective in preventing spam, and they cause administrative problems. The hard line "we don't need e-mail from anyone who can't secure their mail server" attitude might strike a chord with technicians, but is your business really willing to lose clients or customers because their mail is hosted on an open relay? Eliminating 50 percent of the spam and 1 percent of your clients is an easy business decision to make. Spam isn't that important—clients are.

There are a number of other blocking lists: Open Relay Blocking System (ORBS), Spam Prevention Early Warning System (SPEWS), and so forth. These services vary in their listing techniques, but they all ultimately suffer from the same set of problems as open relay blocking: They can't block all spammers, and they will block those who are legitimate mailers, sometimes simply for using the same ISP as a known spammer.

Other predictive blockers use reverse DNS lookup and reject mail from mail servers that don't have names, mail servers from foreign nations that the business isn't commercially involved with, or the client networks of consumer ISPs like dial-up providers and cable-modem systems. Reverse DNS blocking is actually a pretty good way to go if you implement it conservatively: Create your own list, and block only those servers that you've received spam from. While this doesn't eliminate spam, it blocks the majority of it, and it doesn't block legitimate businesses.

While it undoubtedly reduces the amount of spam on the Internet, MAPS and similar services are not completely effective, cannot be completely effective, and can cause serious administrative problems for those who have been blacklisted and their business partners. Don't use black listing services unless e-mail isn't a critical tool for your business.

NOTE

I had a client who suddenly became unable to send e-mail to AOL accounts from their business service. Why? Because AOL decided that anyone whose reverse DNS name resolution included the letters "ppp" must be a consumer Internet broadband subscriber sending spam. Because Pac Bell uses PPP over its business grade T1 circuits, AOL rejected e-mail from my client's server. It took three weeks to get the problem resolved by having Pac Bell change the reverse DNS name of the network.

Spam Filters

Spam filters are e-mail relay services that block spam by recognizing bulk mailings across their list of clients. They don't prevent your servers from being exploited to relay spam, they just protect your users from seeing most of it.

Spam filters work by being listed as your primary MX mail receiver on your company's domain name—all your e-mail goes to them. They scan inbound e-mail messages for spam and relay the non-spam messages to your internal e-mail server.

Spam is easy to detect when you host multiple e-mail domains: Any message that appears in numerous inboxes across multiple clients is considered to be spam and is deleted. The more clients the spam filtering service has, the more effective they become at detecting spam and filtering it.

While spam filters don't reduce the amount of spam congesting the Internet at large, they do keep it from clogging your own circuits. Spam filters are probably the best way to eliminate spam without causing ancillary blocking of mail from open relays. They do require you to trust the filter service, however, and because e-mail is normally not encrypted, that can be a very risky proposition for organizations that are concerned with communications security.

Spam filters vary widely in their effectiveness, and I can't personally recommend them ,because I've never used them. But you can find a number of these services by searching Google for "spam prevention."

SMTP Port Blocking by ISPs

Many ISPs that cater to the end-user market have begun firewalling outbound SMTP traffic, blocking it at the firewall and forcing users within their networks to use the ISPs own SMTP servers if they want to send mail. This prevents their clients from being spammers, because they can't reach servers outside the ISPs network, so they can't send spam. This tactic is now used by every major national dial-up ISP (even by Earthlink, who claims to give you the unfiltered Internet), nearly all cable-modem providers, Satellite broadband providers, and many consumer DSL providers. Business-grade providers never implement SMTP port blocking, because most businesses use their own SMTP servers.

SMTP port blocking is not implemented by ISPs out of some sense of concern for the Internet community; it's implemented to reduce the amount of traffic that the ISP has to carry. While it's effective in preventing the least sophisticated tier of spammers from operating, it only takes a slightly more sophisticated spammer to purchase business-grade DSL for about twice as much as residential cable-modem service, and business-grade DSL won't have SMTP blocking. Spammers trade information about which ISPs do and don't block SMTP, so anyone who cares about spamming will just move to a different ISP.

For you, SMTP port blocking will be an annoyance. Traveling users will be unable to connect to your mail server and unable to transmit mail unless they configure their SMTP server to match the ISP. The easiest way around this problem is to implement a web e-mail interface and teach users how to use it. There are no simple options otherwise.

Review Questions

1. What problems can e-mail encryption cause?

   _____

2. What feature of e-mail causes the majority of security risks?

   _____

3. What is the most commonly implemented form of e-mail encryption?

   _____

4. Besides privacy, what other important security function does e-mail encryption provide?

   _____

5. Why is it possible to forge e-mail?

   _____

6. How common are e-mail viruses?

   _____

7. Can your e-mail server solve all possible e-mail security problems?

   _____

8. What is the most secure method of dealing with attachments?

   _____

9. What is the most practical method of stripping e-mail attachments for most users?

   _____

10. What can be done to provide attachment security for proprietary e-mail servers that cannot be configured to strip attachments?

_____

11. What's the most practical method of attachment security for most organizations?

_____

12. What e-mail clients are more susceptible to e-mail viruses?

_____

13. What is spam?

_____

14. What mechanism does illegal spammers exploit to send spam?

_____

15. How do you close an open relay?

_____

16. What is the problem with spam blocking lists?

_____

17. How do ISPs prevent their clients from sending spam?

_____

Terms to Know
- ❏ Postfix
- ❏ Practical Extraction and Reporting Language (Perl)
- ❏ Pretty Good Privacy (PGP)
- ❏ qmail
- ❏ relay server
- ❏ rooted
- ❏ Secure Multipurpose Internet Mail Extensions (S/MIME)
- ❏ Sendmail
- ❏ Simple Mail Transfer Protocol (SMTP)
- ❏ spam
- ❏ spammers
- ❏ web of trust

Chapter

15

Intrusion
Detection

If someone broke into your network, how would you know? There wouldn't be any muddy footprints. There wouldn't be any broken glass. If you had a strong firewall that has good logging capabilities, you might find evidence of an attack in your logs, but a smart hacker can even get around that.

To see what's really going on, you need an intrusion detection system. These systems watch for the telltale signs of hacking and alert you immediately when they occur. They are a necessary component of any truly secure network.

In this chapter, you will learn about:

 Securing your network against attacks your firewall can't prevent

 Determining when you've been attacked

 Assessing the scope of the damage of a successful attack

 Saving money by using intrusion detection techniques that don't require costly specialized software

Intrusion Detection Systems

Intrusion detection systems (IDS) are software systems that detect intrusions to your network based on a number of telltale signs. **Active IDS** attempt to either block attacks, respond with countermeasures, or at least alert administrators while the attack progresses. **Passive IDS** merely log the intrusion or create **audit trails** that are apparent after the attack has succeeded.

While passive systems may seem lackluster and somewhat useless for preventing attacks, there are a number of intrusion indicators that are only apparent after an intrusion has taken place. For example, if a disgruntled network administrator for your network decided to attack, he'd have all the keys and passwords necessary to log right in. No active response system would alert you to anything. Passive IDS systems can still detect the changes that an administrator makes to system files, deletions, or whatever mischief has been caused.

Widespread hacking and the deployment of automated worms like Code Red and Nimda into the wild have created a sort of **background radiation** of hacking attempts on the Internet—there's a constant knocking on the door, and teeming millions of script kiddies looking to try their warez out on some unsuspecting default Windows or aging RedHat installation.

My company's intrusion detection system routinely logs hundreds of automated hacking attempts every day and at least 10 or so perpetrated by humans.

This means that any intrusion detection system is going to log numerous attempts all the time. You will need to tune your filters to ignore threats that you know you aren't vulnerable to so that you aren't overwhelmed searching through your logs for events that mean that you're being targeted. You might as well not bother with an intrusion detection system if it cries wolf all the time and you learn to ignore it.

Inspectors

Inspectors are the most common type of IDS. These intrusion detectors observe the activity on a host or network and make judgments about whether an intrusion is occurring or has occurred based either on programmed rules or on historical indications of normal use. The intrusion detectors built into firewalls and operating systems as well as most commercially available independent intrusion detectors are inspection based.

intrusion detection system (IDS)
Systems that detect unauthorized access to other systems.

active IDS
An intrusion detection system that can create responses, such as blocking network traffic or alerting on intrusion attempts.

passive IDS
IDS that record information about intrusions but which do not have the capability of acting on that information.

audit trail
A log of intrusion detection events that can be analyzed for patterns or to create a body of evidence.

background radiation
The normal, mostly futile, hacking activity caused by automated worms and script kiddies.

Intrusion detectors rely upon indications of inappropriate use. These indicators include:

⬥ Network traffic, like ICMP scans, port scans, or connections to unauthorized ports.

⬥ Signatures of known common attacks like worms or buffer overruns.

⬥ Resource utilization, such as CPU, RAM, or Network I/O surges at unexpected times. This can indicate an automated attack against the network.

⬥ File activity, including newly created files, modifications to system files, changes to user files, or the modification of user accounts or security permissions.

Inspectors monitor various combinations of those telltale signs and create log entries. The body of these log entries is called an audit trail, which consists of the sum of observed parameters for a given accessed object like a user account or a source IP address. **Auditors** can monitor the audit trails to determine when intrusions occur.

IDS systems always require system resources to operate. Network IDS systems usually run on firewalls, public hosts, or dedicated computers; resource utilization usually isn't a problem, because resources are available on these machines. Host-based IDS systems designed to protect interior servers can be a serious impediment, however.

Inspectors can only detect known intrusion vectors, so new types of intrusions cannot be detected. Auditors stand a better chance of detecting unknown intrusion vectors, but they cannot detect them until after the fact, and there's no guarantee that unknown attacks will be detected.

Inspectors suffer from the same set of problems as virus scanners—you can't detect attacks until their patterns are known. You can think of them as virus scanners for network streams.

However, unlike viruses, useful hacks are somewhat limited in their scope and far more predictable in nature. Contests have emerged among ethical hackers to find new unique hacks and immediately publish their signatures. This sort of preemptory hacking is becoming quite popular as a past time among those who practice hacking as an art rather than a crime, and their product helps to secure networks before they can be hacked.

inspectors
IDS that detect intrusions by searching all incoming data for the known signature patterns of hacking attempts.

auditors
IDS that simply record changes made to a system.

Because of their limitations, IDS systems generally require monitoring by human security administrators to be effective. So much hacking activity occurs as a normal course of business these days that security administrators are really only looking for things they've never seen before or indications that they are being specifically attacked. Countermeasure technology and response systems that temporarily increase the host's security posture during attacks are all in the theoretical research stage. Current IDS systems rely upon alerting human administrators to the presence of an attack, which makes human administrators an active part of the intrusion detection system.

decoys
IDS that detect intrusions by mimicking actual systems and alerting on any use.

honey pots
Decoy IDS, especially those that are sanitized installations of actual operating systems, as opposed to software that mimics actual systems.

Decoys

Decoy IDS (also called **honey pots**) operate by mimicking the expressive behavior of a target system, except instead of providing an intrusion vector for the attacker, they alarm on any use at all. Decoys look just like a real target that hasn't been properly secured.

When a hacker attacks a network, they perform a fairly methodical series of well-known attacks like address range scans and port scans to determine which hosts are available and which services those hosts provide. By providing decoy hosts or services, you can seduce the hacker into attacking a host or service that isn't important to you and which is designed to alert on any use at all.

Decoys may operate as a single decoy service on an operative host, a range of decoy services on an operative host, a decoy host, or an entire decoy network.

TIP

Rather than spending effort on decoy services, you should simply establish an entire decoy host. It's much easier and far more effective at catching actual intrusion attempts.

You can establish an effective decoy host by installing a real running copy of the operating system of your choice on a computer with all normal services active. Using your firewall's NAT port forwarding service, send all access to your public domain name to the decoy machine by default. Then add rules to move specific ports to your other service computers; for example, translate only port 80 to your actual Web server.

When a hacker scans your site, he'll see all the services provided by your decoy host plus the services you actually provide on your Internet servers as if they all came from the same machine. Because the services running on the decoy host include services that are easy to attack, like the NetBIOS or NFS ports, the hacker will be immediately attracted to them. You can then set up alarms to alert on any access to those services using the operating system's built-in tools. You'll be secure in the knowledge that if the hacker intrudes into the system, he'll be on a system that contains no proprietary information. You can then let the attack progress to identify the methods the attacker uses to intrude into your system. I suggest installing an inspector-based IDS on the decoy host so you can keep logs of specific packet-based attacks as well.

Decoy hosts are highly secure because they shunt actual attacks away from your service hosts and to hosts that will satisfy the hacker's thirst for conquest, giving you plenty of time to respond to the attack. The hacker will be thrilled that he was able to break into a system and will be completely unaware of the fact that he's not on your real Internet server until he browses around for a while. You might even consider creating a bogus "cleaned" copy of your Web site on the decoy server to maintain the illusion in the hacker's mind that the actual site has been penetrated. Any desecration performed on the decoy site won't show up on your actual site.

Best of all, decoy intrusion detection costs only as much as a copy of the operating system (Linux can mimic any professional Unix server for free), target hardware, and your existing firewall. You won't have to pay for esoteric software.

TIP

Don't have spare computers lying around? Use VMware (www.vmware.com) to create a virtual intrusion detection host system that runs on your actual host, but absorbs attacks into a virtual sanitized environment that won't affect your main machine. You won't even need a second OS license, because operating systems are licensed per processor and your virtual host will be running on the same processor. Use the host's own NAT service to forward all ports to the virtual machine except those used specifically for servicing legitimate clients. Configure the virtual machine to use non-persistent disk mode so that any changes made by a successful hacker or virus can be eliminated by rebooting the virtual machine—all while your host machine remains online.

Auditors

Audit-based intrusion detectors simply keep track of everything that normal users do (at least those things that concern security) in order to create an audit trail. This audit trail can be examined whenever hacking activity is suspected.

Audit-based intrusion detectors take a number of forms, from built-in operating system audit policies that can be configured to record password changes to software that records changes in critical system files that should never be changed to systems that record every packet that flows over a network.

Sophisticated audit-based systems attempt to increase the value of the audit trail by automatically examining it for the tell-tale signs of intrusion. These vary from system to system, but typically involve looking for **red flag** activities like changing an administrative account password, and then examining the activities that surround that event. If, for example, a password change were followed quickly by a system file change, the intrusion detector would raise the alert.

red flag
A simple detected event that has a very high probability of being a real hacking attempt with serious consequences, as opposed to a normal administrative event or background radiation.

Available IDS Systems

Only a few reliable intrusion detection systems really exist, and that number has only been dwindling in recent years as IDS vendors fail to convince clients that intrusion detection is worth spending money on. The nail in the coffin for commercial vendors is the success of free systems like Tripwire and Snort, which work far better than commercial offerings and are open-source. But what's bad for the industry is good for you, since you can now deploy a robust intrusion detection system for free.

Firewalls with logging and alerting mechanisms are by far the most widely deployed, and the majority of those have no way to respond to an attack in any automated fashion.

Both Windows and Unix have strong logging and auditing features embedded in their file systems. Windows also has an exceptionally strong performance monitoring subsystem that can be used to generate real-time alerts to sudden increases in various activities. This allows you to create simple IDS systems for your servers without adding much in the way of hardware.

auditing
The process of recording the use of resources in an automated system for the purpose of subsequent inspection.

Windows System

Windows has strong operating system support for reporting object use. This support manifests in the performance monitoring and auditing capabilities of the operating system and in the fact that the file system can be updated with date-time stamps each time certain types of access occur. These capabilities make strong inherent security easy to perform.

File System and Security Auditing

Windows has exceptionally strong support for file system and security **auditing**. You can configure Windows using the group policies to create log entries in the security log each time any one of the following events succeeds or fails:

- ◇ Logon attempts
- ◇ File or object access, such as copying or opening a file
- ◇ Use of special rights, such as backing up the system
- ◇ User or group management activities, such as adding a user account
- ◇ Changes to the security policy
- ◇ System restart or shutdown
- ◇ Process tracking, such as each time a certain program is run

What all this means is that you can create your own intrusion detection software simply by configuring Windows to audit any sort of behavior that could indicate an intrusion attempt.

Pervasive audit policies can slow down a Windows server dramatically, so you have to be careful of how wide ranging your audits are in systems that are already under load. Audit unusual events, such as the use of user rights, user logon and logoff, security policy changes, and restarts.

File and object access is a special case in auditing. You have to enable file and object auditing and then use the security tab of each file or folder's property panel to enable auditing for specific files. This allows you to limit the files that you audit. For system files, you should audit for writes, changes, and deletes. For proprietary or secret information you store, you should audit read access.

File and object access occurs constantly, so if you audit a large number of commonly used files, you'll increase the amount of chaff (useless information) in your log files and slow down your computer. Audit only those files that are real intrusion targets, like the system files and your proprietary information.

There is a problem with Windows' audit policy: If a hacker actually gains administrative control of your system, the hacker is free to erase your audit trail after it has been changed.

Tripwire

Tripwire scans files and directories on Unix systems to create a snapshot record of their size, date, and signature hash. If you suspect an intrusion in the future, Tripwire will re-scan your server and report any changed files by comparing the file signatures to the stored records. Tripwire was an open-source project of Purdue University, but it continues development as a licensed package of Tripwire Security Systems, at www.tripwiresecurity.com. The maintained open-source version is at www.tripwire.org.

Snort

Snort (www.snort.org) is an open-source intrusion detection system that relies upon raw packet capture (sniffing) and attack signature scanning to detect an extremely wide array of attacks. Snort is widely considered to be the best available intrusion detection system because of the enormous body of attack signatures that the open source community has created for it. The fact that it's free and cross platform pretty much ensures that the commercial IDS systems won't develop much beyond where they are now. Snort was originally developed for Unix and has been ported to Windows.

WARNING

Snort relies upon an open-source packet capture driver that does not currently support multiprocessor machines. If your public hosts are multiprocessor machines, you'll have to use a dedicated single processor snort host for intrusion detection.

sensor
Intrusion detection software designed to run directly on public hosts and which reports to a central management station.

Configuring snort and writing attack-sensing scripts is no trivial task, but the website provides a wealth of information for the intrepid administrator to plow through. And a Snort community has arisen that allows you to simply download detection scripts for every known hacking methodology there is, much like you would download updates for a virus scanner.

The most important thing to consider when deploying Snort is where to place your **sensors** (Snort installations) to determine when attacks are occurring. You could place them outside your firewall, in your DMZ, on your public hosts, and on the interior of your network. In practice, that's more than you need.

Placing a sensor outside your network is a waste of time, unless you just want to see what's out there for the sake of curiosity. You'll pick up a lot of background radiation that's meaningless because it didn't penetrate your firewall anyway. Avoid looking through a lot of meaningless scripts by not bothering to sense attacks on the public Internet.

You definitely want to place a snort sensor in your DMZ. The best way is to use a hub and attach a dedicated machine running snort along side your public sites. This way, the public machines don't have to run snort, and your dedicated machine can handle everything. If you can't use a hub because of bandwidth constraints, you'll have to run snort on each of your public properties in order to detect intrusions. This is because switches direct traffic to the specific host that is addressed, so a snort sensor on the switch won't see that traffic. It's easier to place a small hub on the firewall's DMZ port and connect only your switch and the snort machine to the hub, which won't affect your switching and will allow Snort to detect intrusions across your entire DMZ.

Finally, you should place at least one snort sensor on a hub inside your network so you can trap any events that make it through your firewall. Even if you used a switched environment, I recommend placing a small high-performance hub between your firewall's private interface and your interior switches so that you can attach a snort sensor in stealth mode. It won't affect your bandwidth since the snort sensor won't be transmitting on the network, and you'll be able to sense everything that makes it through the firewall.

Don't bother placing snort sensors on all of your internal servers. You only need to sense traffic coming in through your firewalls, unless you seriously believe there are hackers active on the interior of your network (as there would be at a university or on an ISP's network, for example).

So, to recap, you only need a snort sensor in your DMZ and in your private network. If you can't use a snort sensor in your DMZ due to switching constraints or because you don't have a DMZ, put a sensor on every public host.

TIP

Snort can be configured as a "Stealth" IDS by simply setting it up on an interface that doesn't have an IP address. This interface will receive traffic that can be sniffed, but won't respond to any IP traffic.

Demarc PureSecure

Demarc PureSecure (www.demarc.com) is a best-of-breed network monitoring and intrusion detection system descended from Snort. PureSecure is a commercial product that uses Snort as its intrusion detector, but it adds typical network monitoring functions like CPU, network, memory, disk load, ping testing, and service monitoring to the sensors that run on every host.

Demarc creates a web-based client/server architecture where the sensor clients report back to the central Demarc server, which runs the reporting website. By pointing your web browser at the Demarc server, you get an overview of the health of your network in one shot.

Demarc can be configured to alert on all types of events, so keeping track of your network becomes quite easy. This is why Demarc's summary page is cool.

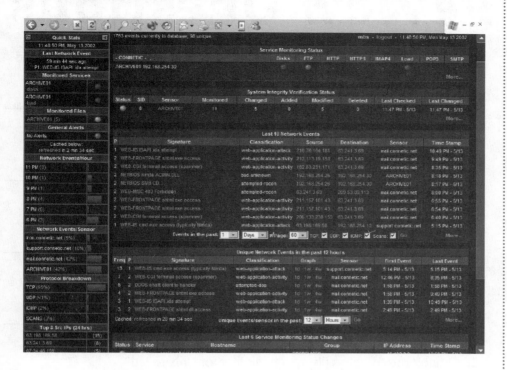

It's quite clever, and well worth its price: $1000 for the monitoring software, plus $100 per sensor.

NFR Network Intrusion Detector

Network Flight Recorder (NFR, www.nfr.com) was one of the first inspector-based intrusion detection systems on the market and was originally offered as a network appliance. Now available as both software and network appliances, NFR has evolved into a commercial product very similar to Snort in its capabilities.

What sets NFR apart from Snort is not the software—it's the company behind it. NFR can consult with you directly to analyze intrusion attempts, to train your staff, and to provide product support for their products. You lose these services when you go with open-source software, because there's no company backing the product.

TIP

NFR provides a free for non-commercial use, simple Decoy intrusion detector called "BackOfficer Friendly" that you can use to catch script kiddies in the act of trying to exploit your home computer.

Review Questions

1. How many automated hacking attempts would be normal against a public site in a 24-hour period?

2. What are the three common types of intrusion detection systems?

3. What common network software are inspectors related to?

4. What software would you use to implement a decoy?

5. What is the common file system auditor for Unix called?

6. What is the most popular intrusion detection system?

7. How many sensors do you need, at a minimum, in an inspector-based intrusion detection system?

Appendix
A

Answers to
Review Questions

Chapter 1

1. Security is the sum of all measures taken to prevent loss of any kind.

2. Security measures fail most often because strong security is an annoyance to users and administrators.

3. Vendors release products they suspect have security flaws because if they spent time to fix it, they would be eclipsed by their non-secure competition who could deliver feature-rich applications faster.

4. Two operating systems make up 90% of the market, Windows and Unix.

5. The number of computer security incidents is increasing at 50% per year.

6. Computers weren't originally designed with security in mind, because security requires compute power, which was precious in the early days of computing.

7. Hacking began to occur in earnest between 1975–1985.

8. Public Key Encryption was invented in 1975.

9. Before the Internet, hackers shared information primarily via bulletin-board systems (BBS).

10. Applications whose creators stop to consider security will come to market more slowly and therefore fail to gain the requisite market share for widespread adoption as a standard.

11. The process of determining the identity of a user is called authentication.

12. The first user is implicitly trusted to be the owner.

13. Biometric authentication is the most secure form of authentication so long as it is implemented correctly and cannot be replayed or spoofed.

14. Permissions-based access control can be circumvented by shutting down the section of the operating system that interprets permissions.

15. Strong encryption-based access control cannot be exploited using computational methods.

Chapter 2

1. The most common type of hackers are script kiddies.

2. The most likely type of hackers to affect a business are disgruntled employees.

3. The most damaging type of hackers are disgruntled employees.

4. Hackers can use direct intrusion, dial-up, Internet, or wireless methods to connect to a network.

5. The Internet is the most common vector used by hackers.

6. The phases of a hacking section are target selection, information gathering, and attack.

7. Scanning enables a hacker to find random targets.

8. A port scan indicates that a hacker has specifically targeted your systems for attack.

9. Worms use service scanning to find targets.

10. Sniffing refers to the activity of examining the uninterpreted contents of packets directly.

11. The simplest type of attack is a denial-of-service attack.

12. There are no security mechanisms employed by e-mail to prevent forgery.

13. A hacker would use a Trojan horse to install a backdoor program that would allow further access.

14. Currently, the most serious hacking threat is the use of buffer overruns in service applications.

Chapter 3

1. Encryption is used to keep secrets.

2. Secret key encryption is considered "symmetrical" because the same key is used on both ends of the communication.

3. A hash is the result of a one-way function that is used to validate the contents of a larger plain text or verify knowledge of a secret without transmitting the secret itself.

4. Hashing algorithms are most commonly used to encrypt passwords.

5. Public key encryption is asymmetrical; it uses two different keys to encode and decode plain text; whereas secret key encryption uses the same key to encode and decode.

6. Public key encryption solves the dilemma of secure key exchange.

7. The major problem with public key encryption is that it is much slower than secret key encryption.

8. A hybrid cryptosystem uses public key encryption to securely exchange secret keys, and then uses secret key encryption for subsequent encryption.

9. Authentication is used to determine the identity of a user.

10. Challenge/response authentication is used to prevent replay attacks.

11. Using unpredictable sequence numbers secures sessions against hijacking.

12. Pseudorandom numbers appear to be random, but occur in a predefined sequence.

13. A digital signature is identity information that can be decoded by anyone but only encoded by the holder of a specific key.

14. A certificate is a digital signature that has been digitally signed by a trusted authority.

15. Biometric authentication includes the use of fingerprints, speech patterns, facial features, retinal patterns, and DNA.

Chapter 4

1. A security policy describes security rules for your computer systems and defends against all known threats.

2. The first step in establishing a security policy is to establish functional requirements, features, and security requirements.

3. Automated security policies avoid the weakness of having to be enforced by humans.

4. An appropriate use policy allows users to understand their security responsibilities.

5. Users should not be required to change passwords often; rather, they should select extremely strong passwords which can be relied upon for much longer periods of time than simple passwords.

6. 8 characters should be the minimum length of a password in today's environment.

7. Enforcing password lockout after failed attempts prevents automated password guessing.

8. Execution environments are dangerous because they can be exploited to propagate viruses and Trojan horses.

9. Java is limited to a sandbox environment, which while not perfect, is far more secure than the unlimited ActiveX execution environment.

10. Digital signatures are only a means of verification; They do not perform any security function beyond attesting that content has not been modified and that it originates from a known source.

Chapter 5

1. Firewalls are derived from routers.

2. The most important border security measure is to control every crossing.

3. Your effective border security is the lowest common denominator amongst the policies enforced by your various firewalls.

4. A DMZ is a network segment with a relaxed security policy where public servers are partitioned away from the interior of the network.

5. It's better to deny by default because a new protocol (used by a Trojan horse) may crop up that you aren't aware of that would then have free access to your network if you only blocked known threats.

6. Packet filtering was the original firewall function.

7. NAT was originally developed to conserve public IP addresses.

8. There's no way to address computers directly since the public address connection has to use the IP address of the NAT itself.

9. Malformed TCP/IP packet attacks are blocked by terminating and regenerating the TCP/IP connection for all protocols that flow through them.

Chapter 6

1. The three fundamental methods implemented by VPNs are encapsulation, authentication, and encryption.

2. Encapsulation is embedding a complete packet within another packet at the same networking layer.

3. VPNs can be established wherever an IP connection to the Internet exists, without the necessity of coordinating with outside organizations.

4. Transport mode does not provide encapsulation, whereas tunnel mode does.

5. IKE enables cryptographic key exchange with encryption and authentication protocol negotiation between VPN endpoints.

6. Use the same (or the fewest possible) ISP for all VPN endpoints.

7. The most common VPN protocol is IPSec with IKE.

8. L2TP separates the physical device used to answer a connection from the device that recreates the original stream.

9. No algorithm is specified for L2TP. Microsoft's implementation uses IPSec to perform the encryption.

Chapter 7

1. VPN connections are potentially dangerous because the VPN endpoint could be exploited, allowing the attacker to use the VPN to penetrate the firewall.

2. Laptops are easy to steal and may contain all the information necessary to connect to the company's network.

3. Laptops the most likely source of virus infection in a protected network because they are frequently connected to other networks that may not be well protected.

4. 57% of corporate crimes have been traced back to stolen laptops.

5. Personal Firewall application software should be used to protect laptops from hacker.

6. Using NAT devices or light firewall devices is the best way to protect home computers from hackers.

7. Encrypting documents stored on the laptop reduce the risk posed by lost information when the laptop is stolen.

8. Storing data on removable flash media in encrypted form that is not stored with the laptop is the best way to prevent the loss of data from a damaged or stolen laptop.

9. No. Opening a single secure protocol to direct access is usually more secure than allowing open access to VPN clients.

Chapter 8

1. Hackers write viruses.

2. No. Pure data can be corrupted by a virus, but only executable code can contain a virus.

3. No. All viruses waste computer resources, but many have no other effect than to propagate.

4. A worm is a virus that propagates without human action.

5. No. Only applications that allow you to write macros and which contain a scripting host powerful enough to allow self-replication are susceptible to viruses.

6. Microsoft Outlook and Outlook Express are susceptible to e-mail viruses.

7. Yes. NT kernel–based operating systems are only immune to executable viruses when run under non-administrative privilege and do not prevent the spread of macro viruses.

8. Inoculators to block an infection and scanners to eliminate dormant viruses are required for total virus defense.

9. You should update virus definitions daily.

10. Anti-virus software is typically installed on clients, servers, and e-mail gateways.

Chapter 9

1. The four major causes for loss are human error, routine failure, crimes, and environmental events.

2. Having a good archiving policy is the best way to recover from the effects of human error.

3. The hard disk is the most likely component to fail in a computer.

4. The hard disk is the most difficult component to replace in a computer.

5. Deployment testing is the easiest way to avoid software bugs and compatibility problems.

6. Using multiple circuits from different ISPs will help you recover from a circuit failure.

7. Strong border security, permissions security, and offline backup are the best ways to minimize the damage caused by hackers.

8. Tape backups are the most common form of fault tolerance.

9. An incremental backup contains all the files changed since the last incremental backup, while a differential backup contains the files changed since the last full system backup.

10. Humans cause the majority of failures in a tape backup system.

11. RAID-0 actually makes failure more likely rather than less likely.

12. RAID-1 and RAID-0 are combined in RAID-10.

13. Since you have to leave 1 disk for parity information, the storage available would be (5-1) × 36GB = 144GB.

14. Physically moving offline backup media to another location and transmitting data to another facility via a network are the two methods used to perform offsite storage.

15. Backup is the process of making a copy of every file for the purpose of restoration. Archiving is the process of retaining a copy of every version of all files created by users for the purpose of restoring individual files in case of human error.

16. The two common types of clustering are fail-over clustering and load balancing.

Chapter 10

1. Mandatory user logon is the foundation of security in Windows.

2. The local computer accounts are stored in the registry.

3. Security Identifiers (SIDs) represent user accounts.

4. The WinLogon process manages the login process.

5. Kerberos is used to authenticate user accounts in Windows 2000 domains.

6. The user's identity is passed to running programs by the inheritance of the access token from the launching program.

7. The LSA compares your access token to the object's security descriptor (Access Control List) in order to determine whether or not you should have access.

8. An object's owner has the right to change the object's permissions irrespective of a user's permissions to the object.

9. The System Access Control List is used too audit various types of access to an object.

10. Rights affect many or all objects, whereas permissions are specific to each object.

11. Inheritance refers to objects receiving of a copy of the containing folder's ACL when they are created.

12. User accounts are stored in the Active Directory.

13. Yes. In Kerberos, trusts transit domain relationships.

14. Group policy is the primary mechanism for controlling the configuration of client computers in Windows.

15. Yes. Early policy changes are overwritten by later policy changes when multiple policies are applied.

16. Yes. Share security works on FAT file system shares.

Chapter 11

1. Unix was originally designed not to include rigorous security in order to solve problems that didn't require high level security.

2. AT&T gave UNIX away in the beginning, because their monopoly agreement with the U.S. government prevented them from selling software.

3. AT&T essentially lost control of its development of Unix when they gave it away to Universities in the 1970's. They also licensed it to numerous hardware developers who modified it as they saw fit. Finally, hackers created their own version using the Internet, and the result is a variety of variations.

4. The file system represents and controls every system object in Unix.

5. File system permissions are the primary security mechanism in Unix.

6. File inodes store permissions in Unix.

7. Unix user account information is stored in the /etc/passwd file.

8. Permissions are not checked for the root user in Unix.

9. The GID of the wheel or superuser group is 0.

10. Read, Write, and Execute are the basic permissions that can be set in an inode.

11. Typically, the chmod and chown commands are used to modify ownership and permissions on an inode.

12. Having an executable's SetUID flag enabled means that it runs under the user account context of the file's owner rather than the logged on user that executes it.

13. Nothing. Daemons are standard executables that run using SetUID permissions.

Chapter 12

1. There is no standard file-sharing mechanism for UNIX, because UNIX was developed before Local Area Networks made file sharing popular.

2. Secure Shell (SSH) is the most secure protocol for remotely logging on to a Unix computer.

3. SMTP has no authentication mechanisms.

4. PAM provides a standardized method for services to authenticate users against a wide array of authentication mechanisms.

5. NIS provides no encryption.

6. Kerberos uses Secret Key encryption.

7. File sharing protocols are capable of transmitting segments of files and allowing multiple users to access files simultaneously. FTP does not have these capabilities.

8. Yes, Samba passwords are encrypted by default in Windows, and encryption can be enabled in Samba and most other SMB implementations.

9. TCP Wrappers provides protection by replacing the service executable with a service that first authenticates the source of the connection, and then allows access to the service.

10. IPChains and IPTables provide TCP/IP packet filtering.

11. FWTK provides protocol level filtering and a proxy service.

Chapter 13

1. Microsoft Internet Information Services and Apache serve over 90 percent of the public Internet.

2. The bugs in the operating system or web server software are the most threatening security problems for public web servers.

3. Closed source and open source operating systems are about equally secure.

4. Apache is both theoretically and operationally more secure than IIS.

5. Websites should only be deployed on dedicated web servers, because general purpose servers are more likely to be exploited, and you could loose valuable information stored by other services if you run public websites on them.

6. Bugs are most likely found in sections of programs that implement rarely used or esoteric features.

7. SSL encrypts web data flowing between the browser and the server.

8. You can secure intranet servers by placing them inside a VPN and not making them public.

9. The universal encrypted authentication mechanism is using SSL to secure basic authentication.

10. Configure Apache by editing the `/etc/httpd/conf/httpd.conf` file.

11. In Perl, taint is a marker that indicates that data has been typed in by a user and should not be trusted.

Chapter 14

1. Encrypted e-mail cannot be stripped of attachments or scanned for viruses by mail servers.

2. Attachments causes the majority of security risk for e-mail systems.

3. Secure Multipurpose Internet Mail Extensions (S/MIME) is the most common implementation of e-mail encryption.

4. E-mail encryption provides authentication in addition to privacy.

5. It is possible to forge e-mail, because there is no standard SMTP authentication mechanism.

6. E-mail viruses are very common. E-mail is the most common propagation mechanism for viruses.

7. Private e-mail servers cannot solve all possible e-mail security problems. Clients that check outside e-mail servers are still a threat.

8. The most secure method of dealing with attachments is to strip them and discard them at the e-mail server.

9. The most practical method of stripping e-mail attachments is to allow only approved types of attachments to be passed through the mail server.

10. By relaying the e-mail through an open-source e-mail server that can be configured to strip attachments, you can provide attachment security for proprietary e-mail servers.

11. Allowing only approved attachment types is the most practical method of attachment security for most organizations.

12. Outlook and Outlook Express are more susceptible to e-mail viruses than other e-mail clients.

13. Spam is unwanted, unsolicited e-mail.

14. Illegal spammers use open relays, relays that will relay mail from any host rather than just hosts within their own domain, to send spam.

15. To close an open relay, require some form of authentication from those who want to send e-mail to a domain other than your own and who originate from outside your network.

16. Spam blocking lists can't block all spam, and they do block a small percentage of legitimate e-mail.

17. ISPs prevent their clients from sending spam by blocking SMTP access to all mail servers except their own.

Chapter 15

1. Hundreds of hacking attempts a day are normal for a public site.

2. Inspectors, decoys, and auditors are common intrusion detection systems.

3. Virus scanners are similar to inspectors.

4. A standard operating system and service software is all you need to implement a decoy.

5. Tripwire is the common file system auditor for Unix.

6. Snort is the most popular IDS.

7. You need at least two sensors in an inspector-based IDS; one in your DMZ and one in your private network.

Appendix

B

Glossary

Access Control Entry (ACE)

An entry in an Access Control List that joins a security identifier to a type of allowed or denied access.

access token

A combination of security identifiers that represents the user account and the security groups that it belongs to. Access tokens are passed from the initial logon to all user-mode programs executed subsequently.

Active Directory

A database that is distributed amongst the domain controllers in a domain or tree that contains user accounts, machine accounts, and other administrative information concerning the network.

active IDS

An intrusion detection system that can create responses, such as blocking network traffic or alerting on intrusion attempts.

ActiveX

An execution environment for the Microsoft Internet Explorer web browser and Windows applications that allow code to be delivered over the Internet and executed on the local machine.

algorithm

A method expressed in a mathematical form (such as computer code) for performing a specific function or operation.

America Online (AOL)

A popular graphical BBS system that has transformed into the largest consumer Internet service provider. Due to its non-Internet origins, AOL uses a proprietary e-mail mechanism that (among other things) does not support true MIME attachments or use standard ports for transmitting e-mail.

AppleTalk

The protocol over which the AppleShare proprietary file and resource sharing mechanism for Apple Macintosh computers ran before Apple adopted TCP/IP. Recent versions of the Mac OS are also compatible with the Windows (SMB) file-sharing protocol.

application

Software that allows users to perform their work, as opposed to software used to manage systems, entertain, or perform other utility functions. Applications are the reason that systems are implemented.

appropriate use policy

A policy that explains how humans are allowed to use a system.

archive marking

A method used by operating systems to indicate when a file has been changed and should thus be included in an incremental backup.

archiving

The process of retaining a copy of every version of files created by users for the purpose of restoring individual files in case of human error.

asymmetrical algorithm

A mathematical function which has no reciprocal function.

Asynchronous Transfer Mode (ATM)

A packet-switched data link–layer framing protocol used for high-speed digital circuits that is compatible across a wide range of physical circuit speeds. ATM is typically used for inter-city and metropolitan area circuits.

attachment

A file encoded in text form for transmission/insertion in an e-mail message, such as a word.doc or picture.jpg file.

audit trail

A log of intrusion detection events that can be analyzed for patterns or to create a body of evidence.

auditing

The process of recording the use of resources in an automated system for the purpose of subsequent inspection.

auditors

IDS that simply record changes made to a system.

authentication

The process of determining a user's identity in order to allow access.

background radiation

The normal, mostly futile, hacking activity caused by automated worms and script kiddies.

benign viruses

Viruses that do not destroy data. Benign viruses simply propagate without performing any other function.

Berkeley Software Distribution (BSD)

A highly customized version of Unix, originally distributed by the University of California at Berkeley.

biometric authentication

Authentication by means of invariant and unique biological characteristics such as fingerprints or DNA.

BIOS (Basic Input/Output System)

The low-level program built into the computer's motherboard that is used to configure hardware and load the operating system.

block devices

Peripherals that transfer mass quantities of information in large units (i.e., processing occurs for each large block of information received, rather than for every byte). Block devices are typically high-speed devices like hard disk drives or local area network adapters.

boot sector

The first executable code stored on a disk, which is used to load the operating system.

brute-force attack

An attack where every possible combination of values is tried in sequence against a password system. Given an infinite amount of time, these attacks will always succeed, but they are impractical against long passwords.

bugs

Errors in programming code.

bulletin-board system (BBS)

Use of a single central computer to which many computers have intermittent access to shared information.

call-back security

Dial-up networking security that is implemented by having the main system call the remote user back, thus ensuring that the user attempting to gain access is an authorized one (so long as the phone system remains secure).

certificate

A digital identity that has been digitally signed by one or more trusted authorities.

333

challenge/response

A method used to prove that a party knows a password without transmitting the password in any recoverable form over a network.

character devices

A class of peripherals that transmit or receive information one byte at a time (i.e., processing occurs for each byte received). Typically, character devices are lower speed devices like keyboards, mice, or serial ports.

cipher

A mathematical function used to transform a plain message into a form that cannot be read without decoding it. Ciphers can encode any message.

circuit

In the context of information technology, a circuit is a data network connection between two points, usually different facilities. The term circuit traditionally applies to high capacity telephone trunk lines.

code

An agreed-upon set of symbols that represent concepts. Both parties must be using the same code in order to communicate, and only pre-determined concepts can be communicated.

combination

A numeric code used to open a physical lock.

commercial Internet exchange (CIX)

One of an increasing number of regional datacenters where the various tier-1 ISPs interconnect their private networks via TCP/IP to form the nexus of the Internet.

computer accounts

Security Identifiers that uniquely identify computers in a domain and authenticate their participation in the domain.

computer policy

The portion of a group policy that is applied irrespective of which user account logs on.

content blocking

A security measure that blocks access to websites based on keywords contained in the content.

content signing

The process of embedding a hash in a document or executable code to prove that the content has not been modified, and to identify with certainty the author of the content.

credentials

Information used to prove identity. Typically, this is a combination of a user account name and a password.

cryptography

The study of codes, ciphers, and encryption.

cryptosystem

A computing system that implements one or more specific encryption algorithms.

daemon

An executable in Unix that runs automatically as a service (i.e., with a unique user context) when the computer is booted. Similar to a *service* in Windows.

data

Information that represents some real-world information, like a novel, a picture, a sound, or a bank account. Data is processed by code to create answers that are themselves represented by data and can be further processed.

Data Encryption Standard (DES)

A secret key encryption algorithm developed by IBM, under contract to the U.S. government, for public use.

decoys

IDS that detect intrusions by mimicking actual systems and alerting on any use.

dedicated leased lines

Digital telephone trunk lines leased from a telephone company and used to transmit digitized voice or data. With a true dedicated leased line, circuits are leased and connected together permanently between two points to form a permanent physical circuit.

demilitarized zone (DMZ)

A security zone with a separate, more relaxed security policy that is used to partition public servers like e-mail and web servers away from the Internal network while providing them firewall protection.

deny ACE

An Access Control Entry that specifically denies permissions, in order to override other permissions that might allow access to the account.

dial-up modem bank

A collection of modems connected to a high-speed network that are dedicated to the task of answering calls from the modems of end users, thereby connecting them to the network.

digital signature

Any identity information encrypted with a private key and therefore decryptable using a public key. Digital signatures are used to prove the validity of publicly available documents by proving that they were encrypted with a specific secretly held private key.

directory

A file that contains the names of other files or directories.

Directory Services Agent (DSA)

The service that communicates between the Local Security Authority and the Active Directory in order to authenticate domain users.

Discretionary Access Control List (DACL)

The Access Control List that is used to allow or deny access to an object.

disk packs

Multiple identical hard disk drives configured to store a single volume in a RAID set.

Distributed Computing Environment (DCE)

An early initiative by the Open Software Foundation to provide distributed login mechanism for Unix and Windows. DCE is supported by many commercial Unix distributions and by Windows.

distributed logon

Any client/server protocol for verifying user identity. The purpose of distributed logon services is to allow users to log on once and use their credentials on any machine within the security domain. This provides the illusion of logging into the network as a whole rather than a single computer.

distributions

A specific packaging of a Unix operating system and associated utility files and applications.

document

A work product created by an application that is intended for human interpretation.

domain

A collection of computers that trust the same set of user accounts. Domain accounts are stored in the Active Directory.

electronic mail (e-mail)

A queued message delivery system that allows users to transmit relatively short text messages to other users over the Internet. The messages wait in a mail queue until they are downloaded and read by the ultimate recipient.

encapsulation

The insertion of a complete network layer packet within another packet of the same layer. The encapsulated protocol may or may not be the same as the encapsulating protocol and may or may not be encrypted.

encryption

The process of encoding a plain text message using a cipher so that it cannot be understood by intermediate parties who do not know the key to decrypt it.

end user license agreement (EULA)

A contract between the developer of software and the users of software. The contract limits the user's right to use and distribute the software as specified by the developer.

Exchange

Microsoft's e-mail and messaging server. Exchange was originally designed for private interoffice messaging, with Internet functionality provided as an add-on. It uses the proprietary Microsoft MAPI protocol for exchanging mail between Exchange servers and clients, SMTP for transmitting e-mail on the public Internet, and can be configured to allow POP3, IMAP, and WebMail access as well.

executable code

Information that represents computer instructions. Lists of code (called programs) are executed by a microprocessor in order to perform a function.

execution environments

Any environment that interprets data as actions and performs those actions. An execution environment might be a microprocessor, a virtual machine, or an application that interprets a script or macro.

export

A directory tree that is published by NFS for remote mounting by NFS clients. Analogous to an SMB share.

extensions

Filename suffixes that identify a document type, so that the operating system (and users) can determine which program should be used to interpret the contents of the document.

fail-over clustering

A fault tolerance method where a server can assume the services of a failed server.

fault tolerance

The ability of a system to withstand failure and remain operational.

file

A sequence of data that is permanently stored on a mass-storage device, such as a hard disk, and referenced by a name.

file shares

A directory tree that is published by SMB for remote attachment by SMB clients. Analogous to an NFS export.

file sharing protocol

A protocol that allows a rich set of semantics for serving files to clients. File sharing protocols are distinguished by their ability to provide small portions of files and provide locking mechanisms so that multiple users can write to the file simultaneously.

file synchronization

The process of comparing files in different locations and transmitting the differences between them to ensure that both copies remain the same. Synchronization is only easy if you can guarantee that the two files won't change on both ends at the same time. If they can, then decisions must be made about which version to keep, and it may not be possible to automate the decision-making process depending upon the nature of the information.

File Transfer Protocol (FTP)

A simple protocol that allows the complete transfer of files between servers and clients. File transfer protocols cannot support simultaneous multiple users. File Transfer Protocol is also the name of the oldest and most widely implemented file transfer protocol.

firewall

A gateway device that filters communications between a private network and a public network, allowing only those that respect the company's security policy.

flash memory

A trade name for Electrically Erasable Programmable Read-Only Memory (EEPROM) that can be erased using the same voltage levels with which it can be programmed. Flash memory is non-volatile permanent storage that is exceptionally reliable, and is now used in almost every computing device on the market to store upgradeable boot loaders or operating systems. Flash memory is also used to make a wide variety of convenient memory storage for cameras, PDAs, and laptops in various form factors.

frame relay

A data link layer packet-switching protocol that emulates a traditional point-to-point leased line. Frame Relay allows the telephone companies to create a permanent virtual circuit between any two points on their digital networks by programming routes into their frame relay routers. This way, "frames" can be "relayed" between two end-points without requiring a dedicated leased line between them.

grass-rooted

A trust system that has no hierarchy, instead it relies upon massive participation to provide a transitive trust mechanism that requires no supporting commercial organization.

group policy

A collection of computer and user configuration policies that are applied to computers based upon their association within an Active Directory container like a domain or organizational unit.

hacker

One who engages in hacking.

hacking

The act of attempting to gain access to computers without authorization.

hard links

Multiple file names for a single inode. Hard links allow a single file to exist in multiple places in the directory hierarchy.

hash

The result of applying a one-way function to a value.

honey pots

Decoy IDS, especially those that are sanitized installations of actual operating systems, as opposed to software that mimics actual systems.

hybrid cryptosystem

A cryptosystem that exchanges secret keys using public key encryption to secure the key exchange and then using the higher speed allowed by secret key encryption to transmit subsequent data.

I/O port

An interface to peripherals, like serial devices, printers, etc.

inherit

To receive a copy of security information from the launching program, containing folder, or other such precursor.

inoculator

Anti-virus software that scans data files and executables at the moment they are invoked and which block them from being loaded if they contain a virus. Inoculators can prevent viruses from spreading.

inode (index node)

A file descriptor in Unix systems that describes ownership, permissions, and other metadata about a file.

inspectors

IDS that detect intrusions by searching all incoming data for the known signature patterns of hacking attempts.

Internet Key Exchange (IKE)

A protocol that allows the exchange of IPSec Security Associations based on trust established by knowledge of a private key.

Internet Mail Access Protocol (IMAP)

A client e-mail access protocol typically used in situations where it's appropriate to allow users to leave e-mail on the mail server rather than downloading it to their client computer.

Internetwork Packet Exchange (IPX)

IPX is the routable LAN protocol developed by Novell for their NetWare server operating system. IPX is very similar to TCP/IP, but it uses the data link–layer Media Access Control (MAC) address for unique addressing rather than a user-configured address, and is therefore easier to configure. IPX routes broadcasts around the entire network, and is therefore unsuitable in larger networks.

interpreter

A programming language application that loads scripts as data and then interprets commands step-by-step rather than by compiling them to machine language.

intrusion detection system (IDS)

Systems that detect unauthorized access to other systems.

IPChains

A stateless packet filtering mechanism for Unix kernels.

IPTables

A stateful packet filtering mechanism for Unix kernels.

Java

A cross-platform execution environment developed by Sun Microsystems that allows the same program to be executed across many different operating systems. Java applets can be delivered automatically from web servers to browsers and executed within the web browser's security context.

kerberized

A service or services that has been modified for compatibility with Kerberos.

Kerberos

An authentication protocol that uses secret keys to authenticate users and machines in a networked environment. Kerberos allows for a transitive trust between widely diverse domains, and is the primary authentication protocol for Windows 2000 and many UNIX distributions.

key

A secret value used to encrypt information.

Key Distribution Center (KDC)

In Kerberos, the authentication server that manages user accounts; a domain controller.

key ring

A database of public keys that have been received by a user.

Layer 2 Tunneling Protocol (L2TP)

An industry standard protocol for separating the data link layer transmission of packets from the flow control, session, authentication, compression, and encryption protocols. L2TP is typically used for remote access applications and is the successor to PPP.

lessons learned

A documented failure analysis that is disseminated to system users in order to prevent the same failure from recurring.

Lightweight Directory Access Protocol (LDAP)

A Protocol for accessing service configuration data from a central hierarchical database. LDAP is frequently used to store user account information in Unix and is supported as an access method by Microsoft Active Directory.

load balancing

A clustering mechanism where individual client sessions are connected to any one of a number of identically configured servers, so that the entire load of client sessions is spread evenly amongst the pool of servers.

local area networks (LAN)

High speed short distance networks existing usually within a single building. Computers on the same local area network can directly address one another using data link–layer protocols like Ethernet or Token Ring, and do not require routing in order to reach other computers on the same LAN. The term is becoming somewhat obsolete as routing within networks becomes more common and long distance technologies become faster than LAN technologies.

Local Security Authority (LSA)

The process that controls access to secured objects in Windows.

Locally Unique Identifier (LUID)

An identifier that is created for each logged on instance of a user account to differentiate it from other logon sessions.

lockdown programs

Software designed to automatically configure the security options of an operating system or other application to be optimal for a specific purpose.

logon prompt

The interface through which users identify themselves to the computer.

macro

A list of instructions embedded within a document and stored as data that is interpreted by a scripting host.

macro virus

Viruses that exist in the interpreted code embedded in Office documents. These viruses are not capable of escaping the confines of their interpreted environment, so they cannot infect executables.

Mail Exchanger (MX) Records

DNS entries that identify the host names of e-mail servers for a specific domain.

mainframe

A large and powerful computer that many users share via terminal displays.

malignant viruses

Viruses that contain attack code that performs some malicious act.

Mean Time Between Failures (MTBF)

The average life expectancy of electronic equipment. Most hard disks have an MTBF of about five years.

mount

To connect a file system on a block device to the operating system. The term comes from the act of mounting a reel of tape on a tape reader.

Multics

A complex operating system developed in the 1960s with many innovative concepts, such as multi-tasking. Multics was the precursor to the simpler and more portable Unix.

Multipurpose Internet Mail Extensions (MIME)

An IETF protocol for encoding and transmitting files along with meta-data that determines how the files should be decoded and what applications should be used to interpret them.

NAT routers

Small routers that provide (typically) just the network address translation function of a firewall. Originally used to share a single IP connection for home users, they have recently become more important for home computer security since they are natural firewalls. These devices are frequently marketed as "cable-DSL routers."

nearline

Data that is stored on offline media that can be automatically mounted and made available in a reasonably short period of time without human intervention.

NetBEUI

Microsoft's original networking protocol that allows for file and resource sharing but which is not routable and is therefore limited to operation on a single LAN. As with any protocol, NetBEUI can be encapsulated within a routable protocol to bridge distant networks.

Network Address Translation (NAT)

The process of rewriting the IP addresses of a packet stream as it flows through a router for the purpose of multiplexing a single IP address across a network of interior computers and for hiding internal hosts.

Network File System (NFS)

A widely supported file-sharing protocol developed by Sun Microsystems for use in Unix environments. NFS allows clients to mount portions of a server's file system into their own file systems.

Network Information Service (NIS)

A simple distributed logon mechanism developed by Sun Microsystems for Unix, originally to support single sign-on for NFS.

New Technology File System (NTFS)

The standard file system for Windows that provides secure object access, compression, checkpointing, and other sophisticated file management functions.

New Technology LAN Manager (NTLM)

The network authentication protocol used prior to Kerberos in Windows NT. NTLM is a much simpler authentication protocol that does not support transitive trusts and stores domain user accounts in the SAM of the Primary domain controller.

No Access permission

See *deny ACE.*

objects

Data structures in a computer environment, such as files, directories, printers, shares, and so forth.

offline

Data that is not immediately available to running systems, such as data stored on tape.

one-time passwords

An authentication method that uses synchronized pseudorandom number generation on both the client and the server to prove that both sides know the same original seed number.

one-way function

An algorithm that has no reciprocal function and cannot therefore be reversed in order to discover the data originally encoded.

online

Data that is immediately available to running systems because it is stored on active disks.

open relay servers

E-mail servers that perform no authentication whatsoever on transmitted e-mail.

open source

Software produced by a free association of programmers who have all agreed to make their work available at no cost along with the original source code. Actual licensing terms vary, but generally there are stipulations that prevent the code from being incorporated into otherwise copyrighted software.

operating system

The program that controls the overall operation of a computer.

Outlook

Microsoft's extremely popular, but poorly secured, e-mail client and personal information manager.

Outlook Express

A stripped-down version of Outlook that handles only the minimum set of features necessary to propagate e-mail viruses.

owner

The user account that created an object or was otherwise assigned ownership. The owner of an object has the right to change its permissions irrespective of user account's permissions.

packet filter

A router that is capable of dropping packets that don't meet security requirements.

PAMed

An application that has been modified to allow for *Pluggable Authentication Modules*.

parent

The preceding process (for programs) or containing folder (for objects, directories or files).

partition

A low-level division of a hard disk. A partition contains a file system.

pass phrase

A very long password consisting of multiple words.

passive IDS

IDS that record information about intrusions but which do not have the capability of acting on that information.

password

A secret key known to both a system and a user that can be used to prove a user's identity to gain access to the system.

permission

An Access Control Entry in an object's Discretionary Access Control List.

permissions

A security mechanism that controls access to individual resources, like files, based on user identity.

personal firewall applications

Software programs that protect an individual computer from intrusion by filtering all communications that enter through network connections.

pipe

An inter-process communication mechanism that emulates a serial character device.

Pluggable Authentication Modules (PAM)

An authentication abstraction layer that provides a central mechanism for connecting various authentication schemes to various network services in Unix. Services trust PAM for authentication, and PAM can be configured to use various authentication schemes.

Point-to-Point Protocol (PPP)

A protocol originally developed to allow modem links to carry different types of network-layer protocols like TCP/IP, IPX, NetBEUI, and AppleTalk. PPP includes authentication and protocol negotiation, as well as control signals between the two points, but does not allow for addressing since only two participants are involved in the communication.

policy

A collection of rules.

port

A parameter of a TCP stream that indicates which process on the remote should receive the data. Public servers listen on "well-known" ports established by convention to monitor specific processes like web or e-mail servers.

Post Office Protocol, version 3 (POP3)

An e-mail client protocol used to download e-mail from mail servers into mail client programs.

Postfix

A popular and highly secure e-mail service for Unix systems.

Practical Extraction and Reporting Language (Perl)

A popular scripting language used in websites and the administration of Unix machines. Windows versions are available.

Pretty Good Privacy (PGP)

A freely available encryption package that supports file and e-mail encryption for nearly all computing platforms.

private key

A secretly held key for an asymmetrical encryption algorithm that can only be used to decode messages or encode digital signatures.

probe

An attempt to elicit a response from a host in order to glean information from the host.

process

A running program.

propagation engine

The code used by a virus to self-replicate.

protocol

An agreed upon method of communicating between two computers.

proxy server

A server that hosts application proxies.

pseudorandom number

A member of a set of numbers which has all the same properties as a similarly sized set of truly random numbers, like even distribution in a set, no predictable reoccurrences, and incompressibility, but which occur in a predictable order from a given starting point (seed).

Pseudorandom Number Generator (PRNG)

An algorithm that generates pseusdorandom numbers.

public key

A publicly distributed key for an asymmetrical encryption algorithm, which can only be used to encode messages or decode digital signatures.

public key authentication

Authentication by means of a digital signature.

public key encryption

Encryption by means of a public key. Public key encryption solves the problem posed by exchanging secret keys by using different but related ciphers for encoding and decoding. Because different keys are used to encode and decode, the public key (encoder) can be widely disseminated without risk.

qmail

A popular e-mail service for Unix systems.

realm

A Kerberos security domain defined by a group of hosts that all trust the same Key Distribution Center.

red flag

A simple detected event that has a very high probability of being a real hacking attempt with serious consequences, as opposed to a normal administrative event or background radiation.

Redundant Array of Independent Disks (RAID)

A family of related technologies that allow multiple disks to be combined into a volume. With all RAID versions except 0, the volume can tolerate the failure of at least one hard disk and remain fully functional.

registry

A hierarchical database local to each Windows computer used for storing configuration information.

relay server

An intermediate e-mail server configured to route e-mail between e-mail servers.

remote access

The process of accessing services on a remote server without executing software directly on the remote machine.

remote logon

The process of logging on to a remote machine in order to execute software on it.

removable media

Computer storage media that can be removed from the drive, such as floppy disks, flash cards, and tape.

replay attack

An attack in which a secret value like a hash is captured and then reused at a later time to gain access to a system without ever decrypting or decoding the hash. Replay attacks only work against systems that don't uniquely encrypt hashes for each session.

requirements

A list of functions that are necessary in a system.

reverse proxy

A web proxy that receives requests for pages from the Internet and passes them through to a one member of a pool of identical web servers. Reverse proxies can be used both for load balancing and security checking.

root

The Unix superuser administrative account. Permissions are not checked for the root user.

Root Certifying Authority

An organization that exists simply to be trusted by participants in order to provide transitive trust. Root CAs certify the identities of all members, so that members who trust the Root CA can trust anyone that they've certified. Root CAs are analogous to Public Notaries.

rooted

A transitive trust system that relies upon a hierarchy that culminates in a single entity that all participants implicitly trust.

sandbox

An execution environment that does not allow accesses outside itself, and so cannot be exploited to cause problem on the host system.

scan

A methodical search through a numerical space, such as an address or port range.

script kiddie

A novice hacker.

scripting hosts

Execution environments that can be called from applications in order to execute scripts contained in the application's data.

secret key

A key that must be kept secret by all parties because it can be used to both encrypt and decrypt messages.

secret key encryption

Encryption by means of a secret key.

Secure Multipurpose Internet Mail Extensions (S/MIME)

MIME with extensions that provide encryption.

secure shell (SSH)

A secure encrypted version of the classic Telnet application. SSH uses public key cryptography to authenticate SSH connections, and private key encryption with changing keys to secure data while in transit.

Secure Socket Layer (SSL)

A public key encryption technology that uses certificates to establish encrypted links without exchanging authentication information. SSL is used to provide encryption for public services or services that otherwise do not require identification of the parties involved but where privacy is important. SSL does not perform encapsulation.

Security Accounts Manager (SAM)

The process that controls access to the user account database in the registry.

security associations (SA)

A set of cryptographic keys and protocol identifiers programmed into a VPN endpoint to allow communication with a reciprocal VPN endpoint. IKE allows security associations to be negotiated on the fly between two devices if they both know the same secret key.

Security Descriptor

Information stored with each object that specifies the owner and contains the Access Control List.

security domain

A collection of machines that all trust the same database of user credentials.

Security Group

A construct containing a SID that is used to create permissions for an object. User accounts are associated with security groups and inherit their permissions from them.

Security Identifier (SID)

A globally unique serial number used to identify user, computer, and security group accounts in Windows.

security principle

A user, computer, or security group account.

seed

The starting point for a specific set of pseudo-random numbers for a specific PRNG.

self-replicating

Something that has the ability to create copies of itself.

Sendmail

The most popular e-mail service, Sendmail is open-source and was originally part of the BSD. Many commercial e-mail services are based on Sendmail.

sensor

Intrusion detection software designed to run directly on public hosts and which reports to a central management station

session

An authenticated stream of related packets.

shadow passwords

A security tactic in Unix that separates password information from user account information while remaining compatible with software written for the earlier combined method.

share

A portion of a file system that the SMB service (server.exe in Windows, samba in Unix) exports for access by SMB clients. Access to the share can be configured on a per-user or per-group basis.

shares

Constructs used by the Server service to determine how users should be able to access folders across the network.

shell

The program launched after a successful login that presents the user environment. Typically, shells allow a user to launch subsequent programs.

signature

A short sequence of codes known to be unique to a specific virus, which indicates that virus's presence in a system.

Simple Mail Transfer Protocol (SMTP)

The Internet protocol that controls the transmission of e-mail between servers. SMTP is also used to transmit e-mail from clients to servers but usually not to receive it, because SMTP requires recipient machines to be online at all times.

Simple Network Management Protocol (SNMP)

A protocol with no inherent security used to query equipment status and modify the configuration of network devices.

single signon

See *distributed logon.*

smart cards

Physical devices that have a small amount of non-volatile memory which stores a random number that is only available to the device. Authentication software can push a value on to the card, which will be encrypted using the random number and returned. Smart cards thereby create an unforgeable physical key mechanism.

sniffing

The process of wiretapping and recording information that flows over a network for analytical purposes.

socket

A specific TCP or UDP port on a specific IP address, for example: 192.168.0.1:80. Sockets are used to transmit information between two participating computers in a network environment. Sockets are block devices.

source routing

A test mechanism allowed by the IP protocol, which allows the sender to specify the route that a packet should take through a network, rather than rely upon the routing tables built into intermediate routers.

spam

Unsolicited unwanted e-mail.

spammers

Those who send spam. Usually, the term is applied to those who steal bandwidth to send spam, as opposed to legitimate e-mail marketers who send spam.

stateful inspection

A packet filtering methodology that retains the state of a TCP connection and can pass or reject packets based on that state, rather than simply on information contained in the packet.

stateless packet filters

Packet filters that make pass/reject decisions based only on the information contained in each individual packet.

stateless protocol

Protocols that do not maintain any information about the client session on the server side. Stateless protocols can be easily clustered across multiple machines without fear of data loss or side effects because it does not matter which server the client connects to from one instance to the next.

symmetrical algorithm

An algorithm which uses the same secret key for encryption as for decryption.

system

A collection of processing entities, such as computers, firewalls, domain controllers, network devices, e-mail systems, applications, and humans.

System Access Control List (SACL)

An Access Control List used to determine how to audit objects.

T1 leased lines

The traditional designator for the most common type of digital leased line. T1 lines operate at 1.544Mbps (as a single channel, or 1.536Mbps when multiplexed into 24 channels) over two pairs of category 2 twisted-pair wiring. T1s were originally designed to carry 24 digital voice lines between a private branch exchange (PBX) and the local telephone company for businesses that required numerous voice lines. Most small to medium-sized businesses rely on T1 lines for their primary connections to the Internet. Outside the U.S. and Canada, the 2.048Mbps E1 circuit with 32 voice channels is most commonly used.

taint

In Perl, a flag indicating that the information contained in the flagged variable was directly entered by a web user and should not be trusted. Taint is copied with the variable contents and can only be removed by interpreting the variable's contents, rather than simply copying the data to a function or another application.

TCP Wrappers

A process that inserts itself before a network service in order to authenticate the hosts that are attempting to connect.

terminal

A remote display and keyboard/mouse console that can be used to access a computer.

ticket

In Kerberos, an encrypted value appended with the time to prove identity to a network service.

Ticket Granting Ticket (TGT)

An encrypted value stored by a client after a successful logon that is used to quickly prove identity in a Kerberos environment.

Top Level Domain Names (TLDs)

The first specific level of the domain name hierarchy, TLDs are used to apportion the domain name system into sections that can be administered by different Internet naming authorities. Each country has it's own country-code TLD (ccTLD) like .us, .ca, .uk, .sp, .fr, .de, and so on. There are also six common general purpose (non-country specific) TLDs (gTLDs): .com, .net, .org, .edu, .gov, and .mil. Some new gTLDs such as .biz, .info, .pro, and .aero have been released, but there has been no significant interest in them. The Internet Corporation for Assigned Names and Numbers (ICANN) administers the TLD hierarchy.

transparent

A proxy server that is capable of automatically proxying a protocol without the client's awareness.

Trojan horse

A program that is surreptitiously installed on a computer for the purpose of providing access to a hacker.

trust provider

A trusted third party that certifies the identity of all parties in a secure transaction. Trust providers do this by verifying the identity of each party and generating digital certificates that can be used to determine that identity. Trust Providers perform a function analogous to Notaries Public.

tunneling

The process of encapsulating packets within IP packets for the purpose of transporting the interior packets through many public intermediate systems. When reassembled at the remote end, the interior packets will appear to have transited only one router on the private networks.

Unix

A family of multi-user operating systems that all conform completely to the POSIX (Portable Operating System Interface for Unix) specification and operate in very similar fashion. Unix includes AT&T UNIX, BSD, Linux, and derivatives of these major versions.

user account

The association between a user account name, a password, and a security identifier (windows) or a user identifier (Unix).

user context

The user identity under which a process executes that determines which files and resources the process will have access to.

User Identifier (UID)

An integer that identifies a user account to the system in Unix

user policy

The portion of group policy that applies to the logged on user.

user rights

Actions that a user account can perform that apply to many or all objects in a system.

virtual directory

A portion of a website with its own specific configuration and security settings. A virtual directory appears as a directory inside the website, but may be located anywhere on the Internet.

virtual host

A web server administration feature that allows a single web server to serve numerous websites as if they were hosted by their own server. The web server inspects the URL header, IP address, or port number from the client connection to determine which virtual host should deliver a specific page request.

Virtual Private Network (VPN)

A packet stream that is encrypted, encapsulated, and transmitted over a non-secure network like the Internet.

virus

Any program which automatically replicates itself.

virus scanner

Software that scans every executable file on a computer searching for virus signatures.

virus scanning

The process of searching a file or communication stream for the identifying signature of a virus. A virus signature is simply a series of bytes that is deemed to be unique to the virus.

VPN software client

A software application for individual computers that creates VPN connections to VPN servers or devices.

web of trust

The PGP grass-rooted transitive-trust mechanism for encrypted e-mail.

web-enabled

Designation for a traditional application that has an HTTP interface, allowing its primary functionality to be used over the Internet.

wide area networks (WAN)

Networks that span long distances using digital telephony trunks like dedicated leased lines, frame relay, satellite, or alternative access technologies to link local area networks.

Windows

A family of single-user operating systems developed by Microsoft for small computers. The most recent version has incorporated enhancements to allow multiple users to run programs directly on the same machine.

Windows Explorer

The shell program in Windows from which most user-mode programs are launched.

Windows Terminal Services

A service of Windows that implements the Remote Data Protocol (RDP), which intercepts video calls to the operating system and repackages them for transmission to a remote user (as well as receiving keystrokes and mouse pointer data from the remote user), thus enabling a low-bandwidth remotely controlled desktop environment in which any applications can be run.

Wireless Access Point (WAP)

An 802.11b wireless network hub.

Wired-Equivalent Privacy (WEP)

A flawed encryption protocol used by the 802.11b wireless networking protocol.

worm

Any program that takes active measures to replicate itself onto other machines in a network. A network virus.

yellow pages (yp)

The original name for NIS.

Index

357

X

Y

From self-study guides to advanced computer-based training, simulated testing programs to last-minute review guides, Sybex has the most complete CompTIA training solution on the market.

Sybex Covers
CompTIA
CERTIFICATION PROGRAMS

Study Guides

STUDY

Designed for optimal learning, Sybex Study Guides provide you with comprehensive coverage of all exam objectives. Hands-on exercises and review questions help reinforce your knowledge.

- In-depth coverage of exam objectives
- Hands-on exercises
- CD includes: test engine, flashcards for PCs and Palm devices, PDF version of entire book

Virtual Trainers™
software

Based on the content of the Study Guides, Sybex Virtual Trainers offer you advanced computer-based training, complete with animations and customization features.

- Customizable study planning tools
- Narrated instructional animations
- Preliminary assessment tests
- Results reporting

Virtual Test Centers™
software

PRACTICE

Powered by an advanced testing engine, Sybex's new line of Virtual Test Centers give you the opportunity to test your knowledge before sitting for the real exam.

- Hundreds of challenging questions
- Computer adaptive testing
- Support for drag-and-drop and hot-spot formats
- Detailed explanations and cross-references

Exam Notes™

REVIEW

Organized according to the official exam objectives, Sybex Exam Notes help reinforce your knowledge of key exam topics and identify potential weak areas requiring further study.

- Excellent quick review before the exam
- Concise summaries of key exam topics
- Tips and insights from experienced instructors
- Definitions of key terms and concepts

Look to Sybex for exam prep materials on major CompTIA certifications, including A+®, Network+™, I-Net+™, Server+™, and Linux+™. For more information about CompTIA and Sybex products, visit www.sybex.com.

Sybex—The Leader in Certification

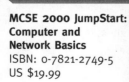

TELL US WHAT YOU THINK!

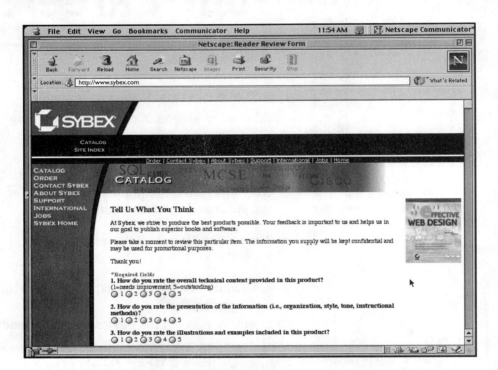

Your feedback is critical to our efforts to provide you with the best books and software on the market. Tell us what you think about the products you've purchased. It's simple:

1. Visit the Sybex website
2. Go to the product page
3. Click on **Submit a Review**
4. Fill out the questionnaire and comments
5. Click **Submit**

With your feedback, we can continue to publish the highest quality computer books and software products that today's busy IT professionals deserve.

www.sybex.com

SYBEX Inc. • 1151 Marina Village Parkway, Alameda, CA 94501 • 510-523-8233